James Oliphant

Victorian Novelists

James Oliphant

Victorian Novelists

ISBN/EAN: 9783337001520

Printed in Europe, USA, Canada, Australia, Japan

Cover: Foto ©Thomas Meinert / pixelio.de

More available books at **www.hansebooks.com**

The Victorian Era Series.

In crown 8vo volumes, cloth, 2s. 6d. each.

The series is designed to form a record of the great movements and developments of the age, in politics, economics, religion, industry, literature, science, and art, and of the life-work of its typical and influential men.

The individual volumes are contributed by leading specialists in the various branches of knowledge treated in the series.

The Rise of Democracy.
By J. HOLLAND ROSE, M.A.

The Anglican Revival.
By J. H. OVERTON, D.D., Canon of Lincoln.

John Bright.
By C. A. VINCE, M.A., late Fellow of Christ's College, Cambridge.

Charles Dickens. By GEORGE GISSING.

The Growth and Administration of the British Colonies, 1837-1897.
By the Rev. W. P. GRESWELL, M.A.

The Free-trade Movement and its Results.
By G. ARMITAGE-SMITH, M.A., Principal of the Birkbeck Institution.

English National Education.
By H. HOLMAN, M.A., formerly Professor of Education in the University College of Wales, Aberystwyth.

Provident Societies and Industrial Welfare.
By E. W. BRABROOK, C.B., Chief Registrar of Friendly Societies.

London in the Reign of Queen Victoria, 1837–1897.
By G. LAURENCE GOMME, F.S.A.

Recent Advances in Astronomy.
By A. H. FISON, D.Sc.(Lond.).

Charles Kingsley and the CHRISTIAN SOCIAL MOVEMENT.
By the Very Rev. C. W. STUBBS, D.D., Dean of Ely.

The Science of Life. By J. ARTHUR THOMSON, M.A.

Tennyson: A CRITICAL STUDY.
By STEPHEN GWYNN.

British Foreign Missions.
By Rev. WARDLAW THOMPSON and Rev. A. N. JOHNSON, M.A.

Victorian Novelists. By JAMES OLIPHANT, M.A.

The Earl of Beaconsfield. By HAROLD E. GORST.

Prospectus containing Press Opinions of each Volume of the Series post free on application.

LONDON: BLACKIE & SON, LIMITED, 50 OLD BAILEY, E.C.
GLASGOW AND DUBLIN.

The Victorian Era Series

Victorian Novelists

Victorian Novelists

By

JAMES OLIPHANT, M.A.

LONDON
BLACKIE & SON, Limited, 50 OLD BAILEY, E.C.
GLASGOW AND DUBLIN
1899

Contents

CHAPTER I
The Novel as an Art-Form - - - - - - 1

CHAPTER II
Scott and Jane Austen - - - - - - - 14

CHAPTER III
Charles Dickens - - - - - - - - 30

CHAPTER IV
W. M. Thackeray - - - - - - - 47

CHAPTER V
Charlotte Brontë - - - - - - - - 64

CHAPTER VI
George Eliot - - - - - - - - 78

CHAPTER VII
George Meredith - - - - - - - - 143

CHAPTER VIII
R. Louis Stevenson - - - - - - - 208

CHAPTER IX
Rudyard Kipling and I. Zangwill - - - 229

INDEX - - - - - - - - 249

Preface

This volume is based on material originally prepared for a course of lectures, and is intended to appeal rather to the general reader than to the expert in literary criticism. It makes no claim, moreover, to historical completeness, many excellent writers of fiction being unmentioned. It was thought that the purpose of illustrating the outstanding features of the English novel during the period of its most noteworthy development could best be fulfilled by the selection of a few representative authors whose work was specially significant. While the treatment is mainly critical, reference is made to biographical facts where these are available, and where it seemed that light could thus be thrown on the character of the writer's work. In the case of the older novelists, where authoritative criticisms were available, they have been taken into account. In the treatment of contemporary fiction the stand-point has naturally been more independent.

J. O.

EDINBURGH, *September, 1899.*

Victorian Novelists.

Chapter I.

The Novel as an Art-Form.

There is very little idea in this country as yet that the pursuit of art in any form, unless as a means of livelihood, may be a serious occupation of one's time. We may no longer consider a theatrical performance in itself sinful, but the cloud in which all kinds of public entertainment were so long enveloped has not entirely lifted, and our newly-acquired tolerance has not yet ripened even into approval, far less into enthusiasm. Even a high-class concert is regarded by many respectable people as a more or less frivolous relaxation, or at best a harmless amusement rather than a means of culture. In this depreciation of art the novel fully shares—indeed, it is depressed even below the other arts in the public esteem. To devote leisure time to pictures or music or poetry is quite respectable; but to be a confirmed theatre-goer or novel-reader lays one open to the suspicion of levity. What justice is there in this distinction? As regards the theatre there is perhaps some ground for it. It is part of the conditions of the drama that it should tend to keep on a comparatively low level. The expense of representation demands an appeal to the popular taste more imperatively than where specially-selected audiences can be addressed, and the opportunities of seeing what is distinctly above the average appreciation are therefore rare. Except in the largest centres, accordingly, to be a frequent theatre-goer means to be easily satisfied. But no such reason applies in the case of novel-reading. Good novels are as much within reach as bad ones. Why is there in some quarters such a presumption against it? It is not only that the constant novel-reader is looked at with suspicion, but one scarcely even says "I have been reading a novel", without feeling that some kind of excuse is expected. The explanation of this must be sought by enquiring briefly: What is the relation of art to life, and what is the place of prose fiction among the arts?

We have as yet no satisfactory philosophy of æsthetics, but whatever be the outer conditions of an impression of beauty, the enjoyment of it is clearly a function of the brain, when affected through the nerves of vision, or one of the other bodily senses. Out of the various influences afforded by the eye, the ear, the palate, there arises a general faculty of perceiving and enjoying beauty, which may be appealed to, not only directly by sensible objects, but by suggestion through the memory and imagination. Such indirect impressions will naturally be less vivid, but they are equally real with those received through the senses. It is not by a mere analogy that we pass from sensuous beauty to what is called intellectual or moral beauty. An outward action is simply a series of visible forms or pictures, and when any such series seems well adjusted to a reasonable end we call it graceful. Here we discover the close relation of the beautiful to the useful. It is a natural extension of this perception of appropriate action to represent to our minds some further end, not immediately present either in space or time, and it is with this conception that we follow any course of events or system of conduct. The enjoyment of beauty is thus brought about by certain sense-impressions, either singly or in combination, either directly or indirectly, through the memory

The Novel as an Art-Form.

or imagination. At this point there emerges the question of art. The desire for the expression of feeling as a relief of surplus energy, a form of action taking rational shapes, but without the justification of any outward end, is shown in every phase of animal life. From the apparently aimless flutterings of the butterfly to the highly-organized games of civilized human beings, we have countless examples of what have been termed the play-instincts, out of which art has certainly had its rise. But expression of feeling only becomes art when it appeals directly to the capacity for enjoying beauty. The precise point when play becomes art is not always easy to determine. Whether the cave-dwellers of the stone ages, who many thousand years ago scratched rude drawings of animals on a reindeer's horn, were consciously ministering to the æsthetic enjoyment either of their neighbours or themselves it would be hard to say; but it is in such efforts as these that the beginnings of art may be traced. We are scarcely entitled, however, to use the word *art* until we have risen beyond the mere reproduction of natural objects, however beautiful, to that selection and arrangement of the material according to a definite purpose, which is known as creative imagination. The mere imitation of nature, as we are often told, is not art; there must also be the transfiguring touch, the idealising power. The extent to which this is necessary or possible varies in the different arts, colour, for instance, being more self-sufficient than form or sound; but there is no art in which the noblest achievements have not been attained by those who were gifted with high imaginative genius. But so far no estimate has been reached of the value of art in relation to life. Its origin in the impulses of play may not seem to testify to its dignity or worth. This, it may be said, is a stern world, a world of work and sorrow and strife, where all our thought and energy are demanded in the struggle for justice, for peace, for progress. A certain amount of recreation may be necessary as oil to the wheels of labour, but it must not trench on the serious business of life. Though necessity may not press hardly on ourselves, are there not wrongs to redress and sufferings to relieve? Shall we be found fiddling while Rome is burning?

But is there not another aspect in which this would appear a narrow and short-sighted view? The true end of life must be to live, as fully and as widely as possible, and though social bonds require that opportunities shall as far as possible be equalised, the doctrine of renunciation which this implies may easily be pushed beyond reasonable limits. A vain endeavour after perfect uniformity of happiness cannot be the final instruction of wisdom for the conduct of life; there is a point where the means may mistakenly be allowed to become the end. Too exclusive a regard for our own chances of living is no doubt an ever-present danger, but the possession of privilege is in itself a trust, to be fearlessly fulfilled. Joy is the flower of life, and if we refuse to pluck it when it is within our grasp we are throwing away our birthright. The pleasures of art are not those which commonly enervate or degrade the character; they are not often purchased at the sacrifice of others' joy. Like mercy, art blesseth him that gives and him that takes; it is a cup of life alike to the artist and to all who can enjoy what he creates. It may indeed be said with truth that the chief end of our life is to enjoy the ideal beauty presented in art.

But if this should be found too hard a saying, a further justification may be sought in the answer to the second part of the original question: What is the place of prose fiction among the arts? In its simplest form, the art of narrative must have arisen insensibly out of the natural use of language for purposes of communication. To relate what has happened, in an effective way, is to take a long step towards the deliberate selection of material for its capacity to please, which is the mark of the artistic process. In a sense, therefore, prose fiction must have been one of the first, if not the first-born, of the arts; but from its earliest form to its latest there has been a transition of the greatest consequence. In its essence the modern novel is a development from the plain unvarnished tale which is no more than a bare record of facts; but it has gathered into its substance the functions and traditions of other arts, and it now fills a place, if not of the highest theoretic importance, at least of the widest and most powerful practical influence. It is not the most ideal of the arts, but it is the most comprehensive, and the most independent of restrictions in the conditions of its appeal. Compared with music, which in its absolute form is the most ethereal of all the arts, the most detached from the elements in nature which gave it birth, prose fiction is composite in its structure, and indirect in its method of addressing the mind. But in these very defects lies its strength. If it does not strike mysterious chords in the soul, telling us of things that we have never known and never shall know, it can yet reflect the significant elements of life with peculiar fulness and fidelity. If it does not minister to the rapturous intensity of appreciation in a highly-specialised sense, it reaches all the wider audience by its catholic use of familiar symbols. It is the most *popular* of the arts, in the highest sense of that term, not because it can readily adapt itself to the taste of the majority—all the arts can make themselves popular in that sense—but because it speaks a universal language, and because it rests on a basis of experience which is in some degree common to all. The beauty which is revealed by one or another of the special arts, the beauty that lies in the forms or sounds or colours of the outer world, and may be wrought up into ravishing dreams for those who have the seeing eye and the ear that can listen aright, is to many of us, alas! but a dim shadow, an alluring phantom that we wistfully gaze at, and see only as through a glass, darkly. But it needs no special faculty to be moved by the record of great deeds, to feel the spirit stirred at the tale of noble courage or heroic endurance, to burn with sympathy for all who wrestle with the powers of darkness. And if these things touch us so nearly in the living world around us, they may be brought no less close to us by the art of the novelist. The truth that lies in the ideal has a reality that transcends all individual experience, and may become more truly a part of our life than any fact of actual occurrence. The thoughts and feelings that reach the sublime in human nature, that form our character and guide our conduct, have rarely been produced from that part of the world's dealings with which we have come directly in contact. We are said to learn only by experience, but that is surely a half-truth. It may be said with equal justice that in our own individual lives we do no more than discover the eternal verities which have been wrought out in the history of the race, and borne in on the spirit of each of us through the types presented in art. In this great service all the arts may share, according to their nature, but on the moral and practical side of life there can be no question that the novelist has a greater wealth of opportunity and freedom of treatment than any other artist. It is his privilege alone to trace in detail the subtleties of cause and effect, to exhibit the development of character with fulness and deliberation, to supply a background of conviction and sentiment to the varied play of motive, insensibly guiding his audience to the lessons of the story. This is, of course, at once more, and less, than a just definition of the function of the novel. But such things are undoubtedly within the province of the artist in prose fiction, and in the highest examples of this art they are all to be found.

Here at least, then, we have ample justification of the supreme place that has been claimed for art in relation to life. If we hesitate to call it in itself the highest *end* in self-realisation, another place of vantage has been established for it as the most efficient *means* thereto. The life of the imagination is at once the exercise of the highest faculties of the mind and spirit, and the instrument by which all the other faculties may be purified.

But we have still to trace the general history of fiction that we may recognize the process by which the novel has attained its recently-acquired place in the forefront of the arts. The first form of the story which seems to have reached a definite artistic standing was the metrical epic, the embodiment of myth and legend in poetic guise, which was probably chanted by the bard to his audience, the art of music being thus summoned to its aid. This was a form of ideal narrative that was well suited to primitive conditions of life. The combination of resources was not beyond the capacity of the more gifted, nor beyond the appreciation of ordinary hearers, and the apparatus of expression was of the simplest. The minstrel with his lyre was self-sufficient, and wherever his wandering steps might lead him, he could be sure of welcome and applause. Out of this composite but rudely-compacted structure which forms the earliest monument of art in the history of almost every nation, there diverged gradually a separate development for each of its elements. Story, verse, and music came to be independent of each other, and could thus receive more careful and persistent cultivation. But the need for a central art-form, which might sacrifice refinements of detail to the need for a wide general appeal, has always asserted itself, and one combination after another was devised to suit the practical requirements, and entered into successful competition with the various arts in their special courses. The epic was succeeded by the drama, which originally harmonized anew the same elements of story and chanted verse, with the important addition of appropriate action. This represents a certain advance in civilization, the necessities of a dramatic performance implying more extended preparation and a high degree of concert among those who take part. The combinations that have been superseded have not necessarily fallen into complete disuse. The epic, in losing its pre-eminent place, lost also its dependence on music, and in a more specialised form lingered on as an academic imitation appealing to the cultivation of the few. Its primitive shape, however, has now become entirely obsolete, and the story in verse survives only in the forms of the idyll and the ballad. The drama has filled the place of honour in the popular esteem for many ages, and if it is now being dethroned to make way for the novel, it has had a place of different, but no less, consideration assigned to it in recompense. After pursuing various lines, religious and secular, its history culminated in the glories of the Elizabethan epoch, but in the form which it then assumed it has held its ground to the present day only by sacrificing its pretensions to poetry. The musical accompaniment with which it had started had been long given up, and the ordinary drama of to-day is only a prose story represented in action. This increasing simplicity and specialism may have helped its development in some aspects, but it has undermined its general supremacy. A new and a glorious future has, however, been opened for the drama in a return to its former composite structure, only under much more complex and perfect conditions of union. Music, poetry, scenery, action, have once more been combined to tell a story in the ideal form of what is known as the music-drama, which has drawn to itself the services of all these arts in a singleness of purpose and a wealth of effect which had never before been dreamt of. But the very strength and richness of such a combination serve to remove it in a sense out of the main channels of appreciation. Its idealism is too far removed from everyday life to appeal to the mass of men, and its demands on the culture of special senses help further to withdraw it from the central currents of imaginative pleasure. The drama has given place to the prose fiction for reasons that are sufficiently clear. As in the passage from the epic to the drama, so in the passage from the drama to the novel there is a mark of progress in civilization. The theatre flourished during the period when people possessed sufficient facilities for meeting in populous centres, in times of festival if not continuously, but before the art of printing and other social advances had made possible the diffusion of education and of the means of gratifying the taste for intellectual food. It represents a phase of culture when the imagination can only be stirred by direct appeal through the various senses. It is not meant that this is a characteristic of the modern comedy, where the refinements of acting have received special cultivation, or of the music-drama, which in its appeal to the senses demands a high degree of proficiency in several arts for adequate appreciation. But it is the distinctive feature of the stage when it is adapted to the average taste, as in the modern melodrama. Since Shakespeare's day the theatre has lost the better part of its audience, who have found a rival attraction in books, and this has inevitably caused a lowering of the artistic standard. The law of supply and demand has in this country at least, where there is no endowment of theatres, discouraged any discriminating appeal to the cultivated classes, who now, for the most part, look on the stage chiefly as a means of killing time. The ordinary dramatic performance is therefore either on the one hand the broad comedy or farce, which scarcely comes within the domain of serious art at all; or it is, on the other hand, the melodrama, which is a means of culture indeed, but a means adapted to a low stage of intellectual and artistic development. To suit this stage the effects must be broad and crude, and very little must be left to the imagination.

The decay of the theatre to such a point that none of our great poets will write for it is no doubt due in part to the influence of the Puritan movement, and to that extent might be successfully resisted, but other causes of decline are more deep-seated, and it would be vain, even if it were desirable, to seek to counteract them. The rivalry offered by books is too powerful under the changed conditions. The indirectness of the impressions gained by reading is atoned for by advantages of various kinds. Convenience and economy may form part of these; a book is easily borrowed or hired, or even bought, though many people think the last a somewhat desperate alternative; it can be taken up or laid down at any time; and it can be read in dressing-gown and slippers at one's own fireside. These materialistic considerations do not, of course, form the chief element in the comparison, but they must not be forgotten. A more important matter, however, is that in the choice of books we can suit our individual likings much more perfectly than in the case of plays. The quality of the dramatic performances that are easily available to most of us is determined by the prevailing taste in the community of which we personally form but an insignificant part, but no one has any say as to the books which we must read. It is no doubt true that in some degree the kind of literature which is produced must be determined by the wishes of the reading public, but there is a great difference in the way in which this demand acts. The manager of a theatre who might think of bringing out a play above the average level knows that he can count on the support of only a limited class, and it is the same with the publisher of a book; but the theatre manager depends on those who are within reach of his theatre, while the publisher can

The Novel as an Art-Form.

appeal to the much larger number throughout the whole country who hold the required standard of taste. With the classes of higher intelligence, moreover, it is felt to be little disadvantage that the sense of beauty should be reached by suggestion, as in poetry or prose fiction, rather than by direct presentation as in the drama. It is not that they are indifferent to the power of sensuous impressions, but the practical limitations of the stage in realising the effects of art are so serious, and there is consequently so great a risk of having one's conception spoilt by inadequate representation, that many of us would prefer to trust to the less vivid but safer suggestions of our own imaginations. We are scarcely willing to accept the embodiment of our ideals from the hands of another, even if he be a true artist working in elements that yield readily to his mastery, as in a picture or in a statue, much less under the restrictions of the stage, which is bound down to the actual at so many points. We would rather fashion our own image of Romeo and Juliet, of Hamlet, or Rosalind, or Cordelia, out of the materials Shakespeare has afforded us, than submit to have these types of beauty or nobility degraded by any living presentation short of the highest. The drama has to attempt so much more than painting or sculpture that its chances of failure are naturally greater. Success is dependent on so many conditions that it is very seldom attained in any satisfying degree.

There is still another respect in which the drama is at a disadvantage compared with the novel, as an art of general appeal. The necessary limit of time in performance to a very few hours, and the absence of opportunity for comment or explanation, since the device of the Greek chorus has been discontinued, make it difficult to develop the story with clearness and effect, and to portray the characters with sufficient fulness of detail. It is of course these very difficulties that give the art its characteristic form, and bring honour when special success is achieved, but for ordinary and general purposes they weigh against it, in contrast with the art of the novelist, who has almost an unlimited freedom in his choice of method.

Such are the chief causes why we have now to look on prose fiction as the central art-form of the present day, if not also of the future. In the use of the word *central* no estimate is hazarded of the relative dignity of the arts. It is not implied that prose fiction must be awarded the highest place on abstract grounds, but only that it is the art that is capable of the widest and most effective influence. Indeed, although prophecies of finality are always of doubtful wisdom, it may almost be said that the evolution which has been traced has now reached its limit, and that it is difficult to see by what form the novel could be superseded. It is time, therefore, that we should revise our current ideas of its worth. Art itself is still undervalued among us in its relation to life; and among the arts that of the novelist is scarcely as yet one of the most highly esteemed. We have indeed got beyond the phase of social opinion when to write romances was to sink below the professional standard of respectability. The novelist has no need now to be so ashamed of his craft that he withholds his name from the title-page, like Sir Walter Scott, who writes: "I shall not own *Waverley*. . . . I am not sure that it would be considered quite decorous for me, as clerk of Session, to write novels. Judges being monks, clerks are a sort of lay brethren from whom some solemnity of walk and conduct may be expected." Scott, no doubt, as the language implies, was half ashamed of being ashamed, but his practice was determined by the fear of losing caste; and if the disability of his successors has become more negative, it is nevertheless still discernible. The very word *novel* suggests something wanting in seriousness, and it is not altogether easy to account for this. There are here none of the associations with an unrestrained manner of life which have unfortunately but naturally depressed the standing of the drama for so long in the opinion of many earnest-minded people. How is the feeling to be explained? The real reason is to be found in the history of the novel previous to the point where it began to supplant the drama. The prose tale had always held a place as a form of art, but before the period when it began to assume its modern shape, a period which in this country may be dated from the publication of Defoe's novels in the beginning of the last century, it had no definite status, no recognized function in relation to natural life. The accepted channels of expression for the highest genius were the metrical epic and afterwards the drama, and the novel had to be content with ministering to tastes that required less elevation of aim. While Dante was putting all that was noble in the thought and feeling of the middle ages into the deathless verse of the *Divine Comedy*, Boccaccio wrote the witty and profligate tales of the *Decameron* to amuse the frivolous leisure of the idle classes. It was through its capacity for reflecting the humorous side of life that the novel won for itself a higher position. For in the hands of a wise and earnest man humour is easily turned to satire, and it was thus used with wonderful effect by Rabelais and Cervantes and Swift. In our own country, however, the novel had to contend with a special disadvantage. It so chanced that the decadence of the drama coincided with the reaction against Puritanism, and the novel thus found its opportunity at the moment when the less serious aspects of life were in the ascendant. This circumstance had a twofold influence. It meant in the first place that irresponsible writers like Smollett, who cared to do little except amuse, had no need for scruple in choosing their methods, and in the second place, that serious writers like Richardson or Fielding, who had the higher purpose of portraying life faithfully, found their necessary material in a debased standard of manners and taste. There were many qualities of greatness in the most noteworthy novels of last century, but it was an unfortunate start for an art-form with a noble destiny before it.

Society rose to a higher level of feeling and conduct before the novel could entirely extricate itself from the conditions of its new birth, and in consequence, at the beginning of the present century the art of prose fiction, in so far as it was associated with genius, was also associated with a coarseness of manners which had been largely outgrown in actual life and in other forms of art. There is still in our day much to do in vindicating for the novelist his true place and function, but the first great steps in the process were taken by Sir Walter Scott.

Chapter II.

Scott and Jane Austen.

Though the annals of fiction for the quarter of a century preceding 1837 are dominated by the prestige of the Waverley novels, it would be an error to regard their author as the founder of a new era in respect of the formal development of his art. Scott's artistic equipment, brilliant as it was on certain sides, was seriously limited in range, while his conception of the novelist's function was in the main conventional. He accepted, both in theory and in practice, the maxim that the natural field of imaginative creation lies in regions that are unfamiliar in place or time, and his reanimation of the past was rather a glorious apotheosis of an outworn tradition than the inauguration of a new *régime*; for without denying the right of the "historical novel" to a place in the art of fiction, we may safely assume that so artificial a product could not claim the pre-eminent position it receives in the Waverley novels. We are sometimes told indeed, by way of apology, that the best of Scott's romances are those where he was dealing with characters and scenes not far removed from his own time, and that he only turned to other lands and bygone centuries when his material was becoming exhausted. But the soundness of this judgment is very doubtful. There is certainly a peculiar charm, especially for Scottish readers, in the masterly delineation of certain national types of almost contemporary interest; but only an untrained artistic intelligence could allow a merely incidental success in characterisation to determine the tone of criticism in regard to the general merits of a work of art that professes to be a whole. Caleb Balderstone is a delightful figure, but *The Bride of Lammermoor* is almost devoid of other interest, the chief characters in the drama having no vitality, and the climax being treated with singular ineffectiveness. Dugald Dalgetty is admirably portrayed, but apart from his appearances *The Legend of Montrose* is dull reading. It may be said generally of Scott's eighteenth-century novels that they are the weakest of the series in point of construction, and that even the characterisation, while excelling in rendering certain phases of life,—mostly of the eccentric type,—falls below the average standard of dramatic realism in the majority of the portraits.

The Heart of Midlothian may be taken as an illustration of the Scottish novel at what is generally considered its highest level, and notwithstanding its many beauties, from an artistic stand-point it is a most disappointing work. Carelessness of execution we find in all the Waverley novels, but in this story, which is often called the author's masterpiece, we may discover how far his judgment could go astray in regard to the elementary conditions of æsthetic effect. His sense of proportion, of climax, was singularly deficient. He did not see that his *motif*, the journey of Jeanie Deans to London to beg a pardon for her sister, was exhausted when that end was accomplished, and that every chapter after that point which helped to spin out the book to the regulation length only served to dilute and dissipate the powerful impression he had already made. It is not only, moreover, that the turning-point in the story is reached too soon in its course, but what follows has not even the merit of being interesting in itself. The characters all suffer from the undue amount of monotonous detail with which they are described after their prosperity set in. Jeanie herself was not one to show to any unusual advantage in the peaceful atmosphere of a country manse, and it was unfair to her that after attracting our sympathy and admiration she should be left so long in our view in a situation that called for no special heroism. Her sister Effie, it may be added, is quite unrecognisable when she reappears as a lady of fashion at the end of the book.

Similar faults of construction and failures in portraiture are evident in every one of the six or eight novels of nearly contemporary Scottish life with which the series began, and that these defects were not due to lack of experience is shown by the fact that they reappear at a later period when the author returned to the same source for his material, as in *Redgauntlet* and *St. Ronan's Well*. It was no conviction that the true function of the artist is to show the ideal significance of the life around him, that determined his choice of subject at the outset; he was merely turning to account the resources that came nearest to his hand, without discerning either what he could do best or what was best worth doing, and without feeling the need for any standard of workmanship. Carlyle may have been too severe in describing him as occupied in "writing impromptu novels to buy farms with", but no one can suppose him ever to have taken himself seriously as an artist, and he was certainly debarred by nature from any conception of the part that might be filled by the interplay of character in imaginative creations. He began by regarding the novel not as an end in itself, but as a medium for the expression of his interest in the picturesque episodes of Scottish history, and as a setting for the portraits of certain national types that had struck his fancy when discovered either in his own experience or in the recollections of older people. In regard to the general mechanism of his stories, therefore, he was content to accept the conventional standard. He seems to have thought it a necessity to introduce into every novel some commonplace and threadbare mystification, and he has not even taken the trouble to provide his readers with a decent variety in this respect. One gets heartily tired of the cheap device of the long-lost child being recovered by a series of coincidences in the person of the hero or the heroine. Scott had neither taste nor faculty for the elaborate weaving together of incidents for the mere sake of unravelling them again, yet he never ventured to discard this device of the traditional romance. It may of course be said that our pleasure in *Guy Mannering*, or *The Antiquary*, or *The Pirate*, is quite independent of the melodramatic *dénoûment*, but such a plea, while paying a tribute to the author's genius in other aspects, gives away the case in the matter of construction. If the interest of a novel does not depend on the subject, it stands condemned as a work of art in the chief head of all, whatever other beauties it may have. This is no small matter in relation to Scott, for it is closely related to another of his greatest deficiencies as a novelist. His achievement in character drawing is limited, not only in range, but in imaginative perception. Admirable as he was in reproducing certain types as he had known them or conceived them in any given circumstances, he is rarely, if ever, successful in tracing the development of character under the discipline of events. His men and women are generally the same at the end of the story as they were at the beginning, or if they have altered, we have only the author's word for it; or else again they are different, but we cannot easily reconcile their last state with their first. He seems, for instance, to have been under the impression that a man might indulge in a prolonged course of violence and debauchery without any unpleasant inward consequences beyond the pangs of remorse. The beautiful moral sentiments expressed by Cleveland and Geordie Robertson come too late in the day; if these reformed reprobates were capable of having such feelings, and acting on them sincerely when they did, they would have done so earlier. Whether Scott recognised his weakness in this respect or not, it probably accounts in a great degree for his being so ready to depend on the ordinary machinery of involved situations. He did not care for these, and it is evident from his want of success that he did not work with them *con amore*, but, failing the development of character, which he instinctively avoided, there was no way left to maintain a progressive interest but to introduce artificial complications into the thread of the story.

Nor is it only in regard to *motif*, to construction, to characterisation, that these comparatively modern novels of the Waverley series belong to the old school rather than the new. Scott stands almost alone among great imaginative writers in his deficient sense of the niceties of style and expression, and he had not even the artistic conscience that would have prompted him to make consistent use of what literary aptitude he possessed. The critical reader will find numerous passages throughout his works quite as faulty as that which moved R. L. Stevenson to the comment, "It is not merely bad English or bad style; it is abominably bad narrative besides. ... A man who gave in such copy would be discharged from the staff of a daily paper." This indifference and obtuseness to the possibilities of subtle suggestion in the choice and arrangement of words must be connected with his very imperfect mastery of realistic dialogue. In his Cuddie Headriggs and Dandie Dinmonts and Nicol Jarvies, figures racy of the soil, and illustrating some foible of human nature or some peculiar influence of national manners, he has little difficulty in making his creations express themselves with dramatic force and appropriateness. The long-winded and pedantic, yet possible, discourses of the Antiquary are equally natural with the homely phrasing of the old bedesman interrupting him with his "Prætorian here, Prætorian there; I mind the bigging o't". But whenever the author gets away from his familiar ground, his hand loses its cunning, and he falls at once into the stilted forms of expression which were supposed in those days to be proper to polite conversation, but which assuredly never, in those days or in any other, were used by rational people in actual life. Did two young people ever discourse together in the following manner?

"'I trust Miss Wardour will impute to circumstances almost irresistible this intrusion of a person who has reason to think himself so unacceptable a visitor.'

"'Mr. Lovel,' answered Miss Wardour, 'I trust you will not,—I am sure you are incapable of abusing the advantages given to you by the services you have rendered us, which, as they affect my father, can never be sufficiently acknowledged or repaid. Could Mr. Lovel see me without his own peace being affected,—could he see me as a friend, as a sister,—no man will be,—and from all I have ever heard of Mr. Lovel, ought to be, more welcome, but—'

"'Forgive me if I interrupt you, Miss Wardour; you need not fear my intruding upon a subject where I have been already severely repressed :—but do not add to the severity of repelling my sentiments the rigour of obliging me to disavow them.'

"'I am much embarrassed, Mr. Lovel,' replied the young lady, 'by your—I would not willingly use a strong word—your romantic and hopeless pertinacity. It is for yourself I plead, that you would consider the calls which your country has upon your talents,—that you will not waste, in an idle and fanciful indulgence of an ill-placed predilection, time, which, well redeemed by active exertion, should lay the foundation of future distinction. Let me entreat that you would form a manly resolution'—"

And so on for another page. We have here no chance infelicity of expression. This is a model conversation between a maiden and her lover; both are supposed to be under the influence of strong emotion, for though the young lady's language may be thought somewhat cold, her affections must have been at least partially engaged, for she was willing to marry the youth later on when he turned out to be the son of an earl. Can anyone imagine such an interview being conducted in these frigid terms and elaborately constructed periods? Directness and lucidity of speech were rarer in Scott's day than they are in ours, but no mortal could at any date have devised such sentences with complex relative clauses, except by writing them down beforehand and committing them to memory. This is one of the chief blemishes of the Waverley novels. There is not one of them where it is not present, and it often forms a most unfortunate barrier to our interest and sympathy with the characters. Who cares anything for the feelings of people who in a momentous crisis of their lives have such unnatural command over themselves as to express their sentiments in a style that would not disgrace the headlines of a copy-book?

But if so many serious deductions have to be made from Scott's greatness as an artist, how are we to account for his abiding popularity, not only with "idle readers lying on sofas", as Carlyle puts it, but with people of taste and discernment? We can understand this only by putting aside what has in recent times been said in praise of the novels of the *Guy Mannering* type and in dispraise of the historical romances. It is really by these latter works, which it is now the fashion to disparage, that Scott's name will live for ever. In spite of the judgment of Ruskin that his pictures of mediævalism, his "knighthood and monkery", ar all false, the final verdict of a posterity that will have reached a sounder basis of æsthetic criticism, will probably be that his masterpieces are, not *The Antiquary, Rob Roy, The Heart of Midlothian, Redgauntlet,* but *Ivanhoe, The Abbot, Kenilworth, Peveril of the Peak, Quentin Durward, The Fair Maid of Perth, Anne of Geierstein.* It is true enough that in these novels he was writing for a public which had not yet begun to study the history of its past with any seriousness, and which therefore imposed no standard of accuracy. His antiquarianism was of an eclectic and dilettante kind, which could make no appearance beside the conscientious spirit of research distinctive of our own generation. He cared little to know how things really were in the middle ages; he only wished to gather from them whatever elements of striking and unfamiliar interest he could combine in vivid contrast, to entertain a curious and uncritical public. It is no business of his whether Rebecca fairly represents the English Jewess of the twelfth century; it is enough that he can imagine piquant situations arising from the presence of such a character in some of the more romantic surroundings of that period. But though *Ivanhoe* and its companion romances are not to be taken as history, nor even as sober illustrations of history, they are sufficiently faithful pictures of past centuries to form an adequate setting to the imaginative creations of a great artist. It is surely a mistake to apply a pedantic standard of accuracy in such matters. The conception that is formed of the conditions of any remote period must always be relative to the point of view of those who are looking back on it, and Scott's pictures will at least have an historical value, if that should be demanded, in showing how the ages of chivalry were regarded by those who first tried to give a semblance of realism to their poetic glamour. The historical novel, though it is only a by-product in the development of prose fiction, is yet a distinct *genre*, and Scott was not only its originator, but one of its greatest exponents. We shall appreciate his achievement aright only by taking him frankly on this level, somewhat short of the highest though it be. It was here that his powers had the freest scope and that his deficiencies were of least consequence. He had a keen eye for the details of scenic effect, which he could turn to full account in displaying the barbaric splendours of chivalry to a generation somewhat less familiar with them than he was himself, but capable of being stirred to an imaginative interest by an idealising touch more vigorous than delicate. The chain of incidents belonging to the historic theme he chose offered a definite guidance to his invention, relieving him of the uncongenial task of weaving artificial complications, while leaving ample opportunity for artistic selection. The chief advantage, however, lay in the portraiture. In the presentation of scenes and events belonging to times of more primitive culture, when feeling and thought were comparatively simple, and the drama of life lay rather in the chances of outward fortune than in the subtle interaction of spiritual forces, Scott's lack of emotional intensity was naturally less obtrusive. At the same time he had the fullest chance of showing his wide and ready sympathy with all sorts and conditions of men whose inner nature was not more elusive than his own. In some quarters he has been thought presumptuous in venturing to bring on the stage monarchs, statesmen, and warriors of note, whom he could not portray with the fullest justice; but it is difficult to acquiesce in such criticisms. In his portraits of outstanding historic figures he has seldom attempted any elaborate characterisation where he would have had to compete with more authentic impressions. His most ambitious efforts, perhaps, were Mary Queen of Scots, James I., and Cromwell, yet in none of these can we say that the endeavour was not justified by the event. The Queen Mary of *The Abbot* is not only very finely imagined, but is probably as trustworthy a portrait as any we are ever likely to get of that enigmatic personality; while the conception of Cromwell was quite as impartial and penetrating as could have been expected before the rehabilitation of the Protector's character had been achieved. Even in regard to dramatic speech, Scott was in a more favourable position in his historical novels. If he had not the same opportunity of rendering with convincing force the vernacular of certain types of marked and recognisable individuality, he at least could attain the even more important though negative virtue of avoiding any palpable failure to be true to nature. The imaginative reproduction of the dialogue of people who lived in a distant time or a foreign country is necessarily so artificial that no precise test of *vraisemblance* can be applied; any approach to contemporary living speech that is judicially flavoured with archaic forms of expression will be accepted by the reader as a satisfactory compromise. Scott's literary skill and judgment were quite sufficient for the purpose, and we are accordingly in the historical novels almost wholly free from any barrier to sympathy in this respect, such as we feel where the setting is comparatively modern. On the whole, it may safely be said that while historical romances have been written since those of the Waverley series, and will doubtless continue to be written, that are based on a fuller and more exact knowledge of the past, and are at the same time executed with more perfect literary workmanship, those of Scott will for long continue to hold the field, not only as the first great examples of their kind, but as the creations of an artist who had a wonderful instinct for the secrets of romantic pleasure in theme and treatment.

But though in regard to this class of fiction which he had the merit of originating, Scott failed to strike the path along which the novel was to travel to reach its highest development, and though his attempts in a more realistic medium were not of a nature to justify us in considering him as the artistic forerunner of the great novelists of the Victorian era, let us not forget to do him honour for one memorable service which he rendered to his art. He it was who raised the English novel to the position of dignity which it now enjoys, and he did this not by making any deliberate claim for the more serious recognition of his calling, nor even by an unconscious vindication of its worth through the attainment of excellence in technique, but simply by the consistent elevation of his treatment and tone. The whole texture of his work is the expression of an individuality in which an abundant sympathy with humanity in all its forms is happily blended with a wholesome solidity of judgment and a moral ideal which has had a great effect on subsequent fiction.

When we seek the true beginnings of the modern English novel, we must turn away from Scott to a group of contemporary writers who were maintaining the older tradition of Richardson and Fielding and Goldsmith, but with certain new and significant features. Of these by far the most memorable was, Jane Austen, whose best work preceded the publication of the Waverley novels, and whose influence on the Victorian writers has been greater than that of Balzac, and George Sand, and Victor Hugo. With but a very moderate equipment in the way of education and culture, and with an outlook restricted to the incidents of an uneventful life, she was yet able to form a high conception of the dignity of her art. By her own definition a novel is "a work in which the greatest powers of the mind are displayed, in which the most thorough knowledge of human nature, the happiest delineations of its varieties, the liveliest effusions of wit and humour, are conveyed to the world in the best-chosen language". Though she made no claim for her own work that it realised this ideal, regarding herself only as a "miniature painter", and though from our present stand-point we must look on her achievement as affording little more than a basis for subsequent developments, we cannot wonder at the extravagant praise of Macaulay and other critics, to whom her work was entirely fresh in design. The importance of her initiative lies in the fact that she was the first consciously to recognise that the dramas of humanity are now for the most part enacted within, through the conflicts of opinion and feeling. It was her mission to point out, even if humbly and inadequately, how entirely what people did depended on what they thought and felt, and how much therefore happiness and unhappiness depend on the interchange of influence and development of character expressed in all the relations of family and social life. It was not necessary that this new type of fiction should begin on a large scale; it was indeed more natural that it should first appear in the delicate and carefully-finished touches of Miss Austen's miniatures. In her own words "three or four families in a country village is the very thing to work on", and it is a proof alike of her genuine power and of the wisdom of her method that out of such limited material she could construct several stories, without lack of variety in character and *motif*, which have won for themselves a sure place among the classics.

It is an ungracious task to call attention to the limitations of an author to whom we owe so much, but the value of Jane Austen's contribution to the art of fiction, as we find it at the beginning of the present reign, can only be appreciated by distinguishing clearly what she achieved from what was left to be achieved by her successors. While justly insisting that the true field of fiction lay in the study of contemporary character and manners, she was shut out by the narrowness of her lot from that breadth of outlook which could alone have made her pictures representative of life as a whole. Notably she excludes all reference to the humbler classes; her characters all belong to her own rank of life, the country gentry and those who were on visiting terms with them; or if any less respectable person appears incidentally, it is only as a dependant or accessory to the upper middle-class society, outside of which she does not seem to feel herself on safe ground. Moreover, it is a somewhat idle and pleasure-loving atmosphere—occasionally almost a sordid atmosphere. Most of the men have several thousands a year and nothing particular to do with them except to enjoy themselves, while the ladies are too often occupied in the soul-destroying pursuit of trying to secure a husband out of the aforesaid men either for their daughters or their sisters or for themselves. Truly, little room for anything heroic in all this! All the greater honour, however, to the artist who, while faithfully representing the life she saw around her, has succeeded so unmistakably in showing us what was worthy in it, as well as what was base and ignoble.

In point of construction, while we cannot reasonably complain of any lack of intricacy or subtlety in the plots, we can recognise certain crudities of treatment in almost all of them. Perhaps *Pride and Prejudice* is the only one where the general design can be almost unreservedly praised, but even in this, which is undoubtedly the finest of her novels, there is one serious defect that is absent in none of them, namely, an inadequate sense of dramatic climax. It may be ungenerous to find fault with the author for the perfunctory manner in which she disposes of the minor figures in her story after the main interest has been exhausted. In this respect she merely followed the tradition which Scott also accepted (though, as it would appear from his occasional apologies, not entirely without misgivings), and we cannot make it a matter of serious reproach that she did not show the discretion of later artists in ringing down the curtain on the most effective situation and leaving the subsidiary issues to resolve themselves in the imaginations of the readers. But it was entirely inexcusable that she should invariably fail to realise the opportunity of making emotional capital out of the supreme psychological moment of her *dénoûment*. Where the principal theme was avowedly the ripening of sentiment and affection by mutual influence between the two characters whose eventual union completed the story, it was a serious error of judgment, if not a lack of artistic courage, which led her always to relapse into frigid narrative at the very point where the leading persons of the drama should have "taken the stage", and admitted the audience to their fullest confidence through the direct impression of living speech under the stress of strong emotion. In *Mansfield Park* what could have been more interesting than a vivid transcript of the scene where Fanny's long-cherished love was first made known to Edmund? But, to use a theatrical term, all this business was done "off", and we merely get a formal intimation that it duly took place. In *Pride and Prejudice*, also, when Darcy renews his offer of marriage after the chastening of his pride, and we are on the tiptoe of expectation to know exactly what Elizabeth will say, how disappointing when the author steps in between us and her characters in the following sentence expressed in perfectly correct but thoroughly undramatic phrases:—

"Elizabeth, feeling all the more than common awkwardness and anxiety of his situation, now forced herself to speak;

and immediately, though not very fluently, gave him to understand that her sentiments had undergone so material a change since the period to which he alluded, as to make her receive with gratitude and pleasure his present assurances ".

Even in the delineation of character, where Jane Austen's chief strength lies, there is one shortcoming that should not escape critical notice. It was inevitable that, writing as she did before the era of organic science, she should betray what we must now hold to be an incomplete conception of the part that is played by the forces alike of heredity and environment in the formation of character. It would be idle indeed even to suggest such a standard if we were merely estimating her historical significance, but when we are asked by Mr. Augustine Birrell to regard her achievement in fiction as greater than that of George Eliot, not relatively to her time but absolutely, we cannot but remember that while the later writer's creations seem all to be *accounted for* in the destiny of their descent and their surroundings, the earlier novelist too frequently presents us with characters that bear no definite relation to their circumstances. All careful readers of Jane Austen's books must have been perplexed by discovering wide differences not merely of temperament but of general tone and type among members of the same family, or between parents and their children, which are not sufficiently explained to make them easily credible. Of course such cases frequently occur in real life, but the artist should illustrate the general truths of nature rather than her exceptional freaks, and the neglect of this maxim, though it should be little noticed in any single novel, may become marked when the writer's work is regarded as a whole.

It is by her gallery of portraits that Miss Austen will live. There is hardly a figure in her books that is not instinct with life; scarcely ever is there any uncertainty or inconsistency in the drawing. She has been accused of exaggeration in some of the characters that are held up to ridicule, but it can scarcely be said that her portrayal of any of these becomes actual caricature. Nor is it possible to agree with the stricture of Sir Walter Scott that the prosing of the foolish people is apt to become tiresome. Indeed the only risk which the author runs of wearying the readers by over-elaboration of analysis and lack of movement in the dialogue, is rather in regard to the characters that are meant to win our sympathy, who sometimes take themselves more seriously than modern taste can find patience to approve. Yet on the whole how admirable these principal figures are! Considering how little opportunity her scheme afforded for introducing variety of circumstance, it is wonderful how much individuality she has been able to impart to her different heroes and heroines—if one may use such terms in reference to stories that tell only of familiar situations and personal interests. It is true that the young men are not all equally worthy of the delightful partners that are mercifully accorded to them, but when we remember how unsuccessful most novelists have been with their youthful heroes, how commonly they have mistaken the conventionally faultless for the truly ideal, we shall be glad to do justice to the memorable achievement of this unpretentious artist. With her heroines she has been happier, and most of these, if not all of them, have a sure place in the select number of original and delightful creations whose existence forms one of the chief pleasures in the life of the imagination. It is in the figure of Elizabeth Bennet that the novelist has put forth all her powers, and we may conjecture that in this maiden's lively but kindly satire, if not also in her more serious qualities, she represented Jane Austen's own disposition and ways of regarding life. In the narrative of the love between Elizabeth and Darcy, which ran smoothly only after a gradual ripening of character on both sides had enabled each to understand the other aright, we come upon an entirely new note in fiction, which has been sounded to wonderful harmonies by the greater artists who followed.

Chapter III.

Charles Dickens.

It is not wholly a matter of mere good fortune that the surroundings of men of letters should so often be well adapted to help them in what they are by natural constitution best fitted to do; the bent of their genius must in part be determined by their outward circumstances, but it will tend also to make a path for itself where it can find the fullest scope. But apart from this mutual reaction, there may be traced in the case of Dickens a special relation between his mental endowment and his experience of the world in his youth and early manhood. He had a marvellous faculty of minute observation which might almost take the place of a systematic education, and this power had an excellent chance of development in the many changes of scene and occupation which the thriftless habits of his father made necessary, while he was freed from the regular schooling which would in most instances be a most desirable preparation for a literary career, but which with him would scarcely have been a preferable substitute for the early struggle with difficulties that fell to his lot. The moral qualities which this hard and bitter conflict with the world developed in him were, as might be expected, self-reliance and energy and perseverance, and he did not succeed in escaping the defects of these qualities, notably self-assertiveness and an intolerance of all advice and control. Although he was an affectionate father, he seems to have ruled with a rod of iron in his own household; and it is difficult to believe that his separation from his wife after twenty years of married life on the professed ground of incompatibility of temper, was not mainly due to his overbearing disposition. A man of this type shows up better in adversity than prosperity, and it would have been safer for Dickens's happiness and for his moral reputation if his success had not been so rapid and so complete. The revulsion from poverty and hardship and obscurity to sudden wealth and consideration was too much for his spiritual equilibrium. He failed to preserve control of himself, and there is good reason to think that his jaundiced view of American life and institutions during his first visit to the New World was due to his own want of patience and temper under the stress of physical weariness. Yet with all his failings there was much that was estimable, and from the accounts of his friends there must have been much that was lovable, about him. His flow of animal spirits made him a most agreeable companion, so long as he was not crossed in his wishes, and he was undoubtedly capable at times of great generosity. He must also be credited with a strong and genuine sympathy with all forms of suffering, and an unflinching courage in attacking cruelty and injustice whenever he found them, or thought that he found them. The shafts that he aimed at various social abuses through the medium of his books were not always wisely chosen, but they give undoubted evidence of a warm heart and a resolute spirit.

On the intellectual side, besides the miscellaneous preparation he gained unconsciously from his various early experiences, he had one course of special training which bore directly on his writing of fiction. His occupation with journalism was indeed so closely related to his later work as a novelist that it not only formed a natural introduction to it, but gave a distinct direction to the form of art which he adopted. It would scarcely be unfair to say that his place in literary fiction is that of a glorified newspaper reporter. He possessed in an intense degree all the gifts which should form the endowment of a special correspondent, and he was somewhat scantily provided with the qualities which are of comparatively little account in that capacity. His readiness and accuracy of observation in all that meets the eye amounted to genius, and its range was only limited by his opportunities. He knew little of the upper class of society, and therefore when he introduces Lord Verisopht and his companions, the picture fails to convince us of its truth. He knew little of the life of the labouring poor, except in certain unusual phases of London experience, and therefore when he tries to deal with it in *Hard Times* there is the same sense of unreality. But no one was ever better acquainted with the ordinary life of the lower middle class, and with such of the characteristic phases of Bohemianism as London offers to this class; and accordingly he is able to present this to us with the fullest confidence. Here his knowledge is admirably supported by his descriptive power. He writes for no special class of readers, and he knows instinctively what the general public wants to hear. He can judge with unfailing correctness what details will make the most vivid impression on the greatest number, and what will interest them most. He has always his hand on the pulse of the man in the street. His prose style also—in so far as it can be called a distinctive style at all—is that of the journalist. The words and phrases are chosen for their immediate effect, without any idea of a more subtle suggestiveness, and the pictures are highly enough coloured to appeal to those who cannot appreciate low tones or the refinements of light and shade. These qualities have had their fitting reward in a rapid and wide popularity, which is not likely soon to pass away.

In certain of the fundamental qualities of a great novelist Dickens was almost entirely lacking. His narrative and descriptive power, along with his keen sense of the broader kinds of humour, fitted him quite exceptionally for a writer of short sketches, such as those with which he began his literary career. *Pickwick Papers* has scarcely even the pretence of being a novel; there is no coherence either in the story or the characters. It was little more than convenience that caused the separate contributions of letterpress to illustrations to be bound up together, and though the author's subsequent works took the more pretentious form of construction, they yet remain in their essence mere collections of single scenes and passages. Their *motifs* are either so indefinite, as in *Dombey and Son*, that they offer no strong interest, or so particular in circumstance, as in *Nicholas Nickleby* or *Oliver Twist*, that their significance passes away, while the chain of incidents has seldom much plausibility, and is often wildly improbable. But the prime defect of Dickens was the lack of insight into character. The inner core of humanity was to him a sealed book. He looked all round it with remarkable acuteness of vision, and any obtrusive features he could reproduce with a rare fidelity; but he failed lamentably in the supreme power of endowing his figures with the individuality which does not overshadow their common heritage of human nature. The child's question, "Was he a good man or a bad man?", is easily answered in Dickens. Most of his characters are either decidedly good or decidedly bad; and there is a further distinction which equally well divides them into two broad classes. Whether they are of the good or the bad order, they have either an individuality so vague that it leaves no strong impression, or an individuality of the crudest kind, marked by the possession of a single quality, or it may be merely by some trick of manner or phrase. He could scarcely represent character except by caricaturing it. He too often sought to enter the world of reality through the doors of broad farce.

Dickens has been called both a realist and an idealist. This is what every novelist ought to be, but the dual character must be carried into every department of his art. With Dickens there was an unhappy alternation. In choosing his subjects, where an imaginative artist would have found some element of universal significance by which the facts around him could be transfigured, he was content to fetter himself to the necessities of representing—or misrepresenting—particular institutions. This is no praiseworthy realism. In his plots, where the impression of probability is the prime requisite, he was wildly imaginative. This is no praiseworthy idealism. In the characters, where everything depends on the success with which the real and the ideal can be blended, his failure was greatest; he imagined where he should have drawn from the life, and when he tried to idealise he entered the world of shadows. In one respect, however, Dickens had scope for the exercise both of his realism and of his undoubted imaginative power. In the descriptive matter with which he surrounded his stories he shows both faculties in a very high degree, and though for a novelist they are used out of proportion, they are great gifts, and are perhaps the chief secret of his power.

Some special criticism may be given to two of Dickens's novels that are generally ranked among his best—*Oliver Twist* and *A Tale of Two Cities*. Ruskin calls *Oliver Twist* his greatest work, and describes it as "an earnest and uncaricatured record of states of criminal life, written with didactic purpose, full of the gravest instruction, nor destitute of pathetic studies of noble passion". Now those who press, or even admit, the claims of fiction to justify and ennoble life, can surely have no ground for anything but satisfaction when a lofty aim is definitely avowed. But the "novel with a purpose" cannot demand

our approval on this ground without some scrutiny. The
highest services of art are attained not by aiming directly
at them, but by fulfilling her laws humbly and faithfully.
Moral influence is not acquired by those who obtrude
their mission in season and out of season. The aim of
a novel, like that of any other work of art, must be the
presentation of ideals, directly or indirectly by contrast.
Its power must be felt through subtle suggestion, not by
cut-and-dry precepts thrust down our throats. Art may
be the handmaid of morality, but she is not to be degraded to the level of a common drudge. Dickens failed
to recognize this distinction. He wished to be a moral
and social reformer as well as an artist, but what he
gained in the one capacity he more than lost in the
other. Even had his notions of reform been wiser
than they were, the immediate gain in impressing
them upon the public ear would not have justified the
means. In the interests of moral and social progress as
well as in the interests of art a protest must be raised
against the novel with a purpose. The schemes of
improvement which moralists and political thinkers de-
vise, can in fairness be presented for general approval
only on their own merits, set forth with whatever skill in
statement they can command. To take the public unawares through an irrelevant appeal to their feelings is
to use an unjust and mischievous advantage. Whatever
principles of conduct or methods of social practice are
still in debate among experts, are dangerous ground to
the artist. If he means to point a moral at all,—which
he would always be wiser to avoid—it should be one of
universal application. His business is to depict what
really exists, idealising of course, so as to submit it to
the conditions of his art, but not falsifying the picture in
the process, or in any degree straining the effect on the
side of his own conviction or feeling. This straining is
too evident in many of Dickens's books. Often it is in
harmony with the sympathies of his readers; sometimes

it is not; but in either case the attempt is to be condemned as inartistic and dangerous in principle. *Oliver Twist* offers an admirable illustration of this mistake. The *motif* consists of two parts. The author wished primarily to attack the administration of the Poor Law, and secondly, to draw a picture of criminal life. The former or didactic part he attempted to carry out in the grossly exaggerated poorhouse scenes, which may afford us amusement, but are too palpably overdrawn to bring any conviction. In the second part, where he had only the genuine artist's wish to represent what *was*, he is singularly successful. The criminal scenes may not be entirely faithful pictures, but they give a greater impression of reality than can be found in almost any other of his books. Nancy is certainly his nearest approach to a heroine, and Bill Sykes, if his wickedness is rather too unrelieved, is still more like a human being than almost any other character he has drawn. And the success is attained simply because in this particular instance he had no theory to illustrate, no lesson to enforce, no scheme to recommend.

As it happened, Dickens's attack on the Poor Law was not only out of place but was unjust and reactionary in its tendency. Three years before, there had been presented to Parliament the memorable Report of the Poor Law Commission, upon which all our subsequent treatment of pauperism has been based. It exposed all the terrible evils of a lax and careless system of relief, and showed the advantages of a stricter application of labour tests, and a more vigorous discipline in the workhouse. The aim of the legislation which arose out of this report was to discourage all dependence on national charity whenever there was capacity for self-help, and though this involved some occasional harshness in its administration, the spirit and methods of the new acts have been heartily approved by all sociologists. Dickens was no thinker, and, carried away by a misplaced sympathy with the pauper, he formed a hasty, superficial, sentimental opinion on the matter, and straightway set about confirming it by scenes and characters evolved out of his own imagination. Could anything be more mischievous? Fortunately for the result, he overreached himself, and failed to exert the influence he intended. But it was painfully bad art as well as bad social politics. Take the following scene, where the Board are bargaining with the chimney-sweep to take Oliver as an apprentice:—

" 'It's a nasty trade,' said Mr. Lumbkins, when Garnfield had again stated his wish.

" 'Young boys have been smothered in chimneys before now,' said another gentleman.

" 'That's acause they damped the straw afore they lit it in the chimbley to make 'em come down agin,' said Garnfield. 'That's all smoke and no blaze; wereas smoke ain't o' no use at all in makin' a boy come down, for it only sinds him to sleep, and that's wot he likes. Boys is wery obstinit, and wery lazy, gen'lemen, and there's nothink like a good hot blaze to make 'em come down with a run. It's humane too, gen'lemen, acause, even if they are stuck in the chimbley, roastin' their feet makes 'em struggle to hextricate themselves.'

"The gentleman in the white waistcoat seemed very much amused by this explanation."

And the Board, after beating down the premium, agreed to let the ruffian have the boy. Now this is all very good farce; but does the novelist wish us to believe that such a conversation was possible? In other cases where he has attempted a direct moral, Dickens has been even more ambitious and equally unfortunate. His greatest failure was in *Hard Times*, where he tried to deal with the whole immense problem of the relation between capital and labour. The worst feature of his attempt was that he had no solution to offer; he had only an unreasoning prejudice to support him, and his attributing all the virtues to the workers and all the vices to the capitalists amounts to little short of dishonesty. These things are a serious set-off against the benefit he may have done in calling attention to the cruelty in boys' schools, or the delays of the Circumlocution Office.

When we pass from the subjects of Dickens's stories to the mechanism of their plots we find little to admire and much to condemn. The most serious fault from the artistic stand-point is their lack of probability. In *Oliver Twist* the series of remarkable coincidences is perfectly absurd. When Oliver goes up to London and falls in with the pickpockets, the first person he comes across is the old gentleman whom he is suspected of robbing and who afterwards befriends him. This turns out to be his father's oldest friend. By a curious chance Oliver is captured by the thieves again and forced to take part in the robbery of a house in the country. He is caught, and the young lady of the house, who befriends him, turns out to be his aunt! Really this is too childish. We allow a novelist a good deal of freedom in arranging his incidents to suit his purposes, but if he cannot manage them in a more convincing fashion than that, the whole illusion is gone. Another unpleasant feature in Dickens's choice of incident is his morbid fondness for scenes of horror. This has been graphically pointed out by Mr. Ruskin:

"In the single novel of *Bleak House*" [he writes] "there are nine deaths carefully wrought out or led up to, either by way of pleasing surprise, as the baby's at the brickmaker's, or finished in their threatenings and sufferings, with as much enjoyment as can be contained in the anticipation, and as much pathology as can be concentrated in the description. . . . And all this, observe, not in a tragic, adventurous, or military story, but merely as the further enlivenment of a narrative intended to be amusing; and as a properly representative average of the statistics of civilian mortality in London."

As to Dickens's failure in drawing character perhaps enough has already been said, but it may be worth while running over the figures in *Oliver Twist*. Mr. Bumble and all connected with the poorhouse may be dismissed at once as not coming within the range of serious portraiture, and in Mr. Fang, the police magistrate, the caricature is carried, if possible, still further. The thieves seem drawn to the life, as far as respectable outsiders are able to judge, and Bill Sykes and Nancy are specially realistic. But the remaining figures are painfully devoid of interest. Monks, the villain, is a mere puppet, without form and void. The Doctor is of the well-known impulsive and benevolent order; Mr. Brownlow has less impulsiveness with equal benevolence and no more individuality, while his friend Mr. Grimwig supplies the inevitable peg to hang a catchword upon, which in this instance is unusually silly and vulgar. There remain the equally inevitable, and as usual wholly colourless, pair of lovers, in whom no one can feel the slightest interest, notwithstanding the author's desperate effort to get up an excitement over the heroine's falling seriously ill, for no particular reason that one can see except to remind us that she is there. A passage from the scene between the lovers just after the illness has subsided will bring out the unsubstantial nature of the whole affair, and will also serve to show the author's style in its worst phase of unreal sentimentality.

"I was brought here" [said the young man] "by the most dreadful and agonizing of all apprehensions, the fear of losing the one dear being, on whom my every wish and hope are fixed. You had been dying, trembling between earth and heaven. We know that when the young, the beautiful, and good, are visited with sickness, their pure spirits insensibly turn towards their bright home of lasting rest. We know— Heaven help us!—that the best and fairest of our kind too often fade in blooming. A creature as fair and innocent of guile as one of God's own angels fluttered between life and death. Oh! who could hope, when the distant world to which she was akin half opened to her view, that she would return to the sorrow and calamity of this!"

The only remaining character of importance, or rather, one should say, of prominence, is that of the boy who gives his name to the book. He is a mere lay figure, and he is so good that it is a great wonder he did not die young—killed for the market, as Ruskin says little Nell was. However, the author made up for this disappointment by introducing little Dick, another little boy, even gooder than Oliver, who did his duty properly by dying very young indeed.

But let us turn for a little to *A Tale of Two Cities*, a novel which, we are often told, is free from the author's characteristic faults, and from an artistic stand-point shows him at his best. There is a certain pretentiousness in the book, from its attempt to deal with the life of a foreign country at a memorable epoch removed from the writer's own time, and we naturally ask first with what success the historical spirit has been assumed. While we cannot say that any fresh light, or even any greater vividness, has been imparted to the scenes of the French Revolution to supplement the flashing pictures of Carlyle, we must yet frankly admit that, in so far as general description goes, Dickens has made good capital out of the stirring events of the period to construct an effective background for the imaginary incidents of the story. What we miss in the historical aspect is any adequate appreciation of the differences in type between French and English character, and the difference in tone of thought and feeling between the eighteenth century and the nineteenth. Dickens had neither the imaginative insight nor the power of dramatic conception that can alone make intelligible to us the conditions of an unfamiliar age and country, and in spite of the outward trappings and surroundings of the figures in this novel

we never feel that we get beyond the atmosphere of the
author's own immediate sphere of observation.

A *Tale of Two Cities* differs from the other novels of
Dickens chiefly in the unusual effort to concentrate
the interest on the fate of a small number of persons,
and this is a feature which can be heartily commended,
for it is one of his artistic sins to crowd his canvas with
figures that have no necessary relation to the main issue,
and in any case have too much attention drawn to them.
But it may be questioned whether in this book the circle
has not been unduly narrowed. The leading characters
are thrown so exclusively into each other's company that
we lose consciousness of their general social relations.
It is implied that in London at least they have each a
more or less independent life, and yet in no case is this
directly suggested, so as to give verisimilitude to the
portraiture. The character of Charles Darnay, for
example, is made perfectly colourless from the absence
of any social setting, and the scientific pursuits and
medical interests of Dr. Manette are assumed too casually
to convince us of their genuineness. This limitation of
the *dramatis personæ* has the further disadvantage of
obtruding the mechanism of the plot at critical moments.
Dickens was always remiss in giving a becoming air of
likelihood to his coincidences, and the fewer the threads
the more difficult it is to avoid the appearance of undue
influence in arranging the desired complication. In
illustration of this stricture may be mentioned first the
absurdly improbable meeting in the wine-shop, at the
crisis of the story, of Sydney Carton, Miss Pross, and
Cruncher, with Barsad the spy, each of them having a
previous knowledge of him quite unsuspected by the
other; and secondly, the far-fetched relationship of
Madame Defarge to the family wronged by the former
Marquis of Evrémonde. Such faults of construction
may be overlooked in the infancy of an art, but they
cannot escape notice when any critical standard is ap-

plied. In this connection it may be further said that the novel before us violates the dramatic unity of time somewhat too grossly. It is difficult to carry the interest of a story over even one considerable gap, and when its various scenes are distributed over a quarter of a century, the difficulty is almost insurmountable. A more accomplished craftsman would have introduced the earlier events either by incidental reference, or frankly by an introductory narrative, presenting the characters only in the final episodes, so that their outlines should not be blurred by the recollection of their earlier appearances.

If no greatness can be claimed for *A Tale of Two Cities*, either as an historical picture or as a well-constructed story, it cannot assuredly be praised for the excellence of its portraiture. There is not a single figure in the book that leaves any impression on the memory. The devotion of Sydney Carton, finding so dramatic a climax on the guillotine,- is of course an outstanding feature, but its pathos gains little or nothing from any sympathetic grasp of the character of the devotee. We may be ready to admit, as the author demands of us, that such types exist, where weakness of purpose destroys the usefulness of a life without making impossible a supreme act of heroism under the impulse of an ideal emotion; but we feel that in the present case the type has not been portrayed with such truth and subtlety that we cannot fail to recognise it. The figure of Dr. Manette has also a certain impressiveness due to his situation in the story, but it is surely incredible that anyone whom an imprisonment of eighteen years had reduced to a condition of imbecility, such as is represented when we first see him, should ever recover his faculties so completely as to carry on successful scientific research. The persons who are intended to express the fierce vengeance of the revolutionary mob are certainly not painted to the life. Defarge is vague and shadowy in outline, and the calculating patience and cold-blooded ferocity of his wife are too inhuman to be credible. The novelist was much more on his own ground in depicting Miss Pross, and Cruncher, and Mr. Stryver, but these are all conceived in the exaggerated vein that places them outside of serious art. Nor is the portrait of Mr. Lorry, the banker, drawn with sufficient consistency to be acceptable. The author may have believed it possible that a man might be absolutely engrossed in business affairs till about the age of sixty without forming any personal ties whatever, and then suddenly develop the most thoughtful sympathy and consideration for others in the most varied and trying relations; but it was his task to reconcile the earlier and the later portraits in the imagination of his readers, and in this he has signally failed. I have left the hero and heroine to the last, not because in contemplating them we can enjoy any sense of contrast with the want of success in the rest of the portraiture, but because they represent the culminating point of failure in the drawing of character. Never were there two figures, intended to fill the most prominent places in the drama, drawn more perfunctorily and conventionally. They are really not presented to us at all; we are practically asked to take for granted about them everything that is good, and so save the author the trouble of bringing them on the stage. In one way this is strange in so tragic a story, for Dickens would seem to have had a high opinion of his skill in emotional dialogue, if we may judge from the evident zest with which he indulges in it on occasion. But we can scarcely regret his abstention when we find how utterly lacking in artistic simplicity of style and in understanding of the heart he has shown himself in the few passages in this novel where he has attempted the actual transcript of a pathetic scene. Take the episode where Lucy, then a girl of seventeen, was taken to the garret to see the father whom she had thought dead, and whom long and close confinement had made almost as one dead. Instead of the few short, broken phrases full of natural feeling, which a young girl would have given utterance to at such a time, she makes a speech, such as she might have prepared the night before, or rather such as she might have had prepared for her by a professional orator. This is what she says. Note the involved periods and the rhetorical refrain.

"If you hear in my voice any resemblance to a voice that once was sweet music in your ears, weep for it, weep for it! If you touch, in touching my hair, anything that recalls a beloved head that lay in your breast when you were young and free, weep for it, weep for it! If, when I hint to you of a home that is before us, where I will be true to you with all my duty and with all my faithful service, I bring back the remembrance of a home long desolate, while your poor heart pined away, weep for it, weep for it! . . . If when I tell you, dearest dear, that your agony is over, that I have come here to take you from it, and that we go to England to be at peace and at rest, I cause you to think of your useful life laid waste, and of our native France so wicked to you, weep for it, weep for it! And if, when I shall tell you of my name, and of my father who is living, and of my mother who is dead, you learn that I have to kneel to my honoured father, and implore his pardon for having never for his sake striven all day and lain awake and wept all night, because the love of my poor mother hid his torture from me, weep for it, weep for it! Weep for her, then, and for me! Good gentlemen, thank God! I feel his sacred tears upon my face, and his sobs strike against my heart. Oh, see! Thank God for us, thank God!"

This passage brings up the general question of Dickens's pathos. And first we must note that it is very limited in subject, being too often founded on one special situation, the death of a child. In a tragedy of the *Barnaby Rudge* order, as described by Mr. Ruskin, there is of course no room for pathos at all, and into the region of sorrow and wrong that is worse than death Dickens has not much power to enter. Only the impressive figure of Mr. Peggotty searching for his little Em'ly saves him from being shut out of it altogether. Even death, which he describes so often and so fully and so variously, does not give him his opportunity, unless he has the help of every circumstance of sadness. The murder of Nancy, which might surely have given him an opening, is spoilt by touches in false taste; and we are really brought down to five episodes, where the same chord is struck—the death of a child. What indeed can there be sadder than this? But that is precisely why we blame the poverty of the artist who has only one string to his lyre, and cannot even play on that till it has been tuned for him to the necessary key. We have, then, the death of Dora, who is after all only a child, of Jo in *Bleak House*, of little Paul in *Dombey and Son*, of little Nell in the *Old Curiosity Shop*, and the visionary death of Tiny Tim in the *Christmas Carol*. In these five scenes Dickens has had very varying success. The two most famous—those of Paul and Nell—are pretty badly done, described with artificial and strained sentiment in place of simple natural feeling and artistic restraint. The deaths of Dora and Jo are very much better, nearly right, but still losing from over-elaboration. The only scene that is entirely successful is that of the fancied death of Tiny Tim, where the conditions of the dream set limits to its length, and gave indirectness to the description. This is surely a very poor record, for with the deepest elements of pathos already provided an artist of very moderate powers should have been able to use them with reasonable success. The great risk in such cases is the risk of saying too much, and this is the snare into which Dickens has almost always fallen.

In humour he stands infinitely higher than in pathos. Like his other qualities, this gift of humour is somewhat rudimentary in character, appealing rather to the natural sense of the ludicrous than to the rarer appreciation of the more subtle elements of mirth or the

delicate shades of irony and satire; but most of it is
quite genuine as far as it goes; and it appears in his
novels in a considerable variety of forms. Indeed there
is too much of it from the artistic point of view; it out-
weighs the serious elements in his fiction. We may
distinguish the different kinds as follows. There is
first the humour of incongruous situations, as when a
respectable elderly gentleman like Mr. Pickwick, be-
guiled into believing that he may prevent an elopement
from a young ladies' seminary, is discovered suspiciously
haunting the place at dead of night, and mistaken for a
robber. There are plenty of these comic incidents in
Dickens, and they are always well contrived and well
described. Next may be mentioned the humour of
exaggeration which is expressed in farcical incidents
and broad caricature of characters. This requires
greater skill, and Dickens has shown himself a master
of it, though he has spoilt almost every one of his
stories by introducing it out of place. He has been
specially blamed, and perhaps justly, for associating
clergymen with such scenes, as in *Pickwick Papers* and
Bleak House. It need not be held that the clergy ought
to have immunity from satire, but Dickens, having
made no attempt to deal sympathetically with the fairer
side of clerical life, had not earned the right even to
satirise them by legitimate means, far less to subject
them to gross caricature. Rising higher in the scale
of humour, we come to those cases where it lies in the
nature of the characters themselves, either unconsciously or consciously. Good examples of unconscious
humour are Mrs. Nickleby and Mrs. Gamp, the latter
of whom is a veritable creation, while by far the most
illustrious instance of conscious humour is the immortal
Sam Weller.

A novelist has still another opportunity for humour,
outside of incident and character, in the reflections which
he offers in his own person from time to time. Dickens

has not made much of this opportunity, his comments being rather serious than humorous, and not particularly impressive or valuable in any way. He was a man who felt strongly, and in general rightly, and who allowed his opinions to determine themselves, partly by his feelings and partly by the moral and religious atmosphere round about him. His convictions, in fact, were either conventional or sentimental.

It is difficult to see that he helped very much in the development of the novel as a work of art. He certainly widened its range by revealing the possibilities of London middle-class and low-class life in yielding suitable material, but he did little to deepen its hold on the realities of human character, and his influence was distinctly unfortunate in making the forms of fiction the vehicles of exaggerated satire. <u>His chief merit, after all, is the indirect one of making the novel a popular institution.</u> His work reached the masses, and continues to reach them, as no other literature of the same degree of excellence ever did before, or probably ever could. In this respect he paved the way for better things.

Chapter IV.

W. M. Thackeray.

Reluctance to have one's biography written may arise from two or three different causes. It may be modesty; it may be a sensitive shrinking from publicity; or it may be the consciousness that there is nothing heroic to tell. In Thackeray's case there was little need for modesty, for there were no great deeds to relate; and besides, he had the irritable hypersensitiveness which is scarcely consistent with true modesty. It is probably in the third of the above reasons, that there was nothing

heroic to tell, that we shall find the chief explanation
of the injunction to his daughter, and here we may gain
a real insight into the character of the man, and the influence of his life upon his work. No one knew better
than Thackeray himself that he was not a hero. He
was dissatisfied with life, and dissatisfied with himself;
and he had some reason for both. Discontent with the
actual may of course be one aspect of a high ideality
which presses on impatiently to better things. To some
extent this was no doubt the case with Thackeray, but
it is not the whole explanation. In his reflection of
human nature two impulses struggled for mastery. The
nobler element in his consciousness of general failure
expressed itself in a repentant optimism, a glorifica-
tion of such elements of good as his unideal characters
were able to show, while the less worthy side had
ampler development in what has been called his cynicism, wherein can be traced a half-unconscious attempt
to justify his own shortcomings by undervaluing the
possibilities of great achievement, and belittling the
significance of life. For certain misfortunes of his own
which tried his philosophy he was not directly responsible, or only partially so. The loss of his fortune when
he had only just reached manhood can scarcely indeed
be looked on as a serious disadvantage, for he certainly
needed the pressure of circumstances to make a path
for himself; and even if he failed at the time to recognise the event as a blessing in disguise, he may at least
have reflected that a part of the catastrophe was due to
his own gambling. No one could mete out heavy blame
to an inexperienced youth who was enticed into such
practices by accomplished swindlers like Mr. Deuceace,
but it is surely not too much to expect of the gambler
that he shall meet his losses like a man, even if they
have been brought on him by unfair means. In the
chief calamity of Thackeray's life, however, he can
fairly claim the fullest sympathy. The mental malady

of his wife, which broke up his home after a very few
years of happiness, was a blow of fate which could not
but greatly affect his whole view of life, and might
naturally darken and sadden his reading of the riddles
of human existence. But though it would ill become
those whose lines have fallen in pleasanter places to
speak pharisaically of the patience he might have shown
in bearing the misfortune, and the reasonableness he
might have possessed in refusing to judge the world by
the measure of his own hard lot, we are entitled to ask
whether any chastening discipline was wrought on him
by his great sorrow,—whether he faced it bravely,
making the best of his life as it was left to him, and
preserving a clear outlook on the realities of the world
around him. It is only with diffidence that one may
venture to pass a judgment on this matter in its personal aspect, for no full record of Thackeray's life has
been given to the world; but we have at least this safe-
guard against injustice, that what materials we have we
owe to his own family and to biographers in whom his
family had confidence. This circumstance has no doubt
another side. We are apt to be suspicious of records
and estimates that have been edited by friendly hands,
and to read between the lines beyond what is justifiable.
It is, to say the least, an unfortunate feature in Thackeray's case that the efforts of his friends have taken so
much the form of an apology. *Qui s'excuse, s'accuse*;
and we often need to pray to be saved from the excuses
of our friends. What Thackeray's apologists seem to
have felt to be chiefly necessary, was to vindicate him
from the implication that in his personal character there
was the same bitterness and cynicism and ill-humour
which many people thought they found in his books.
What the exact nature of this quality, as shown in his
work, really was, we shall have to consider later, but we
are concerned now with what is asserted about his life
and character. The burden of the defence seems to be

that among his intimate acquaintances Thackeray was "the most good-natured man alive". Even this statement, as we shall see, has to bear some qualification; but admitting it in full for the moment, is it a sufficient answer to the question as to how he bore the calamity which changed his life? Let us applaud him that his disposition was not soured, but is there no more to ask? Did he bear his cross manfully, assuming the responsibilities of guardianship, as far as he might, to his motherless children? The evidence is all the other way. For six or seven years after the separation from his wife he left his children to the care of strangers and lived a life about town, frequenting clubs and theatres and taverns. There is no suggestion whatever of any unworthy dissipation or vicious habits, but it is perfectly clear that Thackeray's method of living down his sorrow was that of a superficial self-indulgent man. He tried to drown his care in a whirl of the excitements he loved best. His tastes were too refined to lead him into the coarser gratifications of the senses, but the pleasure of being liked by his peers, or by his superiors in rank, the lazy enjoyments of comradeship in congenial society —these things became for him the chief end in life. For artistic purposes the experiences he thus gained no doubt stood him in good stead, but they were bought at a high price. To sell one's soul consciously for art is a sacrifice with a certain grandeur about it, but Thackeray was scarcely capable of this. He sold his for a mess of pottage, and the artistic reward, such as it was, came to him unawares. He was no doubt an affectionate father, in the sense that when he thought of his children at all, he thought of them kindly and sympathetically. His sensibilities were quick, if not deep, and we read of delightful little letters and little visits to his daughters in their childhood, which seem to disarm criticism of his serious relations with them. But there is surely something even in the tone of these letters which confirms the opinion that thoughts of his duty as a father were only occasional episodes in his experience, and that the exaggerated *empressement* in their expression was due to compunction for neglect. As this conclusion may seem to be strained, and the judgment too severe, the charge of emotional shallowness and self-indulgence must be supported by other evidence, still apart, however, from what may be drawn from his books. And first let us turn to his conduct in regard to Edmund Yates. It may seem scarcely fair to base an estimate of character on any single episode, but we may at least find corroborative evidence in the spectacle of Thackeray, then a man of position and fame, using all his influence to expel from the Garrick Club a young man who had published an ill-considered article on himself, and quarrelling with Dickens for exposing the injustice of such a course. If the mistake had been repented of and expiated, it should have been forgotten. As no redress was ever offered, and the incidental quarrel with an old friend lasted for years, Thackeray must be charged not only with a lamentable want of temper and dignity, but with a self-conceit and indifference to the feelings of others which led him into gross injustice. But the most trustworthy evidence is to be drawn from the annals of Thackeray's later years, when he was able to choose whatever manner of life he pleased. He then mixed a great deal with people of rank and fashion, and he must be held responsible for the influence which this had upon his character. He has been accused of snobbishness in this connection, but the charge is scarcely just. The evidence of his writings is quite enough to show that he was entirely above the littleness of respecting anyone more on account of his birth or social position. He had too keen an insight into reality to make such a coarse mistake as that. But what can fairly be laid to his charge is scarcely less serious. He valued his intimacy with the great, not from any false pride, but simply because it helped him to the social pleasures in which he found the main attraction of life. His chief desire was to have what the Americans call "a good time" and he deliberately bent his steps in the direction where he thought himself surest of it, without that regard to older and more worthy ties which a really great nature would have shown. The seriousness of this accusation is quite recognized by his apologists, but the way in which it is met by his biographer, Mr. Herman Merivale, is rather curious. Admitting that some of Thackeray's old friends found him changed towards them in the days of his prosperity, Mr. Merivale tries to array against these a number of other old friends who found Thackeray the same as ever. This reminds one of the story of the Irishman who, when he was charged with stealing a pig, and five witnesses swore they had seen him do it, undertook to bring fifty witnesses who could swear they hadn't seen him do it. It is not necessary to prove that Thackeray forsook all his old friends; if he neglected even a few of them because his time was too full of social excitements, then he must stand condemned. Miss Martineau may be using too strong a phrase in speaking of his "frittered life and obedience to the call of the great", but there is little doubt that towards the close of his life he was correctly described by several who knew him well, as "*blasé*", spoilt, weary, with overstrung nerves, and that his comparatively early death was mainly due to a prolonged disregard of the conditions of bodily and spiritual health.

Out of the mass of criticism on Thackeray's work two passages may be quoted. Dr. John Brown contributes the following estimate:—

"What a loss to the world the disappearance of that large, acute, and fine understanding; that searching, inevitable inner and outer eye; that keen and yet kindly satiric touch;

that wonderful humour and play of soul! And then such genuine originality of genius and expression; such an insight into the hidden springs of human action! such a sense and such a sympathy for the worth and for the misery of man! such a power of bringing human nature to its essence, detecting at once its composite goodness and vileness. . . . His specific gift was the delicate satiric treatment of human nature in its most superficial aspects as well as in its inner depths by a great-hearted, tender, and genuine sympathy, unsparing, truthful, inevitable, but with love and the love of goodness and true loving-kindness overarching and indeed animating it all. . . . It was his sense of an all-perfect good which quickened his fell insight into the vileness, the vanity, the shortcomings, the pitifulness of us all, of himself not less than any son of time. But, as we once heard him say, he was created with a sense of the ugly, the odd, the meanly false, the desperately wicked; he laid them bare; under all disguises he hunted them to the death." -

There are many to whom this will seem a perfectly just and admirable appreciation of Thackeray, but others will find the praise quite extravagant and the estimate altogether one-sided. Allowance must of course be made for a man of high sensibility and a most sympathetic nature giving utterance to the natural feelings of a personal friend immediately after the great author's unexpected death, but the candid criticism of those who are not under the stress of such an emotion will be expressed much more nearly in the following terms of M. Taine:—

"I open at random his three great works—*Pendennis*, *Vanity Fair*, *The Newcomes*. Every scene sets in relief a moral truth; the author desires that at every page we should form a judgment on vice and virtue; he has blamed or approved beforehand, and the dialogues or portraits are to him only means by which he adds our approbation to his approbation, our blame to his blame. He is giving us lessons; and beneath the sentiments which he describes, as beneath the sentiments which he relates, we continually discover rules for our conduct. . . . Of all satirists, Thackeray, after

Swift, is the most gloomy. Even his countrymen have reproached him with depicting the world uglier than it is. Indignation, grief, scorn, disgust, are his ordinary sentiments. When he digresses and imagines tender souls, he exaggerates their sensibility in order to render their oppression more odious. . . . Thackeray depreciates our whole nature. Almost everywhere, when he describes fine sentiments he derives them from an ugly source. Tenderness, kindness, love, are in his characters the effect of the nerves, of instinct, or of a moral disease. As to the love of the men for the women, if we judge from the pictures of the author, we can but feel pity for it, and look on it as ridiculous. At a certain age, according to Thackeray, nature speaks; we meet somebody; a fool or not, good or bad, we adore her; it is a fever. . . . He relates the history of this passion, as in Major Dobbin's infatuation for Amelia, like an intoxicated man grown sober, reviling at drunkenness. . . . It seems as though he said to his reader, 'My dear brother in humanity, we are rascals forty-nine days in fifty; in the fiftieth, if we escape pride, vanity, wickedness, selfishness, it is because we fall into a hot fever; our folly causes our devotion'. . . . To transform the novel is to deform it; he who, like Thackeray, gives to the novel satire for its object, ceases to give it art for its rule, and the complete strength of the satirist is the weakness of the novelist. . . . When in an ordinary novel the author speaks in his own name, it is to explain a sentiment, or mark the cause of a faculty; in a satirical novel it is to give us moral advice. That Thackeray's lessons are good ones no one disputes, but at least they take the place of useful explanations. A third of a volume, being occupied by warnings, is lost to art. Summoned to reflect on our faults, we know the character less. . . . The character, less complete, is less lifelike: the interest less concentrated, is less lively. . . . The author spoils the character in preaching to us; he does not animate beings: he lets puppets act. He only combines their actions to make them ridiculous, odious, or disappointing. . . . Among all these transformed novels appears a single genuine one, elevated, touching, simple, original,—the history of Henry Esmond, . . . where a powerful reflection has reproduced the manners of the time with a most astonishing fidelity. . . . The style of this work has the calmness, the exactness, the simplicity, the solidity of the classics. . . . The masterpiece is the character of Esmond. . . . It is to be remembered that Thackeray has produced no other; we regret that moral intentions have prevented these fine literary faculties; and we deplore that satire has robbed art of such talent."

The most striking point in this latter criticism, and one where we must entirely agree with M. Taine's judgment, is the distinction drawn between *Esmond* and all Thackeray's other so-called novels. *Esmond* is almost the only example he has given us of a work of art in fiction; the others are simply collections of moral essays or satires, strung on the thread of a story. If we are to judge the author's work as a whole, as an expression of intellectual force, we may of course allow the question of form to sink out of sight for the time, but that is not our stand-point here. We have to consider Thackeray simply as a novelist, and the gifts he may possess outside that capacity can only be taken into account in so far as they help or hinder the effect of those of his books which come before us in the guise of pure fiction. If, like Dickens, he chose his literary form more for the sake of gaining the public ear than because it suited the bent of his genius, his artistic sin has found him out, and his reputation must bear the penalty. If Thackeray had written nothing else in fictional form but *Esmond* and *Barry Lyndon*, and put forth all the rest of his work in the shape of essays and satirical sketches, his fame would deservedly have stood much higher than it does now. As it is, we must judge his books according to the form they profess, and submit them to the same tests as we have hitherto been applying.

Thackeray's subjects may be divided first into two classes, according to their period. Three of them—*Barry Lyndon*, *Esmond*, and *The Virginians*—deal with last-century life, and the other four—*Vanity Fair*, *Pendennis*, *The Newcomes*, and *Philip*—treat of his own times. Now it is a sound general principle that the artist should choose his subjects from contemporary life, but curiously enough the two novels of Thackeray's which have been named as alone worthy of being called finished works of art, both belong to the historical class. Are we to suppose, then, that Thackeray was ill-advised when he sought to represent the life around him, and that his case is an exception to the rule? On the contrary, it may be held that the powers he showed in *Esmond* might have been displayed to even greater advantage in dealing with the more modern subjects, if it had not been for a circumstance more or less accidental. Or rather, the same faults of conception and method which defeated the impression his great intellectual gifts might have produced in the contemporary novels, would also have spoiled *Esmond* and *Barry Lyndon* if it had not been for the accident that these stories are told in the first person. We may call it an "accident", but probably Thackeray was at least partly conscious that he was wise in subordinating his own too obtrusive individuality to the dramatic necessities of this literary form. One proof of the correctness of this explanation lies in the fact that the remaining historical novel, *The Virginians*, which is not told in the first person, is far less successful, and is disfigured by many of the faults of the more modern novels. Our judgment must be, then, that Thackeray, while he was admirably fitted by scholarship, by sympathy, by capacity for careful research, to treat of the eighteenth century in fiction, was not less qualified in these respects, and was even better qualified in others, to deal with the nineteenth century, and that it is not the choice of *period* that is at fault if *Vanity Fair* is to be ranked below *Esmond*. In his case, the advantages of painting contemporary manners rather than those of a bygone age would have been even greater than usual, for he had a faculty of minute observation scarcely inferior to that of Dickens himself, and supported by more interpretative insight. If he had only been content to draw what he really saw, without distorting or selecting the images to make them illustrate his one-sided lessons!

Like Dickens, Thackeray wisely restricted himself mostly to those aspects of life with which he was most familiar, namely, in his case, the upper middle and higher classes of London society; but if the limitation was judiciously determined by his experience, the experience itself was somewhat narrow, and not of the kind most fertile in interest. It is by no means the whole or the best part of English life that is represented by the upper circles of London society; and perhaps if Thackeray's outlook had been wide enough to take in the sounder and more essential elements of our national character, he would have had less occasion to introduce that over-abundant satire which betrayed his artistic instincts.

The mechanism of his plots is generally rather primitive and crude, usually taking the form of recording the personal history of a central figure, the various incidents forming a chain of his successive experiences, and often having little more than a chronological sequence. Where there is any attempt to introduce a mystery, as in *Pendennis*, it is not managed with any peculiar care or skill. In short, it may be said that Thackeray, like Scott, cared little for his plots, and depended on other elements for his success. But though the absence of a central *motif* is to be condemned, it must be admitted that the incidents of Thackeray's stories are not only well described, but seem to follow each other so naturally that any lack of care in their arrangement is scarcely felt. This is a high, and deservedly high, tribute to Thackeray's narrative power, which would serve the purposes of his art admirably if it were not so constantly interrupted by his tendency to moral disquisition.

Turning now to the characters of his novels, we must

first consider the all-important question, Are they real? Are they drawn to the life? This is not the only question that is to be asked, but it is the first. If the characters fail to impress us with a sense of their reality, as is the case of the great majority of Dickens's creations, they are condemned at once. How is it with Thackeray in this respect? M. Taine has pointed out how great the temptation is to a satirist to exaggerate the features which best illustrate his lessons, and there can be no question that in many cases Thackeray has not been able to resist this temptation. In every one of his novels, *Esmond* not excepted, there are figures which are simple caricatures. But his sins in this respect are not to be compared to those of Dickens. The figures in Dickens have either an exaggerated and unreal individuality, or they have practically none at all; he was quite without the gift of lifelike portraiture. In Thackeray, on the other hand, the caricatures are exceptional, and are mostly found among the minor figures, with whom the author did not think it necessary to be careful. No writer ever possessed in a higher degree than he the power of drawing certain types of character with convincing fidelity to nature. If only his range and depth had been equal to his clearness of vision and his faculty of vivid description, we should have had in him another Shakespeare. Unfortunately there are few novelists whose power is so restricted in its scope, and penetrates so seldom below the region of superficial motives. He was only at his best when he was drawing knaves and fools. Even where for decency's sake he has to represent characters that his reader can admire, it is the incidental weakness in them that excites his interest and that he takes pleasure in describing. The estimable qualities may be vouched for by the author, but they are rarely displayed in the action. It is not only that the characters whom we dislike, or despise, or disapprove of, are out of proportion to the number of those whom we can respect. That is a further point. But the worst of it is, that even when the latter are on the stage they are too apt to walk through their parts in a perfunctory manner, leaving no definite impression behind them. When we think of one of Thackeray's novels, which of the *dramatis personæ* is it whose image most readily occurs to us? Take *Pendennis*, which represents a fair average of his work. It is not Laura, or Warrington, or even Mrs. Pendennis that we recall most vividly. It is that excellently drawn embodiment of worldliness, Major Pendennis; or the false, shallow-hearted, sentimental flirt, Blanche Amory; or the supercilious, selfish coxcomb, Arthur Pendennis; or the feeble-minded boor, Harry Foker; or the disreputable fire-eating Irishman, Captain Costigan. It is the doings of these contemptible people, not one of whom touches the ideal at a single point, along with the follies or villainies of Clavering, Altamont, Fanny Bolton, Huxter, Morgan, &c., that Thackeray depicts *con amore*, and that take up the great bulk of his bulky volumes. He shirks telling us what his good characters do and think and feel, as far as he can, and we seem scarcely to understand them any better at the end than at the beginning. There are people who go into raptures about Laura. She is very well as far as she goes, but there is nothing remarkable about her. The scene where she repulses Pendennis's first half-hearted offer of marriage is excellently described, but there is surely nothing very heroic in the position she takes up. One would be sorry to think that most girls of ordinary good sense and good feeling would not have acquitted themselves quite as well. Besides, Laura forfeits her claim to be considered a true heroine by marrying Pendennis in the end, immediately after she had got him out of a scrape which his worldly ambition and unscrupulous selfishness had brought him into, and in which he richly deserved to be left. It may be added that this view of Laura is fully confirmed in the glimpses we get later of her married life in the *Adventures of Philip*. Warrington is the single character in the book who wins our respect, but he is kept so much in the background that his presence scarcely leavens the whole. And if this is the effect of *Pendennis*, what shall we say of *Vanity Fair*? We shake our heads at the cynicism of Carlyle when he says, "There are 1200 million people in this world—mostly fools"; but if we are to believe Thackeray as he speaks to us in *Vanity Fair*, they are all fools together, or else they are knaves.

Thackeray was an immensely clever man and he had many of the gifts of a consummate artist, but in spite of all Dr. John Brown can say, his power of penetrating the highest secrets of human nature was fatally limited by his own spiritual shallowness, and his pictures of life are all irremediably falsified thereby. For it is not only that the good characters are faint and shadowy beside the contemptible ones. Even had they been equally vivid, there would still remain the entirely misleading proportion between the two classes. There are eighteen principal figures in *Pendennis*, and not more than two or three have any moral beauty whatever, while in *Vanity Fair* there is certainly not more than one. Is this an accurate reflection of life? But we shall be asked to turn to *Esmond* for the other side of the picture. While we must share Taine's admiration for the wonderful art shown on many sides in the plan and execution of *Esmond*, we cannot admit that in regard to the present point it forms any marked exception to the general tenor of his other novels. The figure of Esmond himself is certainly fine,—perhaps too fine, considering that he paints it with his own hand. Thackeray called Esmond a "prig" himself, and there may be some truth in the epithet; but even if we grant that this was a modestly harsh judgment on the author's part, the fact remains that there is no other ideal character in the book. Lady Castlewood is certainly too faulty to be so described, and the most graphic and interesting parts of the story are undoubtedly the scenes in which such poor creatures as the three successive Viscounts Castlewood, Beatrix, the Dowager Countess, and the young prince, are on the stage. Nor is Esmond himself drawn with entire consistency. The transference of his affection from the daughter to the mother has been felt by many to be a serious strain on the sympathy, and there is another determining fact in his life which we must have even greater difficulty in understanding. That a man of his noble nature should have been fascinated by a heartless schemer like Beatrix is unfortunately nothing difficult of belief. What cannot be accepted in the picture is that his infatuation should have persisted for years in the absence of any illusion as to the girl's real character, or at least, that he should not have made the slightest effort to kill an emotion which his judgment condemned. Esmond constantly tells us that he saw through Beatrix completely from the first, but though he more than once forced himself to quit the country because of the hopelessness of his suit, it never seems to have occurred to him that a better reason for his taking that desirable step lay in the fact that he was degrading his affection to an unworthy level. Ethel Newcome is another puzzling character; her development seems either unnatural or badly described, for it is scarcely possible to reconcile her last state with her first.

To sum up on this point, it must be granted that while Thackeray was unrivalled in his power of representing all types of character on which it was possible for him to direct his satire, we must place against this great merit three serious considerations — his satirical habit often led him into caricature; he failed entirely in creating types of ideal beauty, lapsing always into vagueness or inconsistency; and finally in number and importance, as well as in truth to nature, the contemptible figures in his portrait gallery are so preponderant that the whole effect is an utter travesty of human life. In a novelist this is an unpardonable sin. The avowed satirist purposely limits his vision, and we accept his pictures with the knowledge that they do not represent the whole truth. But the artist in fiction stands in a different position. He professes to tell us what life is. If it is not necessary that every novel should be a synthesis, the sum of the writer's work must at least give us a reflection of reality that is faithful up to the measure of his capacity. Thackeray was either insincere, or he was blind to the greater part of those elements in life which all of us hold most dear. There is no writer whom it is more delightful to dip into in certain moods; he ministers so admirably to the innate malice of human nature. His books have indeed a more justifiable value than this; as a corrective to conceit, to self-deception, to excess of enthusiasm, his barbed words may often yield a wholesome moral tonic. But as a whole his novels do their readers the greatest disservice that lies within the possibility of any one man's influence upon others. They strike at the root of the noblest sentiment that can animate the human spirit; they would destroy man's faith in man. We never rise from his books with brighter hopes or quickened energies.

One respect in which Thackeray stands supreme among novelists is the perfect naturalness of his conversations. It was perhaps easier for him to attain this, owing to his dealing mainly with the superficial aspects of life, but it is a gift of the highest order, and one which few of the great novelists have possessed even in a moderate degree. In the mouths of his characters as well as in his own person, his style has many of the qualities of the very best prose. It does not rise to the passion and melody of the finest imaginative writers, but it is a model of ease, and purity, and grace. Having such a command of expressive language, and so keen a power of minute observation, it is somewhat strange that he should have attempted so little in the way of description. Very seldom in his novels have we any graphic picture of the outward surroundings of his scenes. The beauties of nature do not seem to have appealed to him strongly. He was a denizen of cities himself; London and Paris formed by far the greater part of his world, and the country was little more than an indefinite background, suggestive rather of dulness than pleasure.

That Thackeray was one of the chief literary figures of our century, and that his individuality has had a marked influence on the work of his successors, there can be no manner of doubt. As a painter of manners, as a satirist, a critic, a stylist, he takes a very high rank, but the qualities which enabled him to excel in these various capacities do not of themselves constitute a great writer of fiction. If he must also be called a great novelist, it is not because he possessed in an eminent degree the special gifts which form the chief glory of the artist, but that his genius in certain faculties which should be subsidiary to the main purposes of creative art, was so forcible as to make him largely independent of the forms of expression he adopted, and to cover his many and serious deficiencies. His influence on the development of the novel has been almost entirely indirect. Following Miss Austen and Dickens in drawing his material from contemporary life, he helped to widen the range by dealing with new phases of society. Following the same writers but reaching a higher success, he touched the limits of realism in dialogue. But he did little to help in guiding the art of fiction into its true channels. In his general methods he has fortunately had no imitators. He sought to turn his novels into vehicles of instruction, and the art he thus treated with indignity has revenged itself on him. With all his wonderful and manifold gifts he stands now in the history of fiction rather as a warning than as a model.

Chapter V.

Charlotte Brontë.

In no instance do we find a closer relation between the life and the work of an artist than in the history of Charlotte Brontë. Not only was there the general correspondence, which we are always able to trace, between faculty and opportunity on the one hand and actual achievement on the other. It was more than the mere turning of experience to artistic account; she put her very self into her books. She could hardly indeed have done otherwise, for it was not given to her to enter into the ordinary world of manifold interests, where material for the imagination to deal with lies in scattered abundance for the selection of the artist. Her lot was cast within singularly narrow limits; there is hardly any kind of restriction which did not press hardly upon her. Those who read the sad record of her short life can only feel wonder and pity that so good and tender a creature could be so remorselessly pursued by misfortune. It may have been little of a personal hardship, though it was undoubtedly an artistic loss, that her experience of the world was so entirely confined to a bleak and solitary Yorkshire village; she and her equally gifted sister Emily may have gained more in the inspiration of nature which they drew from the wild moorland scenery than they lost in their isolation from the centres of human energy. But in the conditions of their family life, in their school experiences, and in their efforts to make a livelihood, they seemed to be the victims of a cruel fate. The early death of their mother, the selfish, masterful temperament of their father, the weak and dissolute character of their only brother, and their struggles with poverty, gave the sisters a home which was lacking in almost all the elements of happiness; and whatever points of contact they had with the outer world seemed only to confirm the painful impressions of life so relentlessly borne in upon them. There are few who would not have sunk under the terrible load of sorrow which Charlotte had to bear when to all these trials was added the unspeakable grief of losing one by one the beloved sisters in whose sympathy she had found almost her only comfort; yet she never lost heart, never failed in the performance of the duties that lay clearly before her, never faltered in her faith to what was good and true.

It is little wonder that a nature which had the strength to triumph over such evil fortune should have possessed qualities remarkable enough to carry her surely into the temple of fame. It may perhaps be called a chance that her moral power was supplemented by a great natural gift of literary expression, but the peculiar merits of her books are too closely related to the character of her spiritual development under sorrow and trial to let us regard the combination of gifts in the light of a coincidence. She was a great novelist because she was a noble, heroic woman: of her it may be said with singular truth, that her creations sprang out of her heart.

It was only to be expected that what her work thus gained in intensity it should lose in breadth and in other elements of artistic excellence. It will be well to refer first to the limitations of her genius, because the final impression of our criticism should be one of high appreciation.

It has been said that she put her own life into her stories as no other writer in fiction has ever done to the same degree. It was not only that she painted almost exclusively from the life with which she came into immediate contact, but she interpreted all that she saw by the light of her own thoughts and feelings. She was no photographer of superficial appearances; she was able to penetrate into the souls of others because her own intensity of feeling gave her a deep sympathy with all keen enjoyment and suffering. She had not, however, the knowledge of the world and the breadth of culture which would have given the true perspective to her impressions, and we therefore find some want of artistic selection in her presentations. It is well for the novelist to draw on his personal experience, but all that he finds there will not be truly representative of life as a whole; he must beware lest he mistake the exceptional for the typical, and the narrower his experience is, the more careful must he be. This was the mistake Charlotte Brontë naturally made; her characters are too often portraits of actual people whom she knew, presented without the idealising touch which should have made them poetic without destroying their reality. This is clearly shown in the children that appear in her books. Her experience of child-life was curiously one-sided, and for the most part unfortunate, and in consequence her pictures are unnatural. There seems indeed to have been a want in her nature on the side of sympathy with children, and it is almost the only trait in her character that is not admirable. It was part of the irony of her fate that her first efforts at gaining a livelihood had to take the form of teaching, where no success is possible without a natural and abundant sympathy with children. It is scarcely possible that her experiences as a governess can have been so uniformly disagreeable as to account for her feeling, without presupposing some defect in herself. But this will not of itself explain the lack of reality in her child creations; they arise mainly from too exact a transcript of a narrow range of observation. It is difficult to believe that there is not some bitterness of caricature in the record of Jane Eyre's early life, drawn from her own and her sister's painful experience of the Yorkshire school to which they were sent; but even if it be a faithful reproduction of events that actually occurred, it is almost too highly coloured for the purposes of art. Taken alone, perhaps it might be justified as throwing light on the heroine's character, but when we place along with it the account of Pauline's childhood in *Villette* and the extraordinary sayings and feelings of the Yorke family in *Shirley*, we are obliged to decide that from natural incapacity Charlotte Brontë failed entirely to understand the natural healthy side of child-life. Her sisters and her brother, like herself, were all remarkably precocious, and the same may be said of the neighbouring family from which the figures of the Yorke family are said to have been drawn. From an artistic stand-point it is no defence that the characters were drawn from actual models. The actual is often ideally untrue, and it was so in this case. Here is an example of one of these children of hers, who are always grown up from their earliest years. Avoiding the preposterous Yorke family, who are confessedly drawn from the life, let us take the figure of Helen Burns in *Jane Eyre*. This young lady, who is in her thirteenth year, delivers the following harangue to her school companion, Jane Eyre, then aged ten:—

"What a singularly deep impression her injustice seems to have made on your heart! No ill-usage so brands its record on my feelings. Would you not be happier if you tried to forget her severity, together with the passionate emotion it excited? Life appears to me too short to be spent in nursing animosity or registering wrongs. We are, and must be, one and all, burdened with faults in this world; but the time will soon come, when, I trust, we shall put them off in putting off our corruptible bodies; when debasement and sin will fall from us with this cumbrous frame of flesh, and only the spark of the spirit will remain,—the impalpable spirit of life and thought, pure as when it left the Creator to inspire the creature."

And so on. This is only the first half of the speech, but it is more than enough to show how extraordinarily far from realism Charlotte Brontë could occasionally travel. For it is not only that the style is painfully inflated; the thoughts and feelings are hopelessly out of place. Helen Burns may really have existed; but if so, she was an infant prodigy whom we do not wish to see in a work of art any more than in real life.

It has seemed worth while to dwell on this matter because it illustrates a vice of method which is not confined to her treatment of children. In other instances as well there is the same apparently slavish adherence to actual experiences. In the eyes of some it somewhat spoils the impression of what is otherwise one of her finest creations, M. Paul Emanuel in *Villette*. Here it takes a rather different form,—that of an excessive realism. The character is described with such an unnecessary amount of almost trivial detail that we sometimes lose sight of its ideal features. And not only in character-drawing, but in method, the same fault appears. Many of the experiences of the two heroines who are understood in some degree to represent the novelist, namely, Jane Eyre and Lucy Snowe, are treated with too great fulness, so that we begin to fancy we are listening to them not wholly because they are of interest, but partly because they actually took place. A wider range of observation would have developed a greater power of artistic selection.

In regard to the sin of improbable incident, Charlotte Brontë is a pretty serious offender, nor is she free from the equally blamable one of providing melodramatic solutions of her plots, which enable the estimable characters to live happy ever afterwards. In illustration of the former fault it may be remembered that Jane Eyre, after leaving Thornfield, arrives as a homeless wanderer at the house of kind people who take her in and afterwards turn out to be her cousins; while Lucy

Snowe has remarkable coincidences of the same sort, arriving by chance at the door of the boarding-school she wished to enter, and afterwards finding that the young doctor, who was the first person she met in the strange city, and who turns up as medical adviser to the boarding-school, is the son of her godmother, whom she had left ten years before. These blemishes are no doubt of less account in novels where the main interest lies in the portrayal of character, but still they are blemishes and cannot be passed by. When the credulity of the reader is taxed to any extent there is a loss of illusion, and the total impression is weakened. The melodramatic device of tampering with the decrees of fate in order to leave the reader in good-humour is resorted to in too palpable and clumsy a fashion in *Jane Eyre*. The burning down of Thornfield Hall, which leaves Rochester a free man, is far too opportune to impose on a cautious reader, and the timely death of the heroine's rich bachelor uncle so as to make her independent is too gratuitous altogether.

There are other signs that Charlotte Brontë had not sufficiently learned her craft. There is a certain crudeness in the arrangement of her *dramatis personæ*. One character is often brought on the stage too evidently to act as a foil to another. Dr. Bretton is intended to contrast with Paul Emanuel, St. John Rivers with Mr. Rochester, and this subsidiary purpose weakens the interest in them for their own sake, not only to the reader but to the author herself, who does not seem to put forth her full power in their delineation. Then there are places where she treads on ground that she is not sufficiently familiar with, as in the group of titled personages at Thornfield Hall, whose insolence and vulgarity are entirely overdrawn.

It may perhaps be thought that if to all these adverse criticisms it be added that Charlotte Brontë had little sense of humour, and that her theory of life was inconclusive so far as it was not purely conventional, there will not be much left to say in her praise. But it is not difficult to prove that with all her faults and deficiencies she has a claim to a distinct place, and a high place, in the history of fiction. And first one or two passages of criticism may be quoted from the little book by Mr. Swinburne entitled *A Note on Charlotte Brontë*.

"If we may attempt some indication of the difference which divides pure genius from mere intellect as by a great gulf fixed, the quality of the latter, we may say, is constructive: the property of the former is creative. Adam Bede, for instance, or even Tito Melema, is an example of construction —and the latter is one of the finest in literature; Edward Rochester and Paul Emanuel are creations."

Swinburne then divides imaginative writers into three classes, describing the marks of each.

"Of the second order," [he says] "our literature has no more apt and brilliant examples than George Eliot and George Meredith. Of the third and highest, there is no clearer and more positive instance in the whole world of letters than that supplied by the genius of Charlotte Brontë. No living or female writer can rationally be held her equal in what I cannot but regard as the highest and the rarest quality which supplies the hardest and the surest proof of a great and absolute genius for the painting and the handling of human character in mutual relation and reaction. . . . The chief gift of which I would speak is that of a power to make us feel in every nerve, at every step forward which our imagination is compelled to take under the guidance of another, that thus, and not otherwise, but in all things altogether even as we are told and shown, it was and it must have been with the human figures set before us in their action and their suffering; that thus and not otherwise they absolutely must and would have felt and thought and spoken under the proposed conditions.

"Such wealth and depth of thoughtful and fruitful humour, of vital and various intelligence, no woman has ever shown,— no woman has ever perhaps shown a tithe of it. In knowledge, in culture, perhaps in capacity for knowledge and for culture, Charlotte Brontë was no more comparable to George Eliot than George Eliot is comparable to Charlotte Brontë in purity of passion, in depth and ardour of feeling, in spiritual force, and fervour of forthright inspiration. It would be little or nothing more or less than accurate to recognise in George Eliot a type of intelligence vivified and coloured by a vein of genius; in Charlotte Brontë a type of genius directed and moulded by the touch of intelligence."

There is a good deal in this criticism which must have entirely failed to commend itself to us. Mr. Swinburne's way of emphasising his praise of one writer by means of dispraising another is in itself far from satisfactory. Even apart from this, however, there is reason to be doubtful about the value of any estimate that is based on fine-drawn distinction between intelligence and genius, or between construction and creation. The term *genius* is one which people are accustomed to use by way of seeming to account for effects that admit of no readily-apparent explanation. The expression has been naturally applied to Charlotte Brontë, because her achievement seemed out of all proportion to her preparation; and there is some reason in applying it in such a case. The truth implied thereby is that intensity of feeling and quickness of sympathy may offer to the imagination a fund of material for poetic treatment not less abundant and stimulating than may be gained from a wide and varied experience of life. But it is indeed a lame conclusion to draw from this fact, that the possession of a liberal culture and a knowledge of the world necessarily detracts from the genius of those who can turn them to account in creative work. Some of the strangeness of genius may have disappeared in the latter case, but not one whit of its greatness: George Eliot had an emotional nature quite as deep as that of Charlotte Brontë, while in every other aspect of an artist's equipment she was head and shoulders above her.

But if we can do Charlotte Brontë no good service by

putting her into competition with her great successor, we can at least try to understand what are the qualities in her work which place her novels in the select body of literature that can never die, and give her a worthy place in the history of fiction. She shares with Hawthorne the merit of discovering the possibilities of what has been called the *motif*. She saw that in the relation between two people there lay a capacity for dramatic development which could scarcely be exceeded by the greatest wealth of incident or complexity of plot. It is true that, as we have seen, she had not the courage to throw aside entirely the more conventional properties of the novelist, but we have also seen that her stories lose more than they gain from these theatrical expedients. It is not the mysterious lunatic in *Jane Eyre* that enthralls our attention; it is simply the relation between Rochester and Jane. We are deeply interested in each of these characters by itself, and in close relation they move us many times more strongly. It seems so natural now for a novelist to depend on a situation of this kind, that we find it difficult to remember how entirely new the idea was when *Jane Eyre* was given to the world. Hawthorne's *motifs* were equally fresh and stimulating, but they were different from Charlotte Brontë's. He dealt mainly with the individual experiences of a human soul struggling with fate, while his English contemporary found her material in the action and reaction of two strongly-marked characters whose interchange of thought and emotion stirs our sympathy to its depths. It is this that constitutes the absorbing interest of her stories, and the discovery that such a firm foundation could be built with such simple materials was of the highest consequence in the development of the art of fiction.

It has been objected, and will no doubt be objected again, that Charlotte Brontë secured this unusually strong interest by attaching an importance to the passion of love which it does not possess, and ought not to possess, in real life, and which it is therefore wrong in a novelist to represent. But in the first place it may be fairly maintained that love, even in this restricted sense, is the most potent factor in human nature, and that if its significance is not realised in actual life as it is in fiction it is because reflection has been so largely and so unfortunately diverted from it. If this all-important element in the evolution of the race were in any adequate sense understood we should not have people marrying and giving in marriage in the hap-hazard and irresponsible and sordid fashion of our undeveloped civilisation. It is Charlotte Brontë's chief claim to greatness that she has ennobled the passion of love by triumphantly proving that it may be independent of physical attraction, and revealing its true basis in the subtle affinities of character. She has idealised love in the truest sense, by interweaving with its self-regarding instincts the golden threads of a spiritual and imaginative sympathy. We have all in some degree experienced, in friendship or in love, the unique delight of meeting a kindred soul whose whole being seems to vibrate in unison with our own. It is then that, in the words of Matthew Arnold:

"A bolt is shot back somewhere in our heart,
 And a lost pulse of feeling stirs again;
 The eye sinks inward, and the heart lies plain,
 And what we mean we say, and what we would we know".

If this mysterious feeling which reveals us to ourselves in the responsive sympathy of our spiritual counterpart, has in any degree been strengthened by communion with the ideal types held together in such a bond in the realms of poetic fiction, we owe a debt of gratitude for the precious gift to the creator of Rochester and Jane Eyre, of Lucy Snowe and Paul Emanuel, of Louis Moore and Shirley Keeldar.

The discovery of the possibilities of such a *motif* would have been of little avail, however, if there had not been in Charlotte Brontë an unusual power of conceiving and representing characters that are at once entirely lifelike and thoroughly interesting. Her portraiture was not always perfect. We have seen that it sometimes became caricature (as it certainly does in the description of the curates in *Shirley*), that in the case of children it was unreal and unsympathetic, that it was apt to err in a too literal transcript of insignificant peculiarities. Even her successes are not always beyond reproach. Fairfax Rochester has been called a woman's man, and it is perhaps true that there are some traits about him that are not entirely drawn as if from within. But as a whole he forms one of the most striking individualities in fiction. We follow all he says and does with the closest interest, knowing that he will constantly surprise us, but also knowing that every fresh revelation will be consistent with what we have already heard. We can have no deeper impression of reality and strength combined than to find our confidence uniformly justified in such a case. There is scarcely the same absolute success in her other heroes. Paul Emanuel certainly comes very near it, and Robert Moore is also thoroughly good, but his brother Lewis is a little shadowy, and his relation to Shirley Keeldar is not perfectly intelligible. There is indeed one mistake that runs through the relations of all the lovers. The assumption of authority on the part of the man, which the authoress supposed to be a proper attribute of the masculine character, and which she represents all her heroines as expecting and approving, is exaggerated till it approaches brutality. In Rochester it takes a specially ferocious form; in M. Paul it is an ungovernable temper; in Robert Moore it is a condescending superiority; in Lewis it is the privilege of a dominie. These are faults not so much in drawing as in the novelist's theory of the relations between men and women. They are to be regretted, but they can be allowed for without seriously interfering with the reader's enjoyment and appreciation. In her heroines Charlotte Brontë naturally achieves an even greater success. Here she had the knowledge of her own thoughts and feelings to guide her, and in two of her heroines, Jane Eyre and Lucy Snowe, she is understood to have largely reproduced not only her own mental experience but many of the scenes and events of her life. In Pauline and Caroline Helstone she drew partly from herself and partly from her sisters, while Shirley Keeldar is believed to be an idealised portrait of her sister Emily, as she might have been had fortune smiled on her. The two figures that most nearly represent the authoress herself are on the whole the most lifelike that she has drawn, and the interest which the novelist naturally takes in them is communicated to the reader. The two resemble each other rather too closely to attain separate and distinct individualities, but the model from which they are both evidently drawn is a perfectly definite as well as an entirely interesting character. She judged rightly when she put herself, literally as well as figuratively, into her novels. The portrait in each case is that of a girl of acute sensibility, made to be very happy or very miserable, but strong enough to bear either lot with firmness and self-control, in whom the discipline of early neglect or unkindness has caused a repression of feeling that might well have engendered bitterness, but has only intensified a noble pride and a stern sense of duty. It is a sad picture to be drawn from the life, this, for which the rule of conduct was the motto, "If you ever really wish to do anything, you may be sure it is wrong", but as material for imaginative treatment it could not easily have been surpassed. We follow the modest fortunes of this plain-looking girl with an absorbing interest, far greater than is called forth by the thrilling adventures of many a beautiful and romantic heroine. The secret of our sympathy lies in our consciousness of the intense capacity of emotion that underlies the calm face and self-contained manner, but it is a notable achievement of art to impress this consciousness upon us without departing from legitimate means of suggestion. Though in both cases the girl tells her own story, the reader is never bored by the confidences of the narrator, and no impression is left of egotism or undue expansiveness. But the most charming feminine characters are to be found, not in these autobiographical books, but in *Shirley*, in the person of the two friends, Caroline Helstone and Shirley Keeldar. Indeed the love episodes in the book are less interesting than the history of the friendship of the two girls. Caroline is perhaps the most charming of Charlotte Brontë's heroines, and this in spite of the fact that here the novelist has been decidedly less successful in endowing her characters with vivid natural speech. Some of the conversations between Shirley and Caroline are expressed in phraseology that is wholly out of keeping with the age and culture of the speakers. This must of course be distinguished from the much more serious error in a dramatic artist of making the characters *act* or *feel* in a way that is inconsistent with their general nature. Charlotte Brontë rarely makes that mistake, but in *Shirley* especially she allows them sometimes to talk more as the mouthpieces of the author than in their own proper persons. In spite of this, however, the relation between the two friends is very finely portrayed, and enlists our sympathies in a high degree. But notwithstanding the excellence of the chief characters, the book as a whole is scarcely equal to *Jane Eyre* or *Villette*. It attempts more. The canvas is larger, and the *motif* is wider, embracing not only the personal relations of the main figures, but the conflict of capital and labour in one of its striking phases. But the success is scarcely in proportion to the greater ambition, and there are more faults of detail than in the other novels. Some of the minor characters, such as Mrs. Prior and Mr. Yorke, cannot be believed in A slight but irritating blemish which runs through all Charlotte Brontë's books may further be mentioned as illustrating curiously the want of taste for which her narrow circumstances were responsible—namely, her constant introduction of French words and phrases where English would have done as well. She had learned French thoroughly during her stay in Brussels, which must have been in many ways the most exciting period of her life, and as her mind was full of it she could not help putting it into her books. It is a mistake to call this affectation; it only proves the absence of a perfectly sure taste.

A study of Charlotte Brontë's novels suggests the judgment that while in all of them there is much that is of high value and interest, there is only one part of one of them that leaves the distinct impression of unmistakable greatness, namely, the relation between Rochester and Jane Eyre. This may seem a small achievement on which to base security of fame, but it is not to be measured by the number of pages in which it is contained. It struck a new note in the history of fiction—a note which has added many grand and subtle harmonies to itself in the works of succeeding writers, and the sweetness and power of which will never die away.

Chapter VI.

George Eliot.

The most remarkable fact in the life of George Eliot is that she, alone of all creative artists who are known to fame, reached middle age without even suspecting the nature of her splendid gifts. This had a marked influence on the quality of her work, for though she came to the exercise of her special powers without having served any apprenticeship, she brought to the task a wealth of equipment which no other literary artist has ever possessed, and which served her purposes better than the practised hand of any professed story-teller. During the first twenty years of her life, spent uneventfully in the country, she was not only unconsciously storing up the material which she afterwards turned to such wonderful account in her pictures of rural manners, but also laying the foundation of that wide and rich culture which afforded so firm a basis for her artistic endeavours. In the next twenty years she had opportunities of enriching her experience by intercourse with many of the leading thinkers of the time, in science, philosophy, and social politics, and her union with George Henry Lewes, while it allowed free play to her emotional nature, gave her the constant stimulus of intimate contact with an active and original mind. Up to the beginning of her career as a novelist there can be little doubt that she enjoyed peculiar advantages of preparation, but whether her outward circumstances after this point were equally favourable to her life-work is not so certain. If in her later novels the reflective habit tended to encroach on her creative powers, this may in part be due to the comparative seclusion required by the indifferent state of her health. She had exhausted in some degree the material she had amassed in the

George Eliot.

earlier period when her lot was thrown among all sorts and conditions of men, and yet was forced to forgo the benefit of fresh and varied opportunities of direct study from the life. The sacrifice, however, was inevitable, and it is useless to lament it.

The essential greatness of her character may perhaps be most clearly recognized in the history of her attitude to religion. The narrow Calvinistic faith in which she was brought up was her only spiritual sustenance until she had reached womanhood, and she embraced it with the fervour of a strong nature in which independent thought had not yet awakened. When contact with the world of reason had given her a breadth of view in which the unsubstantial nature of the primitive doctrine she had at first accepted as essential truth became clear, she was left for a time in the anarchy of belief that with ordinary people has the effect of paralysing moral effort. But in her case not only was the perilous transition from one form of faith to another safely made, but there was no trace of the bitterness of spirit which is too often the accompaniment of religious disillusionment. If the world needed proof that a burning enthusiasm for all that is good does not depend on a belief in supernatural sanctions, and that tolerance reaches its ideal not in indifferentism but in the profoundest sympathy with every earnest endeavour of struggling humanity to understand the truth by which it lives, such proof could not find a more illustrious embodiment than in the life and character of George Eliot.

It is a somewhat hazardous matter to offer an estimate of comparative greatness, especially in the case of writers belonging to our own time when brought into competition with those of earlier periods. There are indeed two different standards which must both be taken into account, but the relative value of which is by no means agreed upon among critics. The final judgment on any author must represent a compromise between his historical significance and his absolute merit. The importance attached to these two elements will differ according to the point of view, but it may be suggested that among scholars the question of the intrinsic interest of a writer is apt to weigh too lightly in the scale. All honour to the pioneers, but those who lead the people out of captivity do not often themselves enter the promised land. In works of art especially, while the critic must never give up the historical stand-point in so far as it helps him to understand how the creations of genius arise, the paramount question is not so much how they came into being, as what they now are in themselves. There is very little question of originality nowadays. It is more profitable to ask, not who has done anything *first*, but who has done it *best*. Those are greatest who have learnt most from their predecessors.

In seeking a true estimate of George Eliot as a novelist we must beware of certain prepossessions. The time is not so long past when her works were regarded with prejudice on account of the shadow on her life, and there are still many whose repugnance towards her as the apostle of a new faith prevents them from judging her dispassionately as a writer of fiction. From such critics we naturally turn aside. But what is more surprising is the qualified tone adopted by others who are entirely free from bias of an irrelevant kind, and whose opinions indeed in most ways would rather dispose them to too favourable a judgment. I refer to such writers as Mr. Leslie Stephen, Mr. Frederic Harrison, and Mr. Henry James, who all knew George Eliot personally, and esteemed her highly, but nevertheless are very much afraid of praising her as a novelist. Mr. Frederic Harrison writes:

" Let us who love the art of George Eliot abstain, if only in obedience to her teaching, from all extravagance of eulogy. Certain that she belongs to the foremost intellectual forces of our time, and seeing that she is a novelist, some are apt to decide that she stands in the very front rank of the artists of the modern world. That is surely to claim a great deal too much. Cervantes, Fielding, Scott, of course, stand immeasurably apart and above, by virtue of their wealth of imagination, their range of insight into manners, and sympathy with characters of every type. Goldsmith, Defoe, Richardson, I think too, Sterne and Lesage, stand again in another class by virtue of their consummate art in producing, in some more limited field, images of pathos, humour, naïveté, or vitality, worthy in their own sphere of the mightiest master's hand. The place of George Eliot will doubtless ultimately be found in the group where we set George Sand, Balzac, Jane Austen, Dickens, Thackeray, and the Brontës. Judging her purely as artist, we can hardly hope that her ultimate popularity will quite equal theirs. That she was immeasurably superior to them all as thinker, teacher, inspirer of thought and purifier of soul, will perhaps be little disputed. As facile creator of types, painter of varied character, veracious chronicler of manners, she has not their range, vivacity, irrepressible energy."

Now as a critic of life and thought there is perhaps no living writer in whom greater confidence may be placed than Mr. Frederic Harrison, yet I submit that in the passage quoted his judgment is entirely astray. His classification of novelists seems to me almost grotesque, and can only be accounted for by presupposing his lack of interest in this department of art. But there seem to be special reasons why he places George Eliot virtually below all the writers he names, as a creative artist, and it will be worth our while to try to distinguish them. In the first place, like most scholars he is probably in fear of losing the true historical perspective, and errs on what he considers the safer side of overvaluing the older authors. In the second place, the value of George Eliot's philosophy and moral teaching has impressed him so powerfully that he has believed too readily what has been said by critics probably unsympathetic to such teaching, namely, that she obtruded it to the serious detriment of her art. And in the third place, he has been over-careful to avoid the partiality of a friend, and perhaps also unable as a contemporary to realise the outstanding greatness of one whose work was so quietly performed. "Can one of ourselves be really worthy of a place among the classics?" This is the unconscious feeling that has damped the appreciation of so many of our trustworthy critics.

I maintain that as an imaginative artist, or, in Mr. Harrison's own words, "as facile creator of types, painter of varied character, veracious chronicler of manners", she is to be placed in the very front rank of novelists, and that her total achievement in fiction is of greater present value than that of any other author. This contention must now be made good by applying the tests of true artistic workmanship.

In choice of subject we shall find that George Eliot has combined all the strongest points in the work of previous writers. The interplay of character which was first treated as a *motif* by Miss Austen and was turned to such excellent account by Charlotte Brontë, and the searching of the individual spirit which Hawthorne was the first to introduce,—these appear in their fullest development in George Eliot's stories, along with the many-sided views of life and manners and the effective treatment of moving incident which are characteristic of Scott, Dickens, and Thackeray. It is not of course implied that she surpassed each of these novelists in their strongest points, but only that not one of these elements of strength is wanting, and that she has found the secret of combining them in an artistic whole. Her predecessors had either worked on a large canvas which they were not wholly able to deal with successfully, or they had attained perfection of finish by narrowing their effort to a smaller scale. She alone has given us pictures that are conceived and executed in the grand style, and at the same time reach the highest degree of excellence in certainty and refinement of touch throughout their entire texture. In her choice of subject she naturally varied her scope from such simple idylls as the *Scenes of Clerical Life*, and the scarcely more ambitious but singularly beautiful tale of *Silas Marner*, to the lofty theme of *Romola*, and the large atmosphere of *Middlemarch* and *Deronda*; but, though there may be adverse criticism to make on minor aspects of treatment, it may confidently be maintained that she has shown no limitation of power in dealing with any form of subject, however narrow or wide its range. On whatever scale the theme may be, it is invariably chosen with the artist's eye for effects of ideal beauty. In the management of her plots, moreover, while it may be possible to find a flaw in one place or another, it will be readily granted that there are no such serious defects as may be found in the case of almost every other previous novelist, by means of which noble works of art have been disfigured and the illusion impaired. It may be that the marriage of Adam Bede and Dinah was a mistaken concession to the desire for a happy ending, or that the death of Grandcourt was too opportune to be wholly probable, but no one can urge that these are felt in any appreciable degree to weaken our interest and our belief in the reality of the story. The only novel of George Eliot's which seems faulty in design is one which in certain other respects may be called her greatest, namely, *Middlemarch*. It contains too many characters—there are fifty of them,—and the interest is distributed so as to affect the unity of structure, while the general impression it leaves is too pessimistic to be consistent with truth. It is not of course to be expected that the author should express her theory of life in every book, but the plan of *Middlemarch* seems to require a summing-up which shall hold the balance fairly.

That George Eliot had an unrivalled power of narrative is beyond dispute, but there is one criticism frequently passed upon her method which may be taken to contradict this, and may therefore be dealt with now. It is objected that the action is not allowed to develop itself, but is constantly interrupted by the comments of the author. Now what is the value of this objection? And first, what does it mean? One difference between a play and a novel is that in the latter the narrator fills up the gaps in the action or the dialogue by explanations which will advance the understanding of the story. The only admissible criticism here is that the comments of the author do not advance the understanding of the story. This is certainly true in the case of Fielding and Thackeray, and sometimes of Scott, but its justice cannot be admitted in the case of George Eliot. It cannot be maintained that she abuses her privilege, like Thackeray, in order to preach to the reader. She never tells you what you are to think of her characters; she lets them act, and she helps you to understand how they are thinking and feeling, leaving you to form your own judgment upon them. In other aspects of narrative capacity no defence is needed. It is not only that she has a firm command of vivid description of events, as in the fight between Adam and Arthur, or the arrival of Hetty's reprieve, but she can invest a simple story, such as that of Silas Marner or Maggie Tulliver, with a wealth of sympathy and imaginative tenderness that brings our hearts close to theirs and to her own. If this is not the supreme magic of the story-teller, where does it lie?

In regard to her drawing of character, attention must first be called to her almost unerring certainty. There may be dispute as to the consistency of one or two figures out of the whole number of her creations, but even were judgment to go against her in these cases it would detract little from our sense of her wonderful success. As has been said, there are fifty characters in *Middlemarch* alone. About a dozen of these are drawn life size, another dozen are not much less prominent, and the remainder are minor figures. But whether principal or subsidiary, there is not one of these fifty characters but is drawn with the most convincing accuracy and presented with unfailing judgment of their effect in furthering the action. Of what other novel of the same proportions could as much be said? Let us turn next to the variety of types she has portrayed. What shall we say of her heroes? Has she overcome the difficulties of presenting types of the *jeune premier*—types that are at once ideal, and human enough to be interesting, and distinct enough to be lifelike? She has not found a figure of this kind to be an invariably necessary element in her stories, and we shall honour her all the more for that; but it is enough merely to mention Adam Bede, Felix Holt, Tertius Lydgate, and Daniel Deronda, to see that she has been able to fill all the above requirements with very high success. There are people who find Deronda too good to be true, but at least his individuality is very distinct from the others, and there is little enough resemblance between Adam and Felix or Lydgate. Even more noteworthy among her characters of men are those that come more obviously short of the ideal in their nature or circumstances, but yet have qualities that command our sympathy or respect. On the higher level of this class come Mr. Gilfil, Mr. Tryan, Seth Bede, Silas Marner, Mr. Irvine, Philip Wakem, Mr. Lyon, Will Ladislaw, Caleb Garth, Mr. Farebrother, and Herr Klesmer; on the lower level are Tom Tulliver, Godfrey Cass, Harold Transome, and Fred Vincy; while we have besides, the powerful but sinister studies of Mr. Dempster, Mr. Bulstrode, Tito Melema, and Mr. Grandcourt. In these last-named figures George Eliot has shown that she can draw villains as well as heroes, but nothing could be further removed from the conventional villain of romance than these wonderfully subtle types of weakness or insensibility developing into brutality and crime. Of the four, Grandcourt is the most powerful; no more striking embodiment of absolute materialism in feeling and conduct is to be found in the whole range of fiction.

In her pictures of women we find, as we might expect, that her vision is no less keen and true, and her hand no less certain. Where else, except in Meredith, shall we find such a gallery of fair women? Esther Lyon, Janet Dempster, Dinah Morris, Maggie Tulliver, Mary Garth, Dorothea Brooke, Romola, are types of beauty that will never fade; yet how entirely different are they in almost every feature! And what a relentless yet sympathetic touch there is in the presentation of such less beautiful figures as Gwendolen Harleth and Rosamund Vincy—the latter a companion figure to Grandcourt in its utter heartlessness under a fair exterior.

It is one of the greatest charms about George Eliot's characters that they almost never fail to talk according to their nature. How many of our great novelists have fallen short in this important point, and how much the effect of their portraits has lost thereby in force and vividness! Scott, Dickens, Charlotte Brontë, succeed only at times in giving us a wholly natural dialogue, relapsing more or less frequently into stiffness and unreality; Jane Austen and Hawthorne never made such gross mistakes in this respect, but there is a certain formality and heaviness of tone running through almost all their conversations; while in considering the novels of George Meredith we shall find how unfortunately the true dramatic quality of his portraiture is obscured by a mannerism of style which cannot readily clothe itself in varied and appropriate forms of expression. Thackeray is the supreme master of vivid, natural speech; but if we cannot recognise in George Eliot's novels quite the same outstanding success, it is only just to remember that the conditions were not the same. It was comparatively easy for Thackeray to record natural conversations, for his range of vision was narrow and superficial. The more complex the relations of human beings are, the more subtle their ideas and emotions, the greater does the difficulty become of representing their intercourse by the ordinary forms of current speech. The scope of George Eliot's portraiture is wider and deeper than that of any novelist who had preceded her; and even had she been far less uniformly successful in her dialogue, she would have deserved credit for overcoming the new difficulties without conspicuous failure. How hard a task it was is very clearly shown by the contrast with George Meredith, whose depth of insight is equal to George Eliot's, and whose breadth of experience is even greater, but whose faculty of dramatic expression has proved unequal to his needs. On these grounds it may be claimed that George Eliot must be placed next to Thackeray among the greater novelists in regard to her skill in making her characters speak with a persuasive naturalness of manner. This is a claim of the kind which it is not easy to justify, for it is scarcely to the point to quote instances of her success. The test is necessarily a negative one; the question must be, how often or how markedly has she failed? There is no outstanding example of failure at all, and it would be easy to bring positive evidence that in all varieties of situation, in every possible relation of two characters, she has shown an undeniable power.

If there is any charm in the author's earlier books that is not to be found in the same measure in *Middlemarch* and *Deronda*, the explanation seems to be suggested in one of her letters, where she writes: "At present my mind works with the most freedom and the keenest sense of poetry in my remotest past, and there are many strata to be worked through before I can begin to use, artistically, any material I may gather in the present". Though the artist may put his fullest power into the expression of the thoughts and feelings that he cares for most, he can hardly hope to be free from some appearance of effort in dealing with themes that he is only in process of mastering. Art is conservative; and while it may find an occasional stimulus in fresh developments of life, it will ever be most at home in the beaten tracks, giving voice to the universal emotions. We may, indeed, be glad to overlook any incompleteness of form for the sake of the larger possibilities that are opened up in the reflection of contemporary manners and ideas; but that is no reason why we should not enjoy to the full the greater simplicity and confidence and spontaneity that mark the artist's treatment of more familiar aspects of life. We may yield to none in admiration for *Hamlet* or *The Tempest*, and yet take a more natural pleasure in *Romeo and Juliet* or *As You Like It*. When George Eliot had worked through the earlier strata of her material, and came to bring into the crucible her own transfigured beliefs and passionate moral convictions, we are inevitably made conscious of the new background, which throws out strong shadows of the intellectual and spiritual conflicts of the time. From this storm and stress the earlier stories, the *Scenes of Clerical Life*, *Adam Bede*, *The Mill on the Floss*, and *Silas Marner*, are comparatively free. In dealing with the scenes of her own youth she is able, out of the strength of her interest, to make us share in the vividness of her impressions.

In drawing attention to the special element in these novels that marked them out as a new departure in fiction, I may begin by quoting a memorable criticism by Mr. Ruskin:

"*The Mill on the Floss* is perhaps the most striking instance extant of the study of cutaneous disease. There is not a single person in the book of the smallest importance to anybody in the world but themselves, or whose qualities deserved so much as a line of printer's type in their description. There is no girl alive, fairly clever, half educated, and unluckily related, whose life has not at least as much in it as Maggie's, to be described and to be pitied. Tom is a clumsy and cruel lout with the making of better things in him, . . . while the rest of the characters are simply the sweepings-out of a Pentonville omnibus."

The greater part of this extraordinary judgment is strikingly opposed by Mr. Swinburne's criticism of the same book:

"*The Mill on the Floss* is on the whole the highest and the purest and the fullest example of her magnificent and matchless powers. The first two-thirds of the book suffice to compose perhaps the very noblest of tragic as well as of humorous prose idylls in the language, comprising, as they likewise do, one of the sweetest as well as saddest, and tenderest as well as subtlest, examples of dramatic analysis. . . . They go near to prove a higher claim . . . on the part of their author than that of George Sand herself to the crowning crown of praise, of 'large-brained woman and large-hearted man'."

There is not of course a direct opposition in these two criticisms, for Ruskin is speaking of the material and Swinburne mainly of the treatment. Yet if we admit the reasonableness of the latter's enthusiasm—and we may think it very little exaggerated—we shall find in it a sufficient refutation of Mr. Ruskin's real contention, which is that the characters were not sufficiently ideal to deserve artistic representation at all. If they were really as commonplace as we are asked to believe, it would be impossible for any treatment, however skilful, to invest them with the absorbing interest which they undoubtedly have for many people not usually satisfied with trivialities. But it will be well to consider this point a little further, for it lies at the root of George Eliot's achievement. It is one of her chief claims to greatness, as truly on the artistic as on the moral side, to have shown how widely diffused are those elements in human nature which call forth our sympathy and respect. To Dickens is due the merit of first introducing into fiction studies of genuine worth appearing in unpromising material, but he too often strained the evidence to suit his purpose, and in any case his endeavour was the comparatively easy one of distinguishing the good in characters outwardly forbidding or ridiculous. George Eliot's was the far harder task of showing that there is no human being, however humble or insignificant or commonplace, whose life is not a battle-ground of good and evil, of joy and misery, and may not therefore attract the sincere interest of all sympathetic souls. Apart from the immense service which her influence has thus rendered to the cause of social morality, this was a wonderful achievement in art, for she has thereby widened the range of imaginative presentation to an almost indefinite extent. In our search for the ideal we are no longer to be confined to types of wholly exceptional or superhuman greatness; the heroic element that lies unsuspected in the bosom of each one of us may be laid bare to the scrutiny of true sympathy. It is not true indeed that Maggie Tulliver's nature and circumstances were as ordinary as Mr. Ruskin asserts; but even if it were, his criticism would be unjust. What triumph in art can be more convincing than the transfiguring touch which turns the dross of ordinary human nature into the purest gold? Even if most of the characters in the book are below the average of intelligence and refinement, they are not exhibited to us, as in Thackeray's novels, that we may laugh at them or hate them, but that we may understand them, and recognize our kinship with them in the realities of their thought and feeling.

In the author's earliest stories there is little attempt at any intricacy of plot. Nothing could be simpler in point of incident than "The Sad Fortunes of the Rev. Amos Barton", and yet what could be a more effective *motif* than the ascendency gained by a clever foreign adventuress over a simple-minded clergyman of no unworthy disposition, but without the sympathetic perception to realise the sacrifice of his devoted and hapless wife? In "Mr. Gilfil's Love-Story" and "Janet's

Repentance" there is more variety of outward incident, and neither is without strong situations, but again the interest lies chiefly in the drama of an emotional and moral development that is rather apprehended through spiritual sympathy than by suggestion to the senses. The limits of these Scenes scarcely admit of full-length portraiture, yet how admirably drawn are the figures, even in the shortest of them! Though in "Amos Barton" and "Mr. Gilfil's Love-Story" we have studies of situations rather than of individuals, there is the utmost certainty of touch in every sketch. The pathos that lies in the fate of Milly Barton and of Caterina is generic in its nature; the fountain of our tears is reached rather through the universal than the particular. But how skilfully the half-tones are suggested in the figures of Amos Barton and Maynard Gilfil! There is surely true poetic realism in the picture of the latter in his declining years with the memory of his youthful romance as his most treasured possession.

So slender a framework was of course possible only in comparatively short tales, and when the author turned to a larger canvas in *Adam Bede*, it was necessary to attempt more elaboration. The novelist or dramatist cannot afford to neglect any opportunity of obtaining a wealth of effect that can be made to harmonize with his design. It may be that the general scheme of his work is not consistent with much variety of movement or subtlety of intrigue. The *Mill on the Floss*, for example, derives its power mainly from its singleness of aim. It might almost be called a study of one character thrown into strong relief by a somewhat neutral background. But a success of this kind cannot be repeated indefinitely, and the artist who works on a large scale must, as a rule, call to his aid all the resources that his medium permits of. *Adam Bede* was George Eliot's first attempt to work in broader effects, and perhaps it leaves some traces of what from a high standard would be considered an unpractised hand. It has been already suggested that the marriage of Adam to Dinah Morris was admittedly a concession to the conventional demand for a *dénoûment* in accordance with poetical justice—a concession made against the author's own judgment. Forty years ago the necessity for a "happy ending" was more imperative than it is now; our taste is becoming more robust. This is not to say that an unhappy ending is essentially more artistic than a happy one, but a reasonable standard of fiction requires that the final impression should be in keeping with the prevailing tone of the story. There is certainly something incongruous, after the sombre tragedy that centres round the fate of Hetty Sorrel, in the sound of the marriage bells at the close. Not that there was anything untrue to nature in this solution of Adam's history; only for the sake of unity of impression the curtain should have fallen a little earlier. Other faults may possibly be found with the structure of this novel. The incident of the reprieve arriving at the last moment is rather a cheap device for rousing excitement; but it is the safe appeal to the popular fancy that is shown in such easily conceivable, if not very probable, conjunctures of circumstances, that has helped to make this the most widely appreciated of all George Eliot's novels. It has of course sterling merits besides, even as regards the conduct of the narrative. Some criticism on points of detail it is scarcely worth meeting. One writer of repute declares the description of the fight between Arthur and Adam to be an offence against art. He would apparently hold that all such violent passages should take place off the stage. Surely this is the extravagance of squeamishness! Another critic of English fiction writes, "As with Scott all interest is subordinated to the dramatic, so with George Eliot all interest converges in the psychological". Now what is really meant by contrasting a psychological, with a dramatic, interest? Is there any necessary opposition between them? Those who think so would seem to associate dramatic quality only with violent gesticulations, loud shouting, and stamping about the stage. Even in the theatre nowadays, where there is naturally a closer appeal to the senses than to the imagination, a cultivated taste disdains the broad effects of melodrama, and finds its interest in the subtler indications of facial expression, tone, and by-play. Much more in the novel are we learning to recognise that it is in the mysteries of psychological development, in the delicate interaction of character, that the only true dramatic action is to be found. Outward events may still be the palpable signs of the inner progress, but they must ever tend to fill a less important part in relation to the emotional and spiritual changes that lie more and more open to imaginative insight. Let us say, if we please, that the power of Scott lay in his command of the drama of outward events, while that of George Eliot lay in the drama of the inner life; but let us admit that the one is as truly a question of dramatic quality as the other.

Adam Bede is a study of the relations between the sexes under two prominent aspects. The more obvious of these, the betrayal of Hetty by Arthur Donnithorne, need not detain us; for though the story is told with a wealth of pathos and a subtlety of insight into the hidden springs of action that give a distinctive character to an only too familiar tale, yet no entirely fresh ground is broken, and the lesson is not a new one. One charge, however, has been made against George Eliot in this connection which must not altogether be passed over. She has been accused of what is termed "moral pedantry" in allowing retribution to fall on wrong-doing with an inevitableness which, it is alleged, is not true to life. In reply to this objection it may be urged that any limitation in the freedom to select instances in point, which a rigid standard of realism would demand from art, should be defended by a clearer instance than this. It may be true that the wicked often flourish like a green bay tree, and that sin is not always followed by suffering either to the evildoer or to those whom he has wronged; but if there be one department of conduct where the lesson of self-restraint may fairly be enforced by encouraging an imaginative perception of consequences, it is surely in those relations of men and women where happiness is guaranteed by a steadfastness of purpose that is far removed from the promptings of vanity and passion.

The other aspect of this relation is shown in the study of Adam's love for Hetty. Here again we have no new situation; but nowhere else shall we find it treated with the same penetration and sympathy. The motive is best expressed in one of the author's memorable comments:

"Beauty has an expression beyond and far above the one woman's soul that it clothes, as the words of genius have a wider meaning than the thought that prompted them; it is more than a woman's love that moves us in a woman's eyes—it seems to be a far-off mighty love that has come near to us, and made speech for itself there; the rounded neck, the dimpled arm, move us by something more than their prettiness—by their close kinship with all we have known of tenderness and peace. The noblest nature sees the most of this *impersonal* expression in beauty, and for this reason, the noblest nature is often the most blinded to the character of the one woman's soul that the beauty clothes."

And again:

"There are faces which nature charges with a meaning and pathos not belonging to the single human soul that flutters beneath them, but speaking the joys and sorrows of foregone generations—eyes that tell of deep love which doubtless has been and is somewhere, but not paired with these eyes—perhaps paired with pale eyes that can say nothing; just as a national language may be instinct with poetry unfelt by the lips that use it "

We may be inclined to think that this apology for the man of strong nature who falls under the fascination of a pretty face, does not represent the last word that is to be said on the matter. But let us at least do the author the justice to recognise that she never seeks to hide from us the deficiencies in her hero's character that would in part account for his blindness. With all his nobility Adam Bede has just the touch of hardness and self-sufficiency that lay him open to the danger of serious mistakes in reading aright his own feelings and the subtler qualities of those around him; so that we are prepared to acquiesce to some extent in Mrs. Poyser's contemptuous deliverance:

"I know what the men like—a poor soft as 'ud simper at 'em like the pictur' o' the sun, whether they did right or wrong. . . . That's what a man wants in a wife, mostly; he wants to make sure o' one fool as 'ull tell him he's wise."

Turning again to *The Mill on the Floss*, we are confronted with Mr. Ruskin's strictures as to the unideal character of most of the figures, but even if this contention were absolutely just, should we not be glad to have so masterly a presentation and analysis, although the types are of the most ordinary kind? I do not say that Mrs. Tulliver, the harmless, helpless, but affectionate woman, whom her husband chose from among the others of her family "because she was a bit weak like"; or Mrs. Pullet, whose interest centred largely in illnesses, deaths, and funerals; or Mrs. Glegg, the strong-minded representative of the family traditions and sentiments in their purest form,—I do not say that these characters would of themselves be enough to justify the production of a serious work of art with any claim to give a true picture of life. In its larger

examples art must choose some ideal element for its
central theme; the partial or transient beauty that may
be disclosed in what is for the most part ugly and
sordid and contemptible cannot be relied on to animate
more than a restricted canvas, or the subsidiary scenes
of a larger unity. But this demand for the highest
kind of artistic interest in the central motive is surely
amply satisfied in the history of Maggie herself, whatever Mr. Ruskin may say, and even as a well-judged
relief from the prevailing sadness of the story, we
should welcome the fearless but kindly satire with which
the aunts and uncles are brought before us. But a
fuller justification still remains to be offered. The
humour of these episodes is only one of their aspects.
They are no mere artificial and incidental devices to
relieve the tension of the main interest; they stand in
organic relation to it. The whole inner meaning of
the story is to be interpreted in the light of Maggie's
struggle to live out a life that could not harmonise
itself with its predominant surroundings, and the pathos
of the conflict lies in the congenital antagonisms that
are involved in the mysteries of heredity. The "little
wench", as her father maintained, was a Tulliver, not
a Dodson, but the cruelty of circumstances compelled
her to grow up under the shadow of the social faith
embodied in the repressive instincts of Aunt Glegg.
The story contains the essence of George Eliot's ethical
teaching in the stress that is laid on the cultivation of
sympathy as the true well-spring of right conduct. In
her hands the importance which modern science attaches
to the effect of surroundings in determining the course
of life, gives a rule for the direction of sympathetic
energy. New vistas of influence are opened, boundless
possibilities of bringing happiness to those around us
whose environment we so largely form. Throughout
this book we find traced with almost passionate insist-
ence the misery of a young life cast in uncongenial

surroundings and wrestling with a hunger for unattainable joys of sense, of knowledge, of emotion. In the author's own words:

"There is no hopelessness so sad as that of early youth when the soul is made up of wants. . . . Maggie was a creature full of eager and passionate longing for all that was beautiful and glad; thirsty for all knowledge; with an ear straining after dreamy music that died away and would not come near to her; with a blind, unconscious yearning for something that would link together the wonderful impressions of this mysterious life, and give her soul a sense of home in it."

Who can read the sorrowful record of unsatisfied yearning, unbroken save by the yet darker shadow of a life whose fruition was but sacrifice, without a sense of quickened sympathy with all noble souls groaning under the bonds of circumstance, of more ardent resolve to do our part in "widening the skirts of light and making the struggle with darkness narrower"?

One further point must be referred to, connected with the general structure and characterisation of this story. It has been suggested that there is an incongruity between the determining act in Maggie's history and her nature as we had been previously led to conceive it. This adverse criticism is expressed in its strongest form by Mr. Swinburne. After praising the earlier parts of the novel, he goes on thus:

"So far all honour; but what shall anyone say of the upshot? If we are really to take it on trust, to confront it as a conceivable possibility, that a woman of Maggie Tulliver's kind can be moved to any sense but that of bitter disgust and sickening disdain by a thing—I will not write a man—of Stephen Guest's; if we are to accept as truth, however astonishing and revolting, so shameful an avowal, so vile a revelation as this, in that ugly and lamentable case, our only remark, as our only comfort, must be that now at least the last abyss of cynicism has surely been sounded."

What is implied by this tirade, and what has been asserted by other critics, is that there is a fatal inconsistency in allowing Maggie to act the part she did in the episode that forms the turning-point in the story,—her letting herself drift away with Stephen, shutting her eyes for the moment to the consequence.

As soon as we look below the surface of the situation we find that the act was supremely natural. Stephen Guest is not the abject creature Mr. Swinburne in his passion of indignation makes him out to be. He certainly possesses no unusual powers of mind or depth of character, but he represents admirably the average qualities of a specially masculine ideal,—good looks, gentlemanly manners, considerable culture, a sympathetic nature, and manly strength. These are the very qualities that would appeal most effectually to a girl like Maggie, starved as her nature had been of all emotional response to the strongest yearnings within her. We are not expected, as some would seem to imagine, to grow enthusiastic over the idea of her falling in love with Stephen; it is simply part of the sadness of her lot that it should be natural for her thus to throw herself away. We are meant to pity her here, as we are in her early sorrows, not only because the happiness she craved was denied to her, but even more because it was unworthy of her had she gained it. And if we grant that her sensibility might be powerfully impressed by a man who, however short of the ideal, yet embodied the qualities of strength and grace in which Philip Wakem was so deficient, is it not much more than conceivable that her conscience should have been partially lulled to quiescence for a brief season under the subtle influence of the situation? Surely there was ample atonement for approaching danger so nearly, in the noble strength of her sacrifice in the severest stress of the temptation,—ample enough to reconcile the final impression to our general conception of her character, and to make good an even stronger claim on our love and sympathy.

Silas Marner relates itself to *Adam Bede* and *The Mill on the Floss*, dealing with the life of rural England in the period that ended within the author's own experience, and choosing its motive from the broader and more general emotions. By critics of conservative temper it is generally held to be the most perfect of all George Eliot's novels. Though this judgment may be in part determined by theories as to the proper sphere of fiction which are open to question, we shall readily sympathise with the feeling on which it rests. There is a simplicity in the motive, and a harmony of treatment, that secure in a high degree that unity of impression which is perhaps the safest criterion of a true artistic success. It was undoubtedly a daring conception to make the bent figure and downcast features of the solitary weaver the centre of imaginative interest. Nothing could be further removed from the ordinary ideal of picturesqueness in the hero of a romance, yet how complete is the triumph of the author in absorbing our attention, and in rousing our sympathy for his cruel wrongs and his redemption from distrust and hopelessness! The material seems at first sight unpromising indeed, but how skilfully we are led to enjoy the subtle contrasts between the hard narrow life of the manufacturing town in which Silas was born and bred, and the no less narrow if more genial conditions of the rural district into which his wandering footsteps led him in his sad exile! It may seem strange enough that we should become so strongly interested in the fortunes of a poor craftsman whose range of vision and capacity were in no way beyond those common to his class, and whose surroundings were of the most restricted order; yet surely the elements of the drama were cunningly chosen. There has been no more delightful picture of the peasants of old times, to whom, we are told, "the world outside their own direct experience was a region of vagueness and mystery; to whose untravelled thoughts a state of wandering was a conception as dim as the winter life of the swallows that came back with the spring; and even a settler, if he came from distant parts, hardly ever ceased to be viewed with a remnant of distrust, which would have prevented any surprise if a long course of inoffensive conduct on his part had ended in the commission of a crime; especially if he had any reputation for knowledge, or showed any skill in handicraft". We may wonder at times what attraction there is to be found for us now in dwelling on a picture of habits and feelings so remote from the spirit of our own times, but it is a sufficient answer that the pleasure lies in the very strength of the contrast. There is an indefinable charm in the consciousness of a secret sympathy with limitations that are almost but not wholly outgrown in our nature. There is no presentment of the past that can move us so powerfully as that of a phase of civilisation which is practically continuous with our own experience. The blending of likenesses and differences offers a potent appeal to imaginative retrospect. The effective background of easy-going rural complacency brings into all the brighter relief the main theme of the book, which may be described in the author's words as a study of "the remedial influences of pure natural human relations". "In old days", she writes, "there were angels who came and took men by the hand and led them away from the City of Destruction. We see no white-winged angels now. But yet men are led away from threatening destruction; a hand is put into theirs which leads them forth gently towards a calm and brighter land, so that they look no more backward; and the hand may be a little child's." The story is so simple that there is little room for criticism of the action. The chief interest lies naturally in the spiritual change that is wrought in Silas, the blessed softening of the heart that had grown hard through cruel wrong and the lack of brotherly sympathy, by the demands of the little foundling on the dried-up fountain of tenderness. But in the subsidiary scenes and character there is much of George Eliot's most delicate workmanship. The most memorable passage in the book is perhaps the wonderful scene in the parlour of the "Rainbow", about which Mr. Leslie Stephen well says:

"One can understand at a proper distance how a clever man comes to say a brilliant thing, and it is still more easy to understand how he can say a thoroughly silly thing, and therefore how he can simulate stupidity. But there is something mysterious in the power possessed by a few great humorists of converting themselves for the nonce into that peculiar condition of muddle-headedness dashed with grotesque flashes of common-sense, which is natural to a half-educated mind."

The beauty and charm of the story, and its perfection as a work of art, have been universally admitted, but it is, of course, an effort on a restricted scale. It is more of an idyll than a drama of life, and though it may be as desirable to achieve success in the smaller as in the larger task, we must be prepared to accord no less admiration where the conditions are more difficult and the success less obvious.

Romola is a dividing point in George Eliot's career. In choosing a theme from another country and another age, and in seeking to clothe with the forms of art characters and events that are known to history, she entered upon an arduous and perilous task which could hardly fail to leave traces on her subsequent work. In her own words, she "began *Romola* a young woman and finished it an old woman"; and though we may not admit all that is implied by this phrase, we can hardly deny that the maturer wisdom, the keener sense of moral difficulties, the deeper spiritual penetration of the later novels, are accompanied by some loss of buoyancy and a less optimistic tone.

In considering *Romola* from a critical stand-point we must bear in mind the imposing scale on which it is planned. Though in one aspect we should be led to doubt whether the achievement has been complete, we may not therefore place the novel on a lower level than one like *Silas Marner*, where a simpler endeavour has been more perfectly carried out. There is such a depth of meaning, such a range of interest, such a breadth of purpose in the book that it claims to be judged by more than a single test. We may bow to the decision of such authorities as Mazzini and Dante Rossetti, when they say that the work is not "native", meaning that it does not accurately represent the true Florentine life of the fifteenth century, yet we may be convinced that it does something else which is quite as good, if not better. "But surely", it will be said, "an avowedly historical novel must not falsify history by giving wrong impressions of the time and place it deals with." Do we then expect to have a picture presented to us which would be accepted as genuine by the characters themselves or their contemporaries? That would be a wholly impracticable ideal. As I have already urged, one age and country cannot contemplate another without its vision being affected by the medium through which it looks. It is an essential part of the transfiguring power which is the special function of art that it should interpret the realities of its subject into a language which can be readily understood by those to whom it appeals. This rule may be difficult to apply with strictness, and it may be capable of abuse, but surely it cannot be ignored. It must not indeed be used to cover any lack of care and insight in filling in the broad outline of the material setting, or in reproducing the leading features of the historical characters and events that are handled. But no one can bring a charge of this kind against the author of *Romola*. She had applied herself with the greatest conscientiousness to the preparation in scholarship that was necessary for her task, and her extraordinary power of assimilation enabled her to take unusual advantage of the opportunities she secured. If the Florence she brings so vividly before us is not the veritable Florence of the fifteenth century, where are we to get a more trustworthy picture? With what are we to compare it? Who will maintain that the portrait of Savonarola is not a true likeness in its main outlines? After all, the opinion that *Romola* in its general tone and atmosphere is not "native"—an opinion often echoed by people very ill qualified to judge,—resolves itself into this, that the characters, or at least some of them, embody the sentiments rather of nineteenth-century English men and women than fifteenth-century Florentines. Now if this charge is well founded, it may be urged against every historical novel. There must always be something artificial in the re-animation of a remote phase of culture, and the artificiality will be most apparent in the outward forms of expression. Does anyone suppose that the Gurth and Wamba of the twelfth-century England discoursed to each other in the least degree as they are represented to have done in *Ivanhoe*? If there was no keen-witted barber in Medicean Florence whose tongue wagged like Nello's, no simple-minded contadina of sluggish temperament who prattled like Tessa, no noble girl whose pride and rectitude gave her the courage to utter great thoughts in pregnant words, even at the hazard of her own peace, such as Romola herself, then at least the world is richer by the creation of these types. There were certainly people there who *felt* more or less as they did, for there are such in every country and in every age. If their speech is not held to be "in the manner born", is it of much moment? The dialogue of fiction is of necessity idealised, even when the surroundings are familiar. Art must have still greater liberty when a bygone time is to be made to live before us. As I conceive it, the only admissible form which an adverse criticism of an historical novel might take, in regard to its verisimilitude, apart from the general accuracy as to persons and events, would be that the picture was not sufficiently vivid to produce an illusion. If this test be applied to *Romola*, I think there can be little doubt of a triumphant acquittal. Is there a single figure in the book that does not impress us with its reality? From the principal actors down to the most subsidiary there is not one that is either shadowy or blurred. Is not this a miracle of art, to bring on the stage characters of so great individuality and of such variety of type, that are sufficiently in keeping with surroundings that are unfamiliar to us, and at the same time are nearly enough akin to us to attract our sympathy?

There are many who hold *Romola* to be the finest of all George Eliot's novels, and there is a great deal to justify their choice. No other has such a variety of aspect, such a wealth of impressions. It may be used as an itinerary of Florence, so clearly does it bring before us the mediæval city. Again, it is a repertory of the characteristic manners and customs of the people, describing their feast-days and processions, their religious rites and their amusements. Then it is an authentic historical record of the larger movement of events, explaining the position of political parties in Florence, in Italy, and in Europe. Further, it offers a special study of the power and weakness of the Church in the career of the great reformer Savonarola. And still we have not come to the chief centre of interest in the work. There are two main themes, which shake themselves free from all historical trappings, and are recognised to be of permanent and universal significance. In the person of Tito Melema we have one of the most masterly psychological studies in the whole realm of history or fiction—a study which has the highest value as an illustration of the author's philosophy of life; while the story of the heroine, besides setting forth a character of ideal beauty, raises in a painfully interesting form certain social problems of great moment. These questions, however, are too large to be discussed at present, and I must be content with calling attention to the remarkable skill with which the general construction of the novel is managed. It is not enough in a work of art that there should be abundant interest in the material; there must be the keen eye for effect, the selective judgment, the wealth and readiness of resource to make the material plastic to the hand of the artist. No one has ever doubted the power of George Eliot to give us wise thoughts and noble lessons of life; few of her readers or critics have failed to do justice to her gifts of characterisation and expression; but it has sometimes been denied that she possesses dramatic skill in any notable degree. To such doubters may be confidently recommended a careful study of the construction of *Romola* simply as a narrative. Let them note the admirable contrast in the various groups as we find them at the outset of the story,—the blind old Bardo and his uncompromising friend Bernardo del Nero, representing the better side of the Florentine nobility, with its stern pride and appreciation of learning; the friends of Machiavelli with their keen interest in politics and their more sophisticated cleverness; the devotees and reformers of the Church as portrayed in the figures of Savonarola and Romola's brother; Tessa and her companions of the market-place, illustrating the substratum of *naïveté* and ingenuousness that forms the bulk of any community. Across these diverse but not incongruous groups the young Greek with the fatally smooth face and facile conscience is suddenly thrust by the combined force of the outward destiny of circumstance and the inner destiny of his own pleasure-loving, superficial nature, and this picturesque thread of connection, subtly woven with the various elements of the story, at once gives life to the picture. As a mere tale of adventure the book holds our interest from beginning to end, and when the dark shadow of Baldassarre, eclipsing the fitful brightness of Tito's fortunes, brings home to us the more terrible reality of his spiritual downfall, the imagination is stirred as it can be only when fiction offers an illusion akin to the impression of actual facts.

Tito Melema is perhaps the subtlest of all George Eliot's creations, and it is scarcely too much to say that the elaborate portraiture of a type at once so distinctive and so natural was a new achievement in fiction. We were only too familiar in the works of the elder novelists with the strong contrasts of hero and villain, all human nature being roughly classified as good or bad. It was a definite approach to a more realistic method when Thackeray, following the lead of Fielding, drew his heroes—I say heroes, for he had no heroines at all—with a sufficient amount of faultiness to appeal to our sympathetic consciousness of defects in ourselves. Other writers, again, have won our interest by bringing out the traits of goodness in characters that are essentially ignoble. All this, however, is simple enough, compared with the exhaustive study of a human being in whom the tendencies for good and evil are up to the time of trial so nearly balanced, that none could foretell with confidence what the issue might be. Tito could never have been a great or noble man; but if his lot had been easier, if no exceptional moral difficulties had crossed his path, he might easily have sustained his part in the world with as much credit as the most of us. And this is not simply because his baseness would never have been discovered; it would really not have existed, except in that form of latent possibility from which none of us can claim to be free. And here it is that the power of the portrait lies in its appeal to our imagination. Though we may hope that Tito was to some extent exceptional in his desire to slip away from everything that was unpleasant, we hardly dare at any point to feel absolutely certain that the same temptation would not have found us equally wanting. It is, as the author reminds us, "an inexorable law of human souls that we prepare ourselves for sudden deeds by the reiterated choice of good or evil that gradually determines character. . . . There are moments when our passions speak and decide for us, and we seem to stand by and wonder. They carry in them an inspiration of crime that in an instant does the work of long premeditation."

The subtlety of the story lies in the masterly analysis of Tito's impulses and mental processes at each stage of his career. If the spiritual degeneration that even a single false step will initiate were at once palpable to the consciousness, we could trust to a healthy reaction of the whole nature that would prompt to repentance and reparation. But the danger of relying on any such guarantee is made clear to us. Even when in the stress of circumstances he had failed to choose an unselfish course, he was not, we are told, "out of love with goodness, or prepared to plunge into vice; he was in his fresh youth, with soft pulses for all charm and loveliness; he had still a healthy appetite for ordinary human joys, and the poison could only work by degrees. He had sold himself to evil, but at present life seemed so nearly the same to him that he was not conscious of the bond. He meant all things to go on as they had done before, both within and without him; he meant to win golden opinions by meritorious exertion, by ingenious learning, by amiable compliance; he was not going to do anything that would throw him out of harmony with the beings he cared for." We know how vain this moral self-complacency was found to be in a nature that had no memories of self-conquest and perfect faithfulness from which he could have a sense of falling, and the whole sad story that touches each one of us so nearly, may be summed up in the simple but moving words in which Romola years afterwards holds out the terrible warning to the youthful Lillo:

"She had taken Lillo's cheeks between her hands, and his young eyes were meeting hers.

"'There was a man to whom I was very near, so that I could see a great deal of his life, who made almost everyone fond of him, for he was young, and clever, and beautiful, and his manners to all were gentle and kind. I believe, when I first knew him, he never thought of anything cruel or base. But because he tried to slip away from everything that was unpleasant, and cared for nothing else so much as his own safety, he came at last to commit some of the basest deeds—such as make men infamous. He denied his father, and left him to misery; he betrayed every trust that was reposed in him, that he might keep himself safe, and get rich and prosperous. Yet calamity overtook him! . . . It is only a poor sort of happiness, my Lillo, that could ever come by caring very much about our narrow pleasures. We can only have the highest happiness, such as goes along with being a great man, by having wide thoughts, and much feeling for the rest of the world as well as ourselves; and this sort of happiness often brings so much pain with it that we can only tell it from pain by its being what we would choose before anything else, because our souls see it is good. There are so many things wrong and difficult in the world that no man can be great—he can hardly keep himself from wickedness—unless he gives up thinking much about pleasure or rewards, and gets strength to endure what is hard and painful. . . . And so, my Lillo, if you mean to act nobly and know the best things God has put within reach of men, you must learn to fix your mind on that end, and not on what will happen to you because of it. And remember, if you were to choose something lower, and make it the rule of your life to seek your own pleasure, and escape from what is disagreeable, calamity might come just the same; and it would be calamity falling on a base mind, which is the one form of sorrow that has no balm in it, and that may well make a man say, "It would have been better for me if I had never been born".'"

No less tragic than the record of Tito's spiritual degradation, and possessing an even more absorbing interest, is the wreck of Romola's happiness. In George Eliot's gallery of fair women, Romola is perhaps not the most attractive figure, but she is the most ideal, the most deserving of worship, and the most cruelly wronged. From the first moment of her appearance on the stage, when the fair-haired girl, "imagining the feelings behind the face that had moved her with its sympathetic youth", comes under the spell of Tito's glance, which had "that gentle beseeching admiration in it which is the most propitiating of appeals to a proud, shy woman, and perhaps the only atonement a man can make for being too handsome", through all the changing phases of misgiving and hope, of self-condemnation and rebellion, to her gradual awakening to her husband's entire alienation, we follow Romola's fortunes with a painful but resistless tension of sympathy, sadly acquiescing in the author's words that—"There is no compensation for the woman who feels that the chief relation of her life has been no more than a mistake; she has lost her crown. The deepest secret of human blessedness has half whispered itself to her, and then for ever passed her by."

It is worth noting that most of the critics of George Eliot's novels have found Romola herself cold and wanting in attractiveness. To my mind this is a superficial judgment, based on a defective sensibility to the finer spiritual relations. It may be granted that we cannot have the same sense of kinship with her as with Maggie Tulliver, but I hold that this slight feeling of distance ought to be no more than is inevitably caused by the wide differences of country and epoch and circumstances; if there is more, then the fault lies in our own moral obtuseness and conventionality. For when we ask what there is to support such an opinion or impression, we find that it seems to rest entirely on the view that no woman who passionately loved her husband could have been so critical of his conduct or so exacting in her ethical standard. This widely-spread feeling is thus expressed in Mr. Oscar Browning's volume in the "Great Writers" series, where he echoes, rather too closely for literary honesty, words that had already been used by Miss Blind:

"A remarkable feature in Romola's character . . . is the suddenness with which her passionate love turns to loathing when she discovers that Tito had been false to her. A woman with more tenderness might have urged him to confession and repentance, and prevented him from falling into his worst crimes."

This charge is none the less serious because it is made almost parenthetically, and as our acceptance of it involves not only our estimate of Romola's character, and of George Eliot's moral insight, but our judgment on one of the most weighty questions in the whole range of social ethics, it deserves some attention. And first I would remark how extraordinary a thing it is that those who take the responsibility of interpreting a great writer to the general public should hazard a pronouncement of the most serious character without even taking the trouble to read carefully the work they are criticising. Whether the critic's view could have been endorsed if the case had stood as he supposed, is very questionable; but we are not called upon to discuss the point, as, so far from there being any suddenness in Romola's estrangement, and so far from its being due to her discovery of Tito's infidelity to herself, the process was a long and gradual one, the various steps of which are described with most searching analysis. We are shown how from the very opening of her married life "her dream of happiness was not quite fulfilled", though the young wife did her very best to believe that the fault lay in herself, or in the nature of things, rather than in the selfishness and insincerity of her husband. But his neglect unconsciously made itself felt, and there had also been ample ground for suspicion as to his relation to Baldassarre before the time when his intimation to Romola that he had sold for his own benefit the library which it had been her father's sacred trust to them both to preserve for the city, roused her passionate remonstrance in the decisive words: "You are a treacherous man!" It was more than two years after this that Romola came to know of the existence of Tessa, and in the dreary time that intervened she had learned to understand her husband's real character only too well. Soon after the first revelation of his inability to realise the sacredness of any obligations that conflicted with his own interest, her keen moral penetration and fearless candour had torn aside the screen that with many of us is put forward by habit and prepossession and cowardice to baffle our scrutiny of the conduct of those nearest to us. In her misery and her hopelessness as to any possible renewal of true sympathy between natures so widely opposed in regard to the profoundest relations of life, she had thought of leaving her home, but had been recalled by the stern message of Savonarola:

"You are turning your back on the lot that has been appointed for you. You are seeking some good other than the law you are bound to obey. But how will you find good? It is not a thing of choice; it is a river that flows from the invisible throne, and flows by the path of obedience."

Romola's obedience to this command, and her patience under the perpetual trial of a bond that could be no true marriage of the spirit, will certainly acquit her of any light or selfish disregard of the claims of society to control domestic relations. Nor was she content with fulfilling the letter of the law. It is placed beyond a doubt that she made every effort to reach a reconciliation with Tito on the only basis that was possible to her, or that ought to be possible to any self-respecting husband or wife, namely, that there should be full and open discussion of their feelings and plans, without the ignominious pretence of peace when there was no peace. "Marriage", says George Eliot, "must be a relation of sympathy or of conquest." Are we to think the less of Romola because to her the alternatives were sympathy or separation?

We shall now hold her acquitted of the cruel charge that her love was killed at a blow by the discovery of the injury to herself as a wife, but we must remember also her persistent efforts for a prolonged period to make the best of the situation, in so far as this was consistent with truth and honour and fidelity to others. How are we to suppose that a woman of more tenderness would have succeeded in "urging her husband to repentance and saving him from his worst crimes"? The position is clearly stated in the following passage:—

"In the first ardour of her self-conquest, after she had renounced her resolution of flight, Romola had made many timid efforts towards the return of a frank relation between them. But to her such a relation could only come by open speech about their differences, and the attempt to arrive at a moral understanding; while Tito could only be saved from alienation from her by such a recovery of her effusive tenderness as would have presupposed oblivion of their differences. . . . He cared for no explanation between them; he felt any thorough explanation impossible; he would have cared to have Romola fond again, and to her, fondness was impossible. She could be submissive and gentle, she could repress any sign of repulsion; but tenderness was not to be feigned."

In the face of this, we are constrained to believe that the so-called "woman of more tenderness" could only mean a woman of a lower ideal, a woman who would sell her soul in blindness to secure a remnant of her privileges.

Felix Holt, which followed *Romola* at an interval of three years, is the novel of George Eliot's which is generally considered the least excellent by critical readers. In some quarters where the critic's judgment is usually entitled to respect, it has even been called a failure. After such masterpieces as *Silas Marner* and *Romola*, it would naturally be difficult to satisfy exacting critics, especially when the work represented to some extent a departure from the author's previous method. It may not have the romantic charm of the earlier stories, or the brilliance of *Middlemarch*, but it has more than one special element of interest to distinguish it, and the general quality of the workmanship is in no way inferior. Undoubtedly, if it had been the only fruit of the author's genius, it would have been enough to secure her immortality of fame and influence. There are two respects in which the book stands apart from its companions: it contains the fullest expression of the writer's social and political philosophy, and it has an unusual intricacy of plot. On the former of these, important though it is, it will clearly be impossible for me to dwell. Even the shortest exposition or criticism of George Eliot's social politics would raise wide controversial questions that cannot with advantage be treated incidentally. Until there is more general agreement as to the laws that govern the progress of societies, the value of any particular thinker's contribution towards the formation of sound political views must be determined according to those individual prepossessions and tastes about which, proverbially, there is no disputing. It must suffice to say, that in so far as Felix Holt, the Radical, may be accepted as the mouthpiece of George Eliot, her conception of social revolution was of a kind which the present so-called "labour party" would hold to be decidedly conservative. Dealing with the period of the first Reform Bill she is animated less by confidence in the benefits of political emancipation than by anxiety lest the people should find themselves possessed of a power which they have not learned to use aright. She has little belief in outward changes that are not accompanied by an inward regeneration, and would rather trust to moral and spiritual influences that are slow but sure, than to the more specious claims of socialistic reforms.

In regard to the second characteristic mark of this novel, the conventional and yet somewhat ambitious nature of the plot, we can understand how in the eyes of some of George Eliot's admirers this should seem to be a matter of regret. After the large and simple issues that were presented in *Adam Bede* and *The Mill on the Floss*, it may appear almost a declension to fall back on the recognized tricks of the ordinary novel-writer, and to try to stimulate interest by introducing the mystery of a disputed inheritance, with the plotting of unprincipled lawyers and other scamps. To this objection, however, it may fairly be replied that there can be no reason why the more sensational forms of intrigue should not play their part in a drama of life, as long as there is no undue reliance on them in proportion to the interest of the characters themselves. It is natural that with a more pretentious plot we should demand exceptional skill in the construction, but in the present case this condition is certainly fulfilled. There are readers who complain that the legal mysteries are not made sufficiently clear, but most people will understand them as well as there is any need for. And surely all will allow that there is no false sense of perspective; that the prevailing impressions we gain from the story do not concern the scheming of Jermyn or Christian, but the terrible penance of Mrs. Transome, the spiritual awakening of Esther Lyon, and the efforts of Felix Holt to realise his noble ideals. The main themes, here as in all the other novels, are taken from the very depths of the human heart, and the lighter web of superficial incident only serves as a material setting for the tragedies of the soul.

In regard to the vitality of its characters, *Felix Holt* is not to be placed below any of the other novels. It was a very difficult task to give a natural presentation of the hero, for the plan and purpose of the work required that he should expound his own views and aims in a way that is somewhat hazardous to a right impression. It is a decided triumph that the author has been able to convince us of Holt's earnestness and sincerity without conveying any suggestion of priggishness. There is really no self-sufficiency in the declaration that sounds the key-note of his character:

"'This world is not a very fine place for a good many of the people in it. But I've made up my mind it sha'n't be the worse for me if I can help it. They may tell me I can't alter the world—that there must be a certain number of sneaks and robbers in it, and if I don't lie and filch, somebody else will. Well, then, somebody else shall, for I won't.'"

The Rev. Rufus Lyon is a singularly interesting figure, and a noteworthy illustration of the author's sympathetic understanding of religious types of every variety. What always strikes one particularly in the delineation of the little minister is the admirably sustained naturalness of his manner of speech. The long sentences, which, in spite of their involved structure, always come out right in the end; the keen controversial habit which leads him to look at every side of his subject, however simple it may be, and yet never tempts him to any real digression; the half-formal but well-chosen terms with which he clothes even ordinary topics—all these qualities are so consistently blended in his conversation as to give a remarkable degree of finish to the portrait. An excellent contrast both to Felix and to Mr. Lyon is afforded by Harold Transome, the clever, fortunate, generous man of the world, whom one cannot help liking, in spite of his self-complacency, his lack of sympathy, and his insensibility to the finer emotions. In a work of art there is properly no question as to any difficulties that arise out of the special circumstances of the artist, but we may be allowed to wonder at the success attained by a woman of a secluded and scholarly life in the rendering of a character which in almost every respect was entirely foreign to her own.

I have reserved to the last any mention of Esther Lyon, whom many will consider to be the most interesting study in the book. Esther is not one of George Eliot's most impressive heroines; she has not the ideal features of Romola, or Maggie Tulliver, or Dorothea Brooke. She was, in the author's words, "intensely of the feminine type, verging neither towards the saint nor the angel": and when we are first introduced to her, before her nature was disciplined by the recognition of larger aims, she was faulty and decidedly human. She is described as having "one of those exceptional organizations which are quick and sensitive without being in the least morbid; she was alive to the finest shades of manner, to the nicest distinctions of tone and accent; she had a little code of her own about scents and colours, textures, and behaviour, by which she secretly sanctioned and condemned all things and persons. And she was well satisfied with herself for her fastidious taste, never doubting that hers was the highest standard." The story of how her innate nobility was gradually roused, and her whole being touched to finer issues, by the "supreme love that gives a sublime rhythm to a woman's life", through that "high initiation" that enables us to choose what is difficult,—all this is told with a moving charm that compels our sympathy at every point.

Middlemarch and *Daniel Deronda* stand apart from George Eliot's other novels, as at once offering distinctive features of interest and showing a culmination of power and achievement. The points of contrast with the earlier works have been generally recognised, but there is a difference of opinion as to whether the later characteristics represent a genuine artistic advance.

Even among those who admit the greater width of vision, the riper wisdom, the deeper intensity of purpose, there is a disposition to regard these qualities as attained at the sacrifice not only of the freshness of the earlier novels, but of other excellences that are even more indispensable to the success of a work of art.

There can be no question that these later works are planned on a grand scale, and this is not, of course, a matter of mere bulk. The dignity of *Middlemarch* is secured by its breadth of purpose, of *Deronda* by the loftiness of its theme. *Middlemarch* is a comprehensive picture of provincial life in England at the Reform period, and may thus be regarded as in some degree a sequel to the author's earlier works. It has been already suggested that the story is open to criticism on the ground of too great a diffusion of interest over the various groups in which the characters range themselves. There are perhaps too many figures to allow a complete unity of plan. As a matter of fact, we know that the work was a combination of two or more distinct subjects which the author had at first intended to treat separately, and though the blending has been accomplished with her usual constructive skill, we may doubt whether complete success was possible. There is, of course, a unity of place, as all the *dramatis personæ* belonged to Middlemarch and its neighbourhood, and their lots are all more or less interwoven in some form of relationship. But the bond is not always sufficiently close to give us a sense of the due subordination of all the minor effects and incidental episodes to some central issue. Mr. Bulstrode is the uncle of Rosamund, and the step-grandfather of Will Ladislaw, and the patron of Lydgate, and his conduct has at one point an important bearing on the fortunes of the main action; but with all that we do not feel that his personality is so intimately bound up with the development of the story as to justify the life-size scale

of the portrait. The same thing may be said of old
Featherstone, of Caleb Garth, of Mr. Farebrother, and
perhaps of one or two others. As individual character
studies they are full of interest and power, but as subsidiary figures in a drama they seem out of place.
There is no room for them in the front of the stage,
yet we cannot be content to regard them as merely
items of the background. Even when we restrict our
view to those who fill the chief parts in the story, we
are conscious of some lack of concentration. The best,
if not the only key to the meaning of the book as a
whole, is to look for its main theme in the history of
Dorothea. In this aspect we can find suitable positions
not only for Casaubon and Ladislaw, for Mr. Brooke,
Celia, and Chettam, but also for Lydgate and Rosamund, whose life-tragedy touches Dorothea's own experience nearly, both through its inner significance and
by the ties of outer circumstance. But we shall still
be at a loss to find a fitting place for the love-story of
Fred Vincy and Mary Garth, the special features of
which seem to have little relation, even in the way of
contrast, to the life-histories that illustrate what we
may suppose to be the central idea. It may be that the
conventional ending in the courtship of Fred and Mary
was intended to relieve the somewhat pessimistic impression of the book, but it is not well adapted for the
purpose. Though Mary Garth is a thoroughly likeable
girl, and attracts our interest strongly in spite of her
plain face and figure, we can hardly feel much sympathy for her partiality to Fred Vincy, who is a poor
creature, always whimpering over the difficulties that
he has not manliness enough to master, and content
apparently with an affection that is altogether independent of respect. There is indeed nothing untrue to
life in such a union. On the contrary, the story is
thoroughly typical, and it is told with all George Eliot's
usual skill, but we cannot see its significance where it

stands. Not only does it stir no enthusiasm to adjust the balance in our estimate of the happiness of marriage, which may well have been disturbed by contemplating the sorrows of Dorothea and of Lydgate, but it offers no lesson to supplement the main teaching of the book.

Indeed this is one of the very few cases where many readers will find it difficult to be convinced that George Eliot's summing up of the situation is conclusive. She surely sounds a note of undue complacency when she writes—

"Mary earnestly desired to be always clear that she loved Fred best. When a tender affection has been storing itself in us through many of our years, the idea that we could accept any exchange for it seems to be a cheapening of our lives. And we can set a watch over our affection and our constancy as we can over other treasures."

We may heartily bow to the wisdom and truth of this last saying, without admitting that the application is just. When ties have not yet been formed, it is surely a doubtful artifice to coerce the freedom of the heart by appeals from duty or reason.

The *motif* of *Middlemarch* is the same as in the *Mill on the Floss*—an appeal for pity and help towards all whose powers fail in due fulfilment owing to the lack of opportunity. It is the practical application of the scientific doctrine which, owing to the teaching of George Eliot and others, is revolutionising all our theories of social progress—the doctrine that our destiny is determined less by the nature we inherit than by the influences of our environment. In one aspect it is a lesson of resignation, but in a wider view it gives the greatest freedom to sympathetic ardour, and encourages a hopeful outlook for the future. If our power to alter our own lot is narrowly limited by the forces that surround us, at least we can all do something—some of us can do a great deal—to improve the lot of those who are near us, whose environment we help to form. If it be urged that in *Middlemarch* it is the less optimistic side of this doctrine that receives greater prominence, the objection is not made because of any indefensible notion that a novel should never give a picture of life that is predominantly dark. We may be entitled, indeed, to protest against any theory of the universe that we believe to be contrary to scientific and historical evidence, and when an imaginative artist like Tourgenieff discovers a background of pessimism behind all his creations, it is a legitimate criticism of his art to doubt the soundness of his philosophy. But the case is different with George Eliot. We know that she called herself a "meliorist", that is, one who believes that life may be made better than it is, and this confidence is visible enough throughout her books, especially in *Daniel Deronda*, which may be taken as her last deliberate utterance. If *Middlemarch* is an exception, then, have we a right to protest? Can we claim that a writer of fiction must present his philosophy in every work? Is he not at liberty to give utterance to what may be a passing mood, a partial truth? Before answering this question I would point out that this is not a matter of tragedy or comedy. Many of the greatest imaginative works—perhaps one might even say all of them—are full of the profoundest tragedy, but their tone is not therefore necessarily hopeless, or even desponding. To take an example from George Eliot's own novels, *The Mill on the Floss* is undoubtedly a tragedy, not only in respect of its pathetic ending in Maggie's death, but in its whole intention, as a transcript of a sad experience of life. But there is nothing in the heroine's history to beget despair of the future progress of the race, or the possibility of happiness. We recognise the causes of Maggie's misfortunes, and while we feel the necessity of the *dénoû-*

ment in the given circumstances, we not only see how such tragedies may to some extent be mitigated or averted, but we are stirred by sympathy to take our share in the work. With *Middlemarch* it is otherwise. The elements of tragedy there seem less due to untoward circumstance than to the nature of things. Besides, we may reasonably expect that in an extended and elaborate picture of provincial life, the good and the evil should be distributed in the same proportion as they exist in the world generally. Among all the fifty characters there are scarcely more than one or two of heroic mould, and even of Dorothea we must agree with the author that the "determining acts of her life were not ideally beautiful". On these grounds we can scarcely help feeling that *Middlemarch*, wonderful and brilliant as it is, scarcely reaches the true poetry of art. But if we can fortify ourselves against the bias of despondency in the final impression, there are valuable lessons that we may learn from it. The dominant note is the misery of an ill-considered marriage, which is illustrated in two terrible examples that have none of the qualifying features of recompense that may be traced in the chastening discipline of Romola, or the saving repentance of Janet Dempster, or the spiritual awakening of Gwendolen Harleth. And here it is worthy of note that George Eliot is the only great novelist who has attempted to portray with fulness the disappointments and failures of married life. The dignity of this task is well justified by her own words:

"Marriage, which has been the bourne of so many narratives, is still a great beginning, as it was to Adam and Eve, who kept their honeymoon in Eden, but had their first little one among the thorns and thistles of the wilderness. It is still the beginning of the home epic, the gradual conquest or irremediable loss of that complete union which makes the advance in years a climax, and age the harvest of sweet memories in common."

It is rather remarkable that even Mr. Meredith, who has done so many original things, for years made no departure from the conventional practice of leading up his story to the marriage of hero and heroine, leaving us with the vague but devout belief that they must have lived happily ever afterwards. Of course, we are familiar enough with the tragedies of married life in the pages of French novelists, but there it is almost invariably a mere record of jealousy and intrigue, not the keen searching analysis of the subtler causes of friction and discord which may wreck the peace of households without any open scandal.

In the two memorable cases before us, there is no ultimate good to be discovered out of the evil, to those who suffer. Neither Dorothea nor Lydgate gains anything by the terrible mistake that each has made. Dorothea's life is saved from irretrievable ruin only by the accident of Casaubon's death, and even then his baneful influence on her fortunes must be held responsible for the reaction that determined her marriage with Ladislaw,—a union that, with all its recompenses, was scarcely an ideal destiny for her. It is true that so bountiful a nature as hers could not altogether fail in its fruition, in spite of meagre opportunity. In the author's summing up we are told that "Her finely touched spirit had still its fine issues, though they were not widely visible. Her full nature . . . spent itself in channels which had no great name on the earth. But the effect of her being on those around her was incalculably diffusive; for the growing good of the world is partly dependent on unhistoric acts; and that things are not so ill . . . as they might have been, is half owing to the number who lived faithfully a hidden life, and rest in unvisited tombs."

We may not undervalue the good of a life like Dorothea's, even if it fulfilled but a remnant of her high hopes; but though her bitter experience may have wrought in her some additional grace, her nature was not one that needed to be purified by suffering, and we miss the consolation of feeling that her loss was in any palpable degree turned into gain. With Lydgate the case is even worse. There could be no sadder picture than that which is conveyed in the few sentences that sum up his destiny at the end of the story. No merciful stroke of death came to relieve him from the millstone he had hung about his neck. The tragic irony of fate was all the more keenly present to him that his career was outwardly prosperous. He gained an excellent practice among fashionable patients and was generally looked upon as a successful man. But "he always regarded himself as a failure; he had not done what he once meant to do".

The errors of Lydgate and Dorothea are lessons of warning, not only enforcing the general importance of wise upbringing and of the influences that determine the formation of sentiment and opinion, but having special reference to the supreme significance of that act which above all others requires care and deliberation, and yet is commonly undertaken under the stress of ill-considered impulse,—the act of marriage. Dorothea's education had been narrow and conventional. She is described as "a girl who had been brought up in English and Swiss Puritanism, . . . whose ardent nature turned all her small allowance of knowledge into principles, fusing her actions into their mould, and whose quick emotions gave to the most abstract things the quality of a pleasure or a pain". Then she had no mother to give her good counsel, and her lot was thrown in idleness and uncongenial surroundings. What wonder that her passionate ideality and unregulated fancy should betray her? The remedy for such mischances may not seem to be readily available. It is easy to say that the education of girls should be planned on broader lines, and that greater freedom of intercourse under thoughtful regulation would give that wider experience and openness to influence that are the best safeguards against a precipitate choice. Perhaps it scarcely needed any special instance to point the way to sound principles of conduct in such cases, and the difficulty will continue to lie in their application to given circumstances.

The lesson of Lydgate's life is similar, but it has features of its own. He also was the victim of a narrow one-sided education, but his mistake was due not to the generous blindness of a strong emotional nature, but to the fact that his sensibilities were uncultivated except in the one direction of his profession. He profoundly miscalculated the place that love insists on claiming even in the lives of those who strive to keep themselves free from its tyranny, and he paid the penalty of his self-sufficiency. That his nature was imperfectly developed is made evident not only by the way that he drifted into marriage, but by the lack of responsibility which allowed him to get into debt. His extravagance was unthinking, but it was related to the less worthy traits in his character. His "tendency", we are told, "was not toward extreme opinions; he would have liked no barefooted doctrines, being particular about his boots: he was no radical in relation to anything but medical reform and the prosecution of discovery". In the rest of practical life he walked by hereditary habit—half from personal pride and unreflecting egoism, and half from that *naïveté* which belonged to preoccupation with favourite ideas. His engagement to Rosamund Vincy was owing partly to his giving very little thought to his personal relations with women, partly to the self-assured obtuseness of feeling which allowed him to trifle with an attractive girl without thought of consequences, and partly to his low ideal of womanhood, which was sufficiently realised by Rosamund's charming but negative personality. In his view, we are told, "if falling in love had been at all in question, it would have been quite safe with a creature like this Miss Vincy, who had just the kind of intelligence one would desire in a woman,— polished, refined, docile, lending itself to finish in all delicacies of life, and enshrined in a body which expressed this with a force of demonstration that excluded the need for other evidence. But after an evening of flirtation, he went home and read far into the small hours, bringing a much more testing vision of details and relations into this pathological study than he had ever thought it necessary to apply to the complexities of love and marriage, these being subjects on which he felt himself amply informed by literature, and that traditional wisdom which is handed down in the genial conversation of men."

With all these faults, which account in great degree for his mistake, Lydgate cannot be held to have fully deserved his punishment, in a lot where there was little room even for expiation. But the terrible force of the tragedy lies in the fact that the rewards and punishments of life are not apportioned to desert.

Let us pass from the general *motif* of *Middlemarch* to consider the character creations on their own merits. This is the supreme test of an artist in fiction. Anyone may sound a note of warning against hasty marriages, but if the lesson is not expressed through living types of men and women in whose reality we cannot help believing, the message of the artist is empty of all true significance. In this aspect *Middlemarch* stands alone among novels. There is probably no other work in the whole range of imaginative literature where so large a number of figures, of so great variety, are presented with absolute fidelity to nature. There is really not a single exception to this wonderful uniformity of success in portraiture. Whatever degree of prominence is assigned to each in the story, one and all are drawn with the utmost clearness of outline, and move before us in the very semblance of life.

Of Dorothea Brooke something has already been said. She is one of the noblest of the author's heroines, but the type was not one that demanded much subtlety of treatment. Yet it is perhaps a more difficult task to sustain the consistency and interest of a character of ideal simplicity of purpose than one that is marked by eccentricities of mental and moral habit. The chief difficulty, of course, was to make it seem natural that a girl of so much intellectual grasp should have been completely deceived in her estimate of Casaubon's character before her marriage. The explanation of this has been already referred to, and it only remains to notice the skill with which every circumstance is turned to account in leading up to the event that beforehand would have seemed too far out of the range of probability. We find it easy in the end to understand how, in the author's words, "She filled up all blanks [in Mr. Casaubon] with unmanifested perfections, interpreting him as she interpreted the works of providence, and accounting for seeming discords by her own deafness to the higher harmonies. And there are many blanks left in the weeks of courtship which a loving faith fills with happy assurance." We follow the process of Dorothea's gradual disillusionment with the keenest pity, and though we feel little enthusiasm in regard to her second marriage, we are constrained to admit that her sympathy with Ladislaw, growing into an attachment that called forth her passion for self-sacrifice, was only the natural sequel to the experiences of her first marriage and the position in which Casaubon had placed her. But the full beauty of her character is better displayed in other relations that are outside her own personal lot. There is no finer scene in this or in any story than her interview with Rosamund, when, full of her own deep sorrow in the belief that Ladislaw has disappointed her trust in his goodness, she puts aside all thoughts of jealousy or anger, and goes to Lydgate's house with the forlorn hope of dispelling some of the clouds of distrust and alienation that were fast gathering between the husband and the wife. It is true that the issue of this visit had a momentous bearing on her own happiness, but no suspicion of this possibility was mingled with the pure and generous ardour of sympathy that led her to Rosamund, and no taint of selfish pre-occupation made her swerve from fulfilling her task to the utmost. It is noteworthy that in this impressive scene the moving power of Dorothea's personality is to be discovered not so much in what she says herself, as in what she makes Rosamund say. Even this shallow-hearted creature was stirred to some faint pulse of candour and generosity by the sympathy of so bountiful a nature.

George Eliot admitted that Rosamund Vincy was a study, the consistency of which she had unusual difficulty in maintaining, owing to the type being so alien to her own nature, but no reader of *Middlemarch* will have the slightest feeling that the character has been drawn with any lack of confidence. Not many of us may have known a Rosamund Vincy in our experience, but we have all felt in some degree in our own self-questionings (or perhaps we have preferred to observe among our more faulty neighbours) one or other of the unobtrusive but terribly potent promptings of a narrow egoism that are here gathered up into so convincing a whole. The author had the same special difficulty to meet as in the case of Casaubon,—the difficulty of endowing a creature so unlovely in her real nature with sufficient attraction to explain Lydgate's falling in love with her. For although the marriage was one of that numerous class that come about more through the stress of circumstances than by deliberate intention on both sides, and though, as we have seen, Lydgate's attitude of mind lent itself readily to the chance of an entanglement against his better judgment, the special features of the tragedy would not have existed if he had not entered upon married life with the high hopes fostered by a genuine affection and the sense of satisfying a fastidious taste. It is in his too tardy discovery how far removed the impulses of an undisciplined affection may be from that passionate sympathy which can alone sanctify a lifelong union, and how inadequate are the assumptions of a superficial taste to the discovery of natural affinities in habits of thought and feeling, that the real pathos of the situation lies. Rosamund is no vulgar adventuress who for her own conscious ends entraps a man of intellectual gifts by means of her physical charms. That is a common enough story, but this is one of far greater complexity and subtlety of interest. Rosamund, as we hear, was "always that combination of correct sentiments, music, dancing, drawing, elegant note-writing, private album for extracted verse, and perfect blond loveliness, which made the irresistible woman for the doomed man of that date. Think no unfair evil of her, pray. She had no wicked plots, nothing sordid or mercenary; in fact, she never thought of money except as something necessary which other people would always provide. She was not in the habit of devising falsehoods, and if her statements were no direct clue to fact, why, they were not intended in that light—they were among her elegant accomplishments, intended to please. Nature had inspired many arts in finishing Mrs. Lemon's favourite pupil, who by general consent 'was a rare compound of beauty, cleverness, and amiability'."

So just, so broadly conceived, is the whole relation of this fair, selfish, shallow-hearted creature to her husband and to her social surroundings, that, in the midst of our acute sympathy with Lydgate in his gradual discovery of her hopeless unreasonableness and lack of generous emotion, we never fail to pity her as well as him. We feel sorry for her even because her nature is so miserably inadequate to the demands upon it.

The scene between Rosamund and Dorothea is a

triumph of art in its revelation of both natures, but it is specially in regard to Rosamund's share in it that we have that peculiar feeling which is the highest effect of imaginative creation—the feeling that, while we could not have anticipated what would happen, we cannot now conceive it differently. The most striking quality in the portrayal of the softening of Rosamund's jealousy and suspicion is the restraint that is shown throughout. The temptation would be to exaggerate the effect of Dorothea's generous ardour, and to make the response more complete than the other's imperfect nature would admit of. This danger is wholly avoided, and we never lose sight of the baser alloy in Rosamund's motives, even when she is prompted by a sympathetic impulse to remove the misunderstanding in regard to Will Ladislaw. A writer with less insight would have made the experiences of this interview a turning-point in her life, but George Eliot makes us realise how much truer to nature it was that there should be no permanent result except in her feelings towards Dorothea. She continued to the end to be her husband's basil-plant, flourishing on his dead brains.

When we compare *Middlemarch* with *Daniel Deronda* we are conscious of the same relation that critics of Shakespeare have traced between the period of *Hamlet* and *Measure for Measure*, and that of *The Tempest* and *The Winter's Tale*. It is natural that every great writer who sees life as it is, should be liable to cynical moods of discontent which will at one time or another find definite expression in his creations, and it is also eminently natural that the period when the darker view of the world prevails most strongly should be when the range of vision is widest and the physical strength is beginning to decline. It is no less probable that this pessimistic impulse, having expended itself in outward forms, should be followed by a reaction, and that the latest efforts should seek to adjust the balance by offering a saner estimate of the meaning of the universe and the destiny of man.

In a superficial sense, it may seem that the position is reversed in the case of George Eliot's two latest works, for while *Middlemarch* abounds in humour of every kind, the prevailing atmosphere of *Deronda* is serious. But when we consider the broader significance of the two works, we shall find that it is to the latter we must look for evidence of the hopefulness and enthusiasm of humanity that we feel to represent the author's deliberate convictions. *Middlemarch*, in spite of its brilliancy and wit, is essentially a tragedy, and a tragedy of a terribly hopeless kind; the wholesomeness of its teaching is felt only indirectly, through the warning of its sad examples and the sting of its incisive satire. In *Daniel Deronda* we are again moving among heroic figures; the tragic events that are so intimately bound up with the central *motif* bring lessons of courage and hope, and the final impression is one of ideal beauty.

If the ordinary novel reader were asked what is the central *motif* of this work he would reply unhesitatingly, "Why, the restoration of the Jews, of course; and a very tiresome *motif* it is". This statement has been so constantly echoed that even more serious students of literary art, who have only read the book once, forgetting perhaps at a distance of some years what their original impressions were, have come to accept it as true, and as constituting a reason for the indefinite postponement of a second reading. Yet everyone who has read *Daniel Deronda* twice, will admit that the Jewish question, so far from being the main subject of the book, is, if not quite episodic, at least entirely subordinate. It will perhaps be a surprise to many to learn that out of over 600 pages, not more than 50 are occupied with this matter; only a twelfth part of the whole!

Even if it were true that the position of the Jews formed the main subject, it would not of course involve condemnation of the book apart from the question of treatment. It can scarcely be denied that a political or social idea may reasonably enough be dealt with in a drama or a story, even as its leading theme, provided in the first place that it is not presented from a one-sided point of view; in the second place, that no precise line of action is obtruded with a propagandist intention; and in the third place, that it does not strain the probability of the narrative or the consistency of the characters.

With the fulfilment of these conditions, George Eliot, if she had chosen, might have made the restoration of the Jews the central theme of her novel, without laying herself open to any adverse criticism on artistic grounds. But the task would have been a hard one, and she has not attempted it. The subject of the Jews cannot in any just sense be called the principal *motif* of *Daniel Deronda*; it is entirely subordinate to the personality of the hero. Even as an important episode, however, it must be tested by its conformity to the conditions named, and it will certainly stand the test successfully. So far from being exhibited in any one-sided aspect, the position and aspirations of the Jews are presented with the utmost breadth. In Mirah and Deronda's mother we have one strongly-marked contrast of type, which in itself would prevent any narrowness of vision; for it is not true, as has sometimes been said, that we are evidently intended to approve of the one character and condemn the other. There is no lack of sympathy in the author's portrayal of the proud passionate Jewess, who, under the consciousness of power to win fame for herself, rebels against the restrictions that her father urged on her from the traditions of her race. The Princess Halm-Eberstein, like Mirah, is accepted as the natural product of special conditions acting on a temperament in no way alien to the general characteristics of so individual a people. The portraiture of Jewish types is admirably completed by the figures of Joseph

Kalonymos, the Cohen family, Mordecai, his father, and Deronda himself. In this group we have represented with the fullest impartiality all the significant varieties of the race, and the dramatic presentation is further implemented by the side-lights of criticism that are to be found in the attitude and opinions of other characters. In this view the discussion at the "Hand and Banner" may find some justification; but the chief vehicle of outside impressions and prejudices is Hans Meyrick, whose standard is that of the acute and satirical but irreverent Philistine.

As to the obtrusion of any propagandist aim, it is enough to point out that the idea of the restoration of the Jewish people to the Holy Land is only indicated as a possible direction for the sympathetic energy natural to a man who has just found the key to his hitherto somewhat purposeless life in the knowledge of his nationality, who is in love with a maiden of his own race, and who has been deeply impressed by the noble aspirations of a gifted enthusiast. It may be held, then, that the Jewish element in this book, while it is strictly subsidiary to the dramatic presentation of the hero and his relations to the other characters, is in itself full of the highest interest, and is treated with the breadth that is demanded by the canons of art. The only objection that there may be some difficulty in meeting, is in regard to the chapter which reports the discussion at Mordecai's club. This has rather too much the appearance of a digression, and though it undoubtedly adds to our understanding of the situation, it should perhaps have been sacrificed to the continuity of the narrative.

But if the question of the future of the Jews is not the central theme of *Daniel Deronda*, in what does it consist? The real *motif* is the spiritual relation of Deronda to Gwendolen Harleth; this is the story that absorbs the chief interest alike of the author and of the reader. It is summed up in these sentences:

"It is hard to say how much we could forgive ourselves if we were secure from judgments by another whose opinion is the breathing-medium of all our joy—who brings to us with close pressure and immediate sequence that judgment of the Invisible and Universal which self-flattery and the world's tolerance would easily melt and disperse. . . . In this way our brother may be in the stead of God to us, and his opinion, which has pierced even to the joints and marrow, may be our virtue in the making. . . . Without the aid of sacred ceremony or costume, Gwendolen's feelings had turned this man only a few years older than herself into a priest. . . . Young reverence for one who is also young is the most coercive of all; there is the same level of temptation, and the higher motive is believed in as a fuller force and not suspected to be a mere residue from weary experience."

This is a special case of the far-reaching truth, enforced with a new emphasis throughout George Eliot's teaching,—that conscience draws its sanction and its compelling force from the social bonds that appeal to our sympathies. There are not many to whom the abstract idea of Duty, even when it is directly associated with the well-being and happiness of the human race, is enough to turn the scale in the conflict of opposing impulses; we all in some degree feel the need for what George Eliot has elsewhere called a "baptism and consecration" in the natures of those who love us, "binding us over to rectitude and purity by their belief about us", and making our sins "that worst kind of sacrilege which tears down the invisible altar of trust". It happens sometimes that this special relationship exists between a man and a woman, where there is little chance or thought of closer personal ties, and the situation has then an added piquancy of interest that supplies an admirable *motif* for a story. To create the desired circumstances it was necessary to have a hero of ideal mould, whom there would be no unfitness in placing in a relation of such high responsibility. It was an acute device of the novelist's art to shroud his parentage in mystery for a time, partly to arouse a natural curiosity in the reader, partly to account for that lack of definite aim in his life which detracts sufficiently from his perfection to make him human, and partly to prepare for the reaction of enthusiasm on his discovery that he belonged to a race with a noble past, and the possibility of a noble future.

The other chief requisite of the situation was a woman faulty enough to stand in great need of the hand that could save her from spiritual death, and yet of fine enough quality to attract the strong interest of the reader. As the presence of a more egoistic affection between the two chief figures would have spoilt the simplicity of the special relation, it was further necessary that the elements of romantic passion should be supplied on other sides, and the two new relationships were skilfully used in the development of the drama, Mirah completing the connection of Deronda's life to the mission of furthering Jewish unity, and Grandcourt providing that element in Gwendolen Harleth's experience which was at once the ordeal of her work and the opportunity of her salvation. Such is the general structure of the novel, and it is to be noted how admirably the plan is devised to combine a wealth of ordinary human interest with the development of the central theme.

If there should be some who are inclined to think that the dignity of a serious work of art which deals primarily with the portrayal of a momentous spiritual relation is lowered by the presence of the love stories, let them listen to the eloquent words with which George Eliot has anticipated such a feeling:

"Could there be a slenderer, more insignificant thread in human history than this consciousness of a girl, busy with her small inferences of the way in which she could make her life pleasant?—in a time, too, when ideas were with fresh vigour making armies of themselves, and the universal kinship was declaring itself fiercely: when women on the other side of the world would not mourn for the husbands and sons who died bravely in a common cause, and men stinted of bread on our side of the world heard of that willing loss and were patient: a time when the soul of man was waking to pulses which had for centuries been beating in him unheard, until their full sum made a new life of terror or of joy.

"What in the midst of that mighty drama are girls and their blind visions? They are the Yea and Nay of that good for which men are enduring and fighting. In these delicate vessels is borne onward through the ages the treasure of human affection."

Before we pass to consider the success of the character drawing in this novel, some reference may be made to criticisms already mentioned in regard to the author's style in her later works. She has been accused of a growing tendency to use scientific terms that are not sufficiently intelligible. This is a matter which one heard a good deal more about some years ago than at the present time. Such expressions were comparatively new then, and were familiar only to cultivated people, whereas now they are the commonplaces of ordinary talk. But in any case are we to lay down the maxim that a novelist must speak in a language that is universally understood? That would be a hard saying if it meant that he may not anticipate in any degree the progress of intelligence in the community as measured by the understanding of new conceptions. The drama is an art of more purely popular appeal than prose fiction, but we should indeed have been sorry if Shakespeare had suppressed all the passages in Hamlet which were not likely to tickle the ears of the groundlings. If it could be said that George Eliot's language as a whole was above the comprehension of the majority, there would of course be ground for complaint, but nothing could be further from the truth than any such contention. The terms that are condemned are of the rarest occurrence, and when you come near them they do not hurt. There was a general howl among the critics when she wrote that there was a "dynamic" quality in Gwendolen Harleth's glance. Well, if the critics of twenty-five years ago did not know the meaning of the word "dynamic", it was either their misfortune or their fault. At any rate we may almost say, to use Macaulay's expression, that every school-boy knows it now. The truth is, George Eliot used occasional terms that were not generally familiar, not from affectation or inadvertence, but because they were the most fitting means of expression for the ideas she wished to convey. Her interpretations of life were those of the new scientific school of thinkers, and it would have been impossible for her to commend their conceptions to her readers, as she has undoubtedly done to a marvellous extent through her artistic creations, if she had been entirely debarred from any extension of phraseology. Her main defence lies in the fact that the objection is felt less and less as time goes on.

But beyond the occasional use of semi-technical expressions, it is said that in *Middlemarch* and *Deronda* the style is altogether less graceful and lucid. No one perhaps has maintained that in *Middlemarch* at any rate there is any decline from the admirably natural *dialogue* of the earlier novels, but even in this book the author's comments are sometimes described as "laboured", while in *Deronda* the fault is said to extend to the sayings of the characters themselves, impairing the clearness and force of their presentation. A candid reader will acquit George Eliot entirely of any such charge so far as the language of her own narrative and reflections is concerned, but will be ready to admit a slight failure in reproducing with sufficient vividness the dramatic speech of one or two characters in *Daniel Deronda*. The general style will be thought laboured only by those who apply a standard of lucidity in expression that takes no account of the ever-increasing complexity of the thoughts and feelings to be expressed. Let us not be deceived by the authority of Milton, when he says that art must be simple. Art *cannot* be simple when life is not simple, and of all forms of art that which best lends itself to the representation of complexity is the novel. That is not to say that there is no room for the simpler forms in fiction as in the other arts, but the finest novel must be one that deals with large issues, where the treatment has the fullest breadth in characterisation, in comment and in expression. *Middlemarch* and *Deronda* are certainly conceived on the grandest scale, and in regard to their style it must be evident that simplicity in the ordinary sense cannot reasonably be demanded. In *Deronda*, however, there is an occasional lapse from perfectly natural dialogue. Sometimes the temptation which every writer must feel, to give the most careful and deliberate expression to every thought, has outweighed the necessity for suggesting the spontaneity and naturalness of unpremeditated talk. The instances that may fairly be cited of this mistake are rare, but they are enough to explain certain charges of failure in characterisation. The figure of Deronda himself has been described as shadowy, unreal, puppet-like, priggish, and it is probable that this impression is due not to any failure in the conception or even in the general presentation of the character, but entirely to an undue elaboration in his speech. The situation was one where a mistake of this kind might very easily be made. It was Deronda's mission to give spiritual help, and it would have been a hard task for him always to avoid the appearance of preaching to his neighbours. Dramatically, indeed, it would have been justifiable for the author consciously to allow him to fall into this mistake, but it may rather be supposed that George Eliot meant her most ideal hero to be free from even so slight a blemish, and that the fault lies in her own execution. It is a pity, for in the few cases where it is noticeable very slight changes of phrase would have made all the difference in our impression. In one of the moving scenes between Gwendolen and Deronda, the latter says:

"That is the bitterest of all—to wear the yoke of our own wrong-doing. But if you submitted to that, as men submit to maiming, or a lifelong incurable disease, and made the unutterable wrong a reason for more effort towards a good that may do something to counterbalance the evil? One who has committed irremediable errors may be scourged by that consciousness into a higher course than is common."

Now much of this passage is excellently put, but there is something that jars on us, that dims our sense of the reality of the scene. Is it not the use of unnecessarily long words at the close? Would the real Deronda, as he existed in George Eliot's mind, have risked the effect of his earnest appeal by the use of so cumbrous a phrase as "committed irremediable errors"? To have said "done grievous wrongs" or "made great mistakes" would have suited his purpose quite as well, and would have brought him into closer sympathy with Gwendolen's feeling. This may seem a small matter, but it is strange how much of life depends on niceties of expression; there is no greater fault of this nature than the suggestion of artificial or formal deliberation, when the utmost directness and simplicity are desirable.

Among the characters in this novel it is the figure of Daniel Deronda himself that has raised most controversy. Mr. Swinburne has called him a piece of waxwork, and many other readers or critics have found or professed to find him wanting in reality, or at least in interest. It has been already suggested that this impression may be mostly accounted for by the occasional lack of simplicity in his speech, where the great difficulty of making him the natural mouthpiece of spiritual guidance and consolation has not always been overcome with success. Beyond this it may be maintained that there is no failure in giving life to the portrait, except what is incidental to every attempt to represent the ideal. The interest we take in the characters of men and women, whether in real life or in the form of imaginative types, is largely due to our sympathetic recognition of their weakness. The further they are removed from the ordinary level of human imperfection, the more finely drawn will be the threads of feeling along which our fancy must travel before it can picture them to the understanding. Every novelist and playwright has felt the difficulty of making the hero at once admirable and interesting; and the inevitable question occurs as to what sort of compromise should be made. Among the older writers of stories it had almost become a convention that the sympathy of the reader should be secured by making the hero err on the side of showing too impetuous a spirit. This was the most venial fault in an age that had scarcely outgrown the traditions of an aggressive militarism, and it does service even up to our own day. Meredith himself, with all his originality, has seldom got far beyond the beaten track in this respect; Richard Feverel, Evan Harrington, Harry Richmond, Nevil Beauchamp, Carlo Ammiani—all these are but variations of the familiar pattern, where a generous ardour and high courage are held in more esteem than wisdom or self-restraint or disinterested enthusiasm. It is one of George Eliot's chief claims to greatness as a creative artist that she has done so much to break down this convention by recommending to our sympathy heroic types of a kind more in harmony with what is noblest in our modern civilisation. In drawing such figures as Adam Bede, Felix Holt, and Daniel Deronda she has challenged our appreciation on a higher moral plane, and if in this new sphere the strain on our imperfectly developed sympathies should sometimes be too perceptible, at whose door is the blame to lie? It is on the portrait of Deronda that George Eliot has put the greatest venture. The sense of nobility in Adam Bede and Felix Holt is sufficiently tempered by our recognition of their redeeming defects and of the limitations in their lot, but in the case of Deronda no such sop is held out to us. He is frankly presented as an ideal figure, offering no concession to our envious cry for signs of weakness that will bring him closer to us, for the shadows that are thrown round his life only make the purity and strength of his nature shine forth more radiantly when they disappear. Are we to confess that this is an imaginative height to which our emotional interest cannot attain? And in such a case are we to condemn the over-generous confidence of the artist, or acknowledge our own restricted vision and hardness of heart?

In drawing the character of Gwendolen Harleth, George Eliot had to meet the difficulty already pointed out of making the woman who depended on Deronda's help sinful enough to give point to the situation and at the same time attractive enough to win our sympathy, and she has surmounted it in a singularly intrepid fashion. It would have been comparatively easy to paint the ordinary model of a woman whose crucial fault is her loving "not wisely but too well", and whose good qualities have won the reader's good favour before there is any question of her forfeiting his respect. Gwendolen is frankly presented as a girl who, before her trial, compels admiration without esteem, whose intrinsic moral worth is at first not simply hidden, but almost non-existent. It was a bold thought to make the heroine of the book out of such material, to bespeak our interest in a girl without tenderness or generosity, who loves and thinks of no one but herself, and who marries not only from sordid ambition and love of ease, but in disregard of other claims that she had pledged herself to respect. We should have said beforehand that such a woman richly deserved her fate, whatever it might be, and that our enthusiasm could scarcely be roused by any repentance she might be found capable of. If there are people in whom this anticipation is justified, who remain untouched by the issue of Gwendolen's ordeal, surely they must be very few. So terrible is her punishment that we cannot withhold our compassion, and at length our sympathy is called out in spite ot ourselves for her efforts under Deronda's influence to work out her redemption from evil impulses and selfish coldness. Her confession to Deronda after her husband's death makes one of the most masterly scenes that George Eliot has written. There is nothing in it that we feel to be inconsistent with her previous character, nothing that has not been sufficiently accounted for by her little experience; and yet what a new light it throws on her nature! Far more than any violent revulsion does it impress on us the blessed possibilities of good that lie in even the most unpromising material.

Much as we may admire the workmanship in the portraiture of Deronda and Gwendolen, we are impressed even more strongly by the figure of Grandcourt, which is a veritable triumph of art. There is no other villain at all like him in the whole of fiction, yet who can call him unreal? From the social stand-point he is an irreproachable gentleman, and though there may be ugly secrets in his past history, it is not by hypocrisy that his position is secured. He has enough to recommend him without any concealment of unpleasant facts. "Whatever he had done," we are told, "he had not ruined himself; and it is well known that in gambling, for example, whether of the business or holiday sort, a man who has the strength of mind to leave off when he has only ruined others, is a reformed character." According to conventional standards, Grandcourt's behaviour is perfectly decorous, and even one who was intimate with every

detail of his private life would have found it difficult to
accuse him to society, yet no words are too strong for
the detestation we come to feel for him. We almost
dread to read of his entries into the story; his blighting
presence seems to infect our own lives, all the more that
his malignity is negative, lying not in his intention but
in his nature. He will remain the incarnate expression
of all that is most baneful in the characteristics of modern
upper-class civilization: the unrestrained desire for mastery; the narrow contempt for any motive outside the
range of a cold, passionless self-seeking; the utter lack
of any sympathetic or generous impulse; the *blasé* complacency of a nature that has sucked all experience dry
without satisfying any healthy appetite or developing
any wholesome taste.

Mirah, like Deronda, has been found wanting in realistic charm, but in her case again a defence of the author's
portraiture may be offered. She may seem colourless in
contrast with the striking features of Gwendolen Harleth
and Deronda's mother, but just as the happiest nations
have no history, it may be said that the best women have
no strongly-marked idiosyncrasies. That is as much as
to say, of course, that it is difficult, if not almost impossible, to make them the subjects of romance. Much will
depend, however, on the circumstances in which they
are placed. The less there is of unusual interest in the
character, the more must the artist depend on romantic
elements in the surroundings. This condition is amply
fulfilled in Mirah's case. If her nature is too simple
to tax our powers of penetration or appeal to our
curiosity, at least her experience was full of moving
incidents, and we can scarcely read the account of her
sufferings without a feeling of strong sympathy. Her
self-control and devotion to her ideals may seem too exalted to be natural to one whose upbringing had been so
unhappy, but those who have recognized the wonderful
tenacity of purpose that distinguishes the Jewish race

will find little here to cavil at, and even her somewhat prim and formal modes of expression will be accepted as the outcome of her peculiar education.

Chapter VII.

George Meredith.

The estimate formed of Meredith as a novelist must depend entirely on the theory we accept as to the true place and function of prose fiction. If the novel is no more than a means of diversion, an irresponsible product from which nothing is to be demanded except that it shall titillate jaded nerves, or while away an idle hour, then Meredith is at once to be ruled out of court. But if we hold that prose fiction is a serious form of art, amenable to the canons of æsthetic criticism in general, and to certain definite conditions proper to itself, then it may be safely asserted that, judged on this higher level, Meredith is one of the greatest artists of our time,— indeed the only living writer of English novels who can be ranked unhesitatingly among the giants.

That prose fiction is one of the fine arts, worthy of serious study and capable of producing powerful emotional impressions, will not now be explicitly denied by many intelligent people. The burden of proof may fairly be left with those who would deliberately degrade the novelist from the status of an artist to that of a public entertainer. Yet there is a good deal of current criticism—or perhaps it should rather be called comment—on Meredith in which we can detect a vague assumption that any novel which makes an unusual demand on the capacity or attention of the reader stands condemned on that ground alone. The question can be best considered *apropos* of Meredith's style, about which we constantly hear things said that require some careful examination.

When his writing is described as unintelligible, what is exactly meant? To begin with, unintelligible to whom? Do we expect any work of art to be understood and appreciated equally well by all who come within its influence? Does not each take from it up to the measure of his own nature? It may be said that though some will get more than others, none should be sent away empty-handed. There may have been a time in the childhood of the world when such a universal appeal was possible, at least in certain of the arts and under certain chosen conditions. It is not always possible now. In every art there are realms that are only open to the initiated, and literature, though it may not have the exclusiveness of music, for example, finds a growing need for some limitation in the area of its appeal. We are sometimes told indeed that the artist who deals with words, the accepted medium of communication between man and man, has not the excuse of those who work with less familiar material. But surely this is shallow reasoning. How much is there really in common between the current forms of everyday speech and the "winged words" of the poet, the philosopher, the novelist? If a writer sets himself only to tell a plain tale, which he that runs may read, it is natural to expect him to make his meaning clear to all who speak his own tongue; but the novel in its most complex and therefore its highest form differs as widely from a simple narrative of events as a Wagnerian music-drama from an oratorio of Handel's, and it cannot be made a ground of reproach that there are some—it may even be many —who lack the intelligence, or the sensibility, or the mental energy, that can alone admit them into the charmed circle of appreciative readers. No doubt the esoteric tendency may be pushed to an extreme. Though a writer may for his own part be content, like

Landor, to "dine late with guests few and select", we are unwilling to call him great if the sphere of his influence has been really narrow. But no such difficulty can arise with Meredith. In his own lifetime, and before he has laid down his pen, the sale of his books has reached a point that would almost justify us in describing him as a *popular* author. There are evidently enough of people to whom his novels are on the whole intelligible, and if we refuse him the rank of a great artist, it cannot be because the area of his appeal is too restricted.

It may be said, however, that though his readers understand him sufficiently to reap a balance of satisfaction, the effort demanded from them by his mode of presentation is so great as to affect seriously their judgment of his artistic eminence. "He might have been a great novelist", we are told, "if he had only possessed lucidity of style." Now, how far is this a reasonable criticism? That Meredith is lacking in lucidity of expression no one of course will deny, but in the first place what is exactly meant? Intelligibility, it has been urged, is a purely relative term. Are we on firmer ground if we call him obscure? It may be doubted if there is a single passage in all his novels where the meaning cannot be, at least superficially, discerned by anyone of average intelligence and cultivation, if not at first sight, at least after a second or possibly a third reading. It is the general testimony of all who have made the experiment, that not only in regard to individual passages but to each novel as a whole, there is no writer of fiction who repays a careful study more bountifully. Difficulties alike in construction and in expression that seem as mountains to the cursory or unprepared reader dwindle to mole-hills, if they do not disappear altogether, as one becomes accustomed to the lights and shadows of the new atmosphere. The difficulty of Meredith's style and manner has been greatly exaggerated, and is felt to be a serious impediment to appreciation only by those who have not the patience to apply themselves to the study of the higher fiction with the same ardour that they would deem necessary in the case of any other art.

Apart from this defence, however, there will surely remain something fatuous in the statement that but for his style Meredith might have been a great novelist. As well say that if he had not been himself he might have been someone else. Can anyone conceive Meredith without his distinctive style? It is too closely associated with many of his rarest qualities. When we find thoughts as deep, emotions equally subtle and intense, imaginations of such a bold and varied flight, visions of life as mature and sane as his, expressed in language that is not only forcible and suggestive, but also lucid and persuasive,—when we find such things done, if we ever do, it will then be time enough to speak harshly of the failures of those who were the first to attempt them. No one has ever tried to make words convey so much meaning as Meredith, and very few have had so much meaning to express.

But though it may be idle to speculate on what his style might have been when judged by the standard of other writers, it is fair enough to mark the course of its development and compare its successes with its failures. It would be beside the mark to point to *The Shaving of Shagpat* in illustration of what Meredith could have done throughout his works if he had only liked, for the manner of that brilliant extravaganza is hardly suited to the treatment of realistic themes, but in *Richard Feverel* and *Rhoda Fleming* we have good examples of the author's early style. There is in these little failure in lucidity, but along with the absence of positive defects we miss the characteristic flavour that makes up so much of the charm of the later works. It may be said of his writing generally that the smaller the unit of style the greater is the success. He is surpassed by none in the variety and appositeness of his use of individual words. His phrase-making is no less wonderful, but is less uniformly happy. His sentences have for the most part little pretension to perfect ease and balance, while few and far between are the passages where there is any attempt at sustained eloquence or flow of melody. With the publication of *The Egoist* in 1879 there is a marked change of style which is accentuated in the novels that succeeded it,—a change that is partly for the better and partly for the worse. The expression becomes more finished in detail, less satisfactory in its broader effects. There is a more fastidious choice of words, an increasing command of felicitous phrases, a more persistent attempt to put the fullest significance and suggestiveness into every sentence. But these qualities have their related defects. When the higher aim misses its mark, the failure is sometimes painfully obtrusive; we get an impression of artificiality, of affectation, of lack of taste. And often when the effort is successful, we cannot think it well judged. The fault is almost always on the side of overloading language with ideas. Each word, each clause, may be right, but the general effect is lost from an excess of meaning.

The most serious consequence of this surrender to the fascination of epigram is its interference with the dramatic presentation of the characters. In the earlier books the terse sayings were confined to the narrative and explanatory portions, or were put into the mouths of characters to whom they were appropriate. But in the later novels there are times when one and all of the people in the story begin to talk in the same compressed, elliptical, metaphorical fashion. The dialogue becomes a war of wits, and a war carried on under impossible conditions, for the epigrams that are fired off in rapid succession are generally such as only the most exceptionally gifted minds could have devised with less preparation than at least two minutes for each. In such circumstances we have difficulty in distinguishing the individuality of the figures, and the author does them injustice in representing them as straining after a sententious brevity of phrase. Fortunately the failure in dramatic discrimination is but skin-deep. If the characters do not always present themselves to us in lucid and fitting speech, at least they invariably think, and feel, and act in keeping with their conception, and thereby prove themselves to be veritable creations.

This question of style has demanded some attention, for it is a matter of frequent strife between Meredith's admirers and those who are repelled at the threshold of their acquaintance with his books, but surely it is not a point of such high importance as is commonly asserted. After all, style is by no means the chief part of the artistic equipment of a novelist. His mastery of technique involves far more than the command of verbal expression. It is in his choice of *motif*, his arrangement of the plot, his handling of the narrative, his conception and portrayal of the characters, his idiosyncrasies of tone and treatment, that we shall find the main part of the evidence on which our judgment of his artistic rank must be formed.

There are certain aspects of Meredith's work that are more open to adverse criticism than his style. We cannot but take into account the proportion of an author's achievement which represents him at anything like his best, and it may be said of Meredith that his period of full maturity was long in being reached, and was too soon over. There would be little value in weighing the merits of one novel against those of another if it were not possible to discover some principle of growth or decay on which criticism can be directed. There are two tendencies discernible throughout Meredith's work that to a considerable extent interfere with his artistic success. He is too frequently possessed by a spirit—the spirit of comedy; and he yields too much to the fascination of a *tour de force*. On the former point he has been at no small pains to anticipate criticism. Two of his books are frankly described as comedies, a third suggests the same in its title, in one or two others there are explanatory digressions of a defensive kind, and the author has even thought it well to publish a separate essay on comedy. *Qui s'excuse, s'accuse*; but while the case is hardly made out, full justice must be done to the position. It is no less true in the realms of thought and feeling than in the material world that we can often see a thing better by looking at something else. In the literature of fiction Meredith is the great master of the indirect. He has demonstrated in many and divers ways how immensely we may add to our knowledge of persons and events by studying their significance in a reflected light. He contends that though in one sense men and women may be more truly understood in their determining moments, yet in another aspect they lay themselves more unreservedly open to our vision when they are not in any assumed pose, when they are, as it were, in moral undress. The spirit of comedy disguises the seriousness of its quest under a mask of levity, and is thus able to take its victims unawares. But there is a snare in this attitude of aloofness. The guise of cynical indifferentism that the author sometimes assumes cannot deceive those who have learned to penetrate below the surface of his manner to the hidden depths of generous pity and ardour that animate his message as a whole; but such an understanding does not come without some initiation. Unfortunately it is in his earliest works, which are naturally read first, that he has laid himself open to misconstruction in this respect. *Richard Feverel* and *Sandra Belloni* especially suffer from the influence of a tone of reflection that seems out of keeping with the seriousness of the issues. It is no doubt due to his belief in the efficacy of a borrowed light. In his quest for truth he dreads the narrowness of vision that belongs to a single point of view, however earnest and intense the scrutiny may be, trusting more to the independent play of a vagrant humour that allows no significant trait in human nature to escape its notice. This is a method which in general terms we can heartily approve of, but it is liable to abuse in the application. In his earlier days Meredith seems to have worked under a morbid fear of taking himself and the world too seriously, and thereby contracting his vision. It was perhaps even the keenness of his sensibility that led him by a natural reaction into what we must almost call the affectation of being moved only to a smile and a shrug of the shoulders by the power of the tales he relates, however serious or pitiful they may be. A good example of this misplaced lightness of treatment, which is mistaken for heartlessness by those who do not recognise that it is the defensive attitude of a nature only too open to the appeals of pathos, may be found in the description of Richard Feverel's wedding, where the tone of easy-going banter is apt to seem unsympathetic. That Meredith became conscious of the risk he was running of being misunderstood, is pretty clear from the defence he offers near the close of *Sandra Belloni*, when he is nevertheless preparing to suit himself to the epic dignity of *Vittoria*. He playfully refers to the dispassionate, purely observant element in himself as the "garrulous, super-subtle, so-called Philosopher, who first set me upon the building of 'The Three Volumes'". . . .

"In vain I tell him" [says the author] "that he is making tatters of the puppets' golden robe,—illusion; that he is sucking the blood of their warm humanity out of them. He promises that when Emilia is in Italy he will retire altogether; for there is a field of action, of battles and conspiracies, nerve and muscle, where life fights for plain issues, and he can but sum results. Let us, he entreats, be true to time and place. In our fat England, the gardener Time is playing all sorts of delicate freaks in the hues and traceries of the flower of life, and shall we not note them? If we are to understand our species, and mark the progress of civilisation at all, we must. Thus the Philosopher. Our partner is our master, and I submit, hopefully looking for release with my Emilia, in the day when Italy reddens the sky with the banners of a land revived."

Meredith is here making a golden bridge for himself, and most of his readers will be glad to let him escape on these easy terms from what is certainly a weakness of inexperience. It is to be noted that though the satiric, philosophical partner reappears in some of the later works, particularly in *The Egoist*, he does not again obtrude himself with the maladroitness that somewhat disfigures *Richard Feverel* and *Sandra Belloni*. Even where the story treats of "fat England", with its abundant material for comedy,—in such books as *Beauchamp's Career* and *One of Our Conquerors*,—there is no return to the habitual tone of tolerant mockery. The imps of humour cross our path now and again when they see their chance, but they are no longer allowed to run riot.

The second detraction from Meredith's artistic greatness is somewhat more serious. It is his inclination to attempt a *tour de force*, for this is the description which applies in a greater or less degree to nearly half of his novels. We may be quite ready to grant that it was from no vulgar desire to display his ingenuity, but merely from the artist's love of setting himself a difficult task, that he was led to choose such themes as those of *Evan Harrington*, of *Harry Richmond*, of *Diana of the Crossways*, of *The Amazing Marriage*, and we may almost add, of *The Egoist*. But however we may admire the skill of the craftsman, and however little we may feel inclined to contest the success of the *dénoûment*, the nature of the situations inevitably gives an impression of artifice that to some extent destroys the dramatic illusion. Moreover, the success is not always triumphant. There is sometimes a strain on our sense of probability, and there is occasional reliance on scenes that border on farce, and on characters that are within measurable distance of being caricatures.

It is possible to make these admissions without taking refuge in any such paradoxical position as that announced by a recent writer in the *Fortnightly Review*, who states that he is more attracted by Meredith than by any other novelist, while he considers him to violate every canon of art that prose fiction is bound to observe. He is to be placed in the front rank of novelists, not because he is a philosopher and a poet and a wit, though undoubtedly he is all of these in no mean degree, but because he has the supreme gift of creating types of character that are at once ideally representative and essentially true to the realities of life. It is by his gallery of portraits that the novelist, as distinguished from the mere romancer, must stand or fall. If he has succeeded in imparting a living interest to a large number of figures through a variety of nature and circumstances, penetrating with power and certainty to the hidden springs of their being, as it may confidently be claimed that Meredith has done, then all the other important constituents of his art are virtually included. If the chief *dramatis personæ* are of heroic mould and have had ample scope to present themselves in their full stature, that is all the evidence we need that the theme has been worthy of ideal treatment, that the construction of the story has been sufficiently skilful, that the background of comment has been in keeping with the subject, and even that the dialogue has not departed unduly from the *vraisemblance* of living speech. The one unpardonable sin of the novelist is to play fast and loose with his characters, to allow their outlines to be blurred or distorted in order to suit the exigencies of the plot. Whatever deficiencies Meredith may have, this charge can scarcely be made good against him, and there are few novelists indeed of whom so much can be said.

Considered as the work of a man under thirty years of age, *The Ordeal of Richard Feverel* is certainly a wonderful production, even though in its present form it may show the benefit of the author's later revision. While not many students of Meredith would call it his best novel, it has yet many qualities recommending it to popular favour which some of the best of his novels possess in much less abundant measure. The most noteworthy of its merits in contrast with the later stories are the lucidity of the narrative and the naturalness of the conversations. There is here none of the bewildering rapidity of movement in the record of events that sometimes takes away our breath in *Harry Richmond* or *Vittoria*, none of the indiscriminate endowment of all the characters with aphoristic gifts, that perplexes us at times in *The Egoist* and *One of Our Conquerors*, little or none of the exaggeration approaching caricature that in some degree disfigures the portraiture in *Sandra Belloni* and *Lord Ormont*. In addition to these negative excellencies, *Richard Feverel* has the advantages of a *motif* of strong and wide interest, a plot full of movement and variety of incident, and a group of admirably-contrasted figures for the *dramatis personæ*. The true moral of the story is not, as the satire of the author might lead us superficially to suppose, that in the determining crisis of life instinct is a safer guide, and chance a more bountiful dispenser of happiness, than the loving thought and care of those who are nearest to us, but rather that parents in the training of their children must search their own hearts and expel every trace of self-conceit and prejudice and doctrinaire complacency. This is a strong *motif*, and it is worked out with great skill, if not with entire success. The crucial factor in the story is the portrayal of Sir Austen Feverel. It is his acts that determine the course of the narrative and bring about the tragic *dénoûment*. The delineation of his character shows undoubtedly the hand of the master that afterwards drew Sir Willoughby Patterne, that most elaborate and wonderful of portraits. In some respects, indeed, Sir Austen is a companion figure to Sir Willoughby. The former has a native sincerity and unselfishness that are wanting in the Egoist, but he has the same narrow self-confidence and sensitive vanity.

The character of the hero himself is little or no less faithful to reality. When he reaches the critical period between youth and manhood he inevitably chafes at the moral despotism which is the result of his father's preoccupation with abstract theories, to the neglect of that sympathetic guidance and openness that would have secured his son's confidence as well as his affection. The tragedy begins in Richard's concealment of his thoughts and feelings from Sir Austen's too exclusively scientific scrutiny. The golden opportunity once lost of establishing a bond of feeling between them, we are prepared for the gradual alienation that in the end so hopelessly destroys the happiness of both. The great difficulty, however, in the plan of this story is to account for the magnitude of the catastrophe. We have a right to protest against our feelings being harrowed by any degree of sadness in the ending that is not shown to be inevitable. In our struggle to disbelieve in a too painful *dénoûment* we are always on the look-out for some loophole of escape from the pressure of events. This we may find in one of two ways: we may be able to say either that such and such a character at some important crisis would not have acted in the way represented, or that a certain conjunction of circumstances was too far beyond the bounds of probability to be accepted. At a first reading of the novel one is inclined to fancy that an escape is offered by a serious inconsistency in the action of the hero. It is not to be supposed, of course, that heroes must invariably act with perfect consistency in fiction any more than in real life, but it is the business of the novelist to prepare us for any improbable event, and when it bears a tragic issue in its train, the task of bringing conviction to the reader is all the harder. The crisis of the story turns on Richard's remaining away so long from his young wife on the somewhat unreasonable suggestion that he should propitiate his father by going up alone to London and awaiting his pleasure there. We cannot but admire the skill with which the author has woven the threads of his plot so as to lead up to this situation. It is not only that the cruel scheming of Lord Mountfalcon and his associates is so carefully conceived and executed, but we are constrained to admit the success of the devices by which all the leading characters are consciously or unconsciously made accessories to the deed. Sir Austen's prolonged absence is quite in keeping with his character, while in London the influence of Mrs. Doria Forey and of Adrian Harley is in each case directed towards the same sinister end without the need to assume any motive beyond those that were eminently natural to them. All this may be granted, and yet we may remain unsatisfied that Richard, being what he was, would have allowed himself to become the victim of a combination of influences, however potent and malign, when there were such strong reasons for his breaking away. This is the difficulty that many readers have felt, but a closer study of the novel does not support the superficial judgment. Though the tragic ending may not have the absolute inevitableness that could alone reconcile us to its terrible sadness, Meredith must be acquitted of obtaining his strongest effects by the cheap device of playing fast and loose with his characters. A more careful analysis of the impulses that were powerful with Richard Feverel at this crisis of his fate—an analysis which we may make from the material supplied by the author—will discover the true efficient cause of the catastrophe where, according to the highest artistic canons, it ought to be found, namely, in the imperfect discipline of the hero's own nature. This view of the matter may involve a sacrifice of those aspects of his character that would best deserve to be called heroic, but after all it is little derogation to Richard to say that not until his soul had been purified by suffering was he in any way worthy of a high destiny. Before his ordeal he was no true hero, as he came to realize for himself only too completely. The cause of his transgression lay deeper than the wiles of his enemies and the selfish folly of his friends could explain. He was not wholly to blame that he had to pass through the valley of humiliation before he came to a saving knowledge of himself; he could not but be conscious that his father had failed him when his need of guidance and sympathy had been sorest. But he rose to his full moral stature only when he was able to take upon himself the full responsibility for his own deeds, when the pride and arrogance and impatient self-confidence that made him unworthy of his noble wife had given place to a reverent humility. Oh the pity of it, that his self-revelation came too late! Who can read the final scene between Richard and Lucy before he goes to fight his duel, and the letter of Lady Blandish to Austen Wentworth telling how it all ended, without being stirred to a pang of sympathy that is almost too deep and painful for tears? It is little wonder if in self-defence we passionately refuse to believe that Lucy really had to die before she could even understand that she was on the threshold of a new chastened happiness that gave promise of a lifelong endurance. But the author was right. Lucy must have died, and it is a proof of Meredith's courage as an artist that he told the truth boldly as he saw it, when every consideration of mercy towards himself and his readers would have prompted him to stay his hand.

Is there, then, no respite from the terrible conclusion? While no serious flaw can be found in the consistency of the character-drawing,—the chief difficulty is in believing that Richard after his fall could have destroyed all his letters from home without reading them—the tragedy at the close has not the highest degree of inevitableness. The fault therefore, if there is one, must lie in the way that the incidents are treated in the development of the plot. It is a somewhat ungracious task to look for defects in the mere arrangement of circumstances when we are satisfied that the general lesson of the story is just, and that the characters in whom it is expressed are true to life. But if criticism is to be trustworthy it must be uncompromising in searching out the weak places wherever they may be found. Perhaps we cannot say that Meredith in this book has strained probability at any definite point, but it is, to say the least, unfortunate that in one or two important junctures momentous issues are made to turn on events that are too much of the nature of coincidences. Curious coincidences are occurring every day, and often have grave consequences, but it is hazardous for a novelist to hang too much upon them, for he at once sets us to constructing a new story in our own minds where these coincidences did not happen, and so everything turned out quite differently. Each of the two events that caused the fatal misunderstanding between Sir Austen and his son in regard to the latter's marriage was in itself sufficiently unlikely, but the chances against their both occurring together were so very great that we cannot but feel that we have here the weak link that affects the strength of the whole chain.

Evan Harrington is the lightest of all Meredith's novels. He describes it by the same title that he afterwards more explicitly gave to *The Egoist*, as a comedy, and it will be worth while to note what is suggested by this term. A comedy on the stage we understand to be a drama that is serious in so far as it aims at a consistent development of its material, and is yet a more or less artificial product, in respect that the material itself is chosen to illustrate only the lighter aspects of life. That is broadly the sense in which Meredith takes the expression, but in casting two at least of his stories into this form he has so definite a purpose in view that it may be well to hear his justification. In the prelude of *The Egoist* he writes:

"Comedy is a game played to throw reflections upon social life, and it deals with human nature in the drawing-room of civilized men and women, where we have no dust of the struggling outer world, no mire, no violent crashes, to make the correctness of the representation convincing. . . . The Comic spirit conceives a definite situation for a number of characters, and rejects all accessories in the exclusive pursuit of them and their speech. For, being a spirit, he hunts the spirit in men; vision and ardour constitute his merit: he has not a thought of persuading you to believe in him. 'Follow, and you will see.'"

And again we are told that Comedy, while "watching over sentimentalism with a birch-rod, is not opposed to romance".

We have here a definition that disarms criticism at some points. We are asked to accept the characters and situations of a story like *Evan Harrington* without the rigorous scrutiny of their *vraisemblance* that would be demanded in a record of tragic passion. The tests that have been applied to *Richard Feverel* would be out of place in such an atmosphere. While we are far from consenting to any irresponsible juggling with probability for the sake of piquant effects such as form the essence of farce and burlesque, we allow ourselves to be so absorbed in the wider significance of the incidents as they appeal to us in the language of genial humour and tender pathos, that our sense of a true scientific perspective is lulled to sleep. We are satisfied if the chief figures show a general adherence to the laws of nature without enquiring too closely into the secrets of their mechanism. We shall not call out that they are puppets as long as they are cleverly manipulated.

Even at the risk of estimating *Evan Harrington* on a lower level than might successfully be claimed for it, it will be safer to keep to the vantage-ground of regarding it as in some degree a *tour de force*. Let us for once grant to the novelist a little of the licence that is claimed by the playwright to make up for the necessary limitations of a stage performance. Let us be tolerant if the mechanism of the plot is more artificial than we should be satisfied with in a work of professed seriousness. What if, after the manner of Dickens, a benevolent and eccentric gentleman is introduced as a *deus ex machina* to account for developments that would otherwise be wanting in likelihood? It is all a part of the play. What if we are conscious of a somewhat palpable device to bring all the characters together in the final scene? Is not this a pardonable concession to the wishes of a gratified audience to take a last look at their entertainers before the fall of the curtain? Thorough-going devotees of Meredith's will indignantly disdain the need of any such justification of so brilliant and interesting a book as *Evan Harrington*, but it is no true homage to any artist to try his work by a more exalted standard than is claimed for it.

In the spirit of Comedy we may be willing to accept the situations that are offered to us in this book, and confine our judgment to the treatment of the characters in these situations without complaining that the scheme of the story is not something entirely different. A recent writer has based a violent attack on the novel on the supposition that the author intended to deal with the weighty problem of the fusion of social classes in matrimonial alliances. This is a lamentable misunderstanding of Meredith's purpose. Evan was of course never intended to be a typical tradesman, as Felix Holt was a veritable artisan. If he had been, there might have been a story, but assuredly it would not have in the least resembled that which we now possess. George Eliot's *motif* may be the finer of the two, but it is idle to compare achievements so different in their nature. The interest, so far as the hero is concerned, lies in the struggle of a youth of natural refinement and high spirit, who has been brought up in the associations of a class above his own position, to reconcile his tastes and inclinations with the straightforward acceptance of responsibilities that are enforced on him by his sense of honour, and yet seem hopelessly inconsistent with the success of his love-suit. Evan is no sturdy democrat defying social prejudice in the passionate claim to marry the girl he loves in whatever class she may be found; he is simply a gentleman in habit and culture, who finds himself pressed by the irony of fate into the position of a tailor at a time when he has the strongest reason to avoid the shafts of conventional prejudice. The problem is serious enough certainly, and it is solved in a perfectly serious and satisfactory way. To assert, as has been done, that the treatment of the story is "utterly lacking in common dignity and manhood", on the ground that "Harrington finds salvation not in paying off his father's debts by working, but by the old, old snobbish expedient of marrying an heiress", is simply a disingenuous perversion of the facts. No healthy social sentiment is outraged by the *dénoûment*, even though the hero's path is smoothed out for him by a turn of good fortune that saves him from an uncongenial occupation. His moral salvation is effectually wrought out when he abandons all pretence to the future in which his happiness seems involved, and accepts courageously the humble career marked out by duty and honour. Surely we may be satisfied with this, without demanding in the interests of moral realism that Evan shall remain at the cutting-board all his life.

Although the formal *motif* of this novel is the effort of Harrington to submit himself to the destiny that fate has appointed for him, our interest is no less strongly centred on two other themes that are interwoven with it. The romantic element that is supplied in the courtship of Rose Joceleyn is not only highly effective in its emotional appeal, but has a deep psychological significance. The history of Evan's relations with the brave-hearted, impetuous English maiden is told with that keen penetration into the subtleties of the hearts of women which may be claimed as the outstanding feature of Meredith's power as an artist. Even more distinctive and important, however, is the study of the Countess de Saldar, the brilliant and unscrupulous lady whom the pressure of events has driven to adopt the *rôle* of an adventuress, but whose desire for the social advancement of her brother rather than of herself almost wins our sympathy in spite of our disapproval of her methods. The Countess and Richmond Roy are probably the most subtle studies of the type they represent that could be found in the whole of fiction; beside them Becky Sharp and Barry Lyndon are coarse commonplace schemers.

Rhoda Fleming is on the whole a finer novel than *Richard Feverel*. If it does not rise to the same high level of beauty in description, and does not sparkle with wit in the same degree, it is yet a more perfectly-balanced whole, challenging less criticism in point of construction. In regard to simplicity and strength of handling, moreover, it may almost be placed first of Meredith's novels, while it has a further distinctive interest in its confutation of the charge that its author apparently does not think life has any seriousness except for those who are "clothed in purple and fine linen, and fare sumptuously every day". We may admit that he has drawn his material more largely from the life of the upper ranks of society, and that in his treatment of humbler characters, especially servants, he has sometimes aimed rather at reproducing their oddities and weaknesses than representing their inner nature with complete faithfulness; but that he is shut out from a sympathetic understanding of the life of the people is amply contradicted by the portraiture in this book alone. The creator of Farmer Fleming, and Rhoda, and Robert Eccles, cannot be accused of any want of insight into the thoughts and feelings and manners of speech of the sons and daughters of the soil. The heroine is not of course a typical farmer's daughter. In character and upbringing she may be above her station, but she is none the less an unsophisticated country girl, whose strong and simple nature is wholly foreign to the artificial conventions of society.

Though the consistency and power of the portraiture in this novel are generally admitted, there are several points at which doubts may arise as to the author's entire success. But even if judgment should go against him in two or three instances, we shall at least have the compensating satisfaction of admiring the wonderful skill in dramatic penetration and psychological analysis which creates so complete an illusion that we scarcely venture to trust our critical reflectiveness in contradiction to our first impressions. The most serious question is as to whether Rhoda would really have insisted on her sister marrying Sedgett in spite of her repugnance, even after she knew that Edward was willing to make Dahlia his wife. This is a point which it is impossible to decide on abstract grounds. We have to take into account not only the strenuousness of Rhoda's conviction as to right and wrong, but the narrowness of experience that explained her unreasonable mistrust of Edward's repentance. The author's treatment of the situation may not bring conviction to every reader; but no one will maintain that at the worst her action was so improbable as to interfere materially with our conception of her character.

One or two minor defects may be admitted in passing. The freak of the money-demon in urging Antony Hackbut to rob the bank is too much like a freak of Meredith's imagination, and the convenience of the episode in relation to the exigencies of the plot form no valid excuse for it. We may admire the resource of an artist who can justify his inventions with such aplomb as is undoubtedly shown in this instance, but we shake our heads nevertheless. There are many masterly portraits in the book, but there are one or two that do not stand out quite clearly. Major Waring is something of a lay-figure, but the least successful presentation is that of Margaret Lovell. The mixture of good and evil in her composition is too little explained; we do not seem to reach the springs of her character.

These blemishes, however, are more or less incidental, and scarcely detract from our appreciation of the power and beauty of the story. The strongest passages in the novel, those that impress the imagination with something of the elemental force of Shakespeare's creations, deal with the relations of Rhoda and Robert. The whole of the fourteenth chapter is a monument of spiritual analysis expounded with the finest sense of dramatic effect. It is scarcely possible to quote from it, but some idea of the passionate fervour which the proud, self-sacrificing nature of the heroine could inspire may be gathered from her lover's colloquy with his friend:

"'She saw you, did she? Did she colour when she heard your name?'

"'Very much,' said Major Waring.

"'Was dressed in—'

"'Black, with a crimson ribbon round the collar.' Robert waved the image from his eyes.

"'I'm not going to dream of her. Peace, and babies, and farming, and pride in myself, with a woman by my side—there! You've seen her—all that's gone. I might as well ask the east wind to blow west. Her face is set the other way. Of course the nature and value of the man is shown by how he takes this sort of pain; and hark at me! I'm yelling. I thought I was cured . . . but here's the girl at me again. She cuddles into me,—slips her hand into my breast and tugs at things there. I can't help talking to you about her, now we've got over the first step. I'll soon give it up. She wore a red ribbon? If it had been spring, you'd have seen roses. Oh what a staunch heart that girl has! Where she sets it, mind! Her life where that creature sets her heart! But for *me*, not a penny of comfort. . . . Will you believe I thought those thick eyebrows of hers ugly once—a tremendous long time ago. Yes, but what eyes she has under them! And if she looks tender, one corner of her mouth goes quivering! and the eyes are steady, so that it looks like some wonderful bit of mercy. I think of that true-hearted creature, praying and longing for her sister, and fearing there is shame. That's why she hates me. I wouldn't say I was certain her sister hadn't fallen into a pit. I couldn't. I was an idiot. I thought I wouldn't be a hypocrite. I might have said I believed as she did. There she stood, ready to be taken—ready to have given herself to me, if I had only spoken a word! It was a moment of heaven, and God the Father could not give it to me twice! The chance has gone.'"

Sandra Belloni, or *Emilia in England*, as it was originally named, was written and published before *Rhoda Fleming*, but it may best be considered along with *Vittoria*, to which it forms an introduction. Judged apart from its splendid sequel, *Sandra Belloni* must be held to belong to the lower rank of Meredith's novels. It is one that is not likely to be adequately appreciated until one has become well accustomed to the author's idiosyncrasies of style and method. The diction, indeed, has the comparative clearness of the earlier works; the passion for aphoristic expression is still kept under control. But there is a peculiar quality of satire in the general tone of the narrative that might readily be misunderstood. The three Misses Pole, who "supposed that they enjoyed exclusive possession of the Nice Feelings, and exclusively comprehended the Nice Shades", were certainly legitimate objects of satire, but it is difficult for anyone to believe that these young ladies could ever have existed as they are represented. It is admirable caricature, but it is not serious art, and greatly detracts from the impressiveness of the book. Nevertheless, there are admirers of Meredith who are not repelled by it. Miss Hannah Lynch, who has written an interesting little book on the novelist, finds *Sandra Belloni* "entrancing", and places it in the front rank of his works. And apropos of this fact, it is interesting to note that there is no general agreement among those who know and love Meredith's books as to which of them are the best. This is a high tribute to his many-sidedness, as well as to the abundance and force of the impressions he never fails to supply. *Sandra Belloni* suffers considerably from the lack of moderation in the portraiture of the Misses Pole, for they form a good part of the background of the story; but in spite of this fault, it is a great book, with more of interest and value in it than even in most novelists' masterpieces.

Vittoria is to be placed in the forefront of Meredith's achievements. It is one of the great novels of the world. In the liberation of Italy the author found a theme that roused his enthusiasm to the highest pitch, and gave him a matchless opportunity for a sustained elevation of tone and treatment. But it is not only in its earnestness of purpose that the novel stands out from the rank of its fellows; it has scarcely a trace of Meredith's characteristic faults, and it displays his command of the resources of the novelist's art with unusual fulness and certainty. The atmosphere of war and rebellion and conspiracy, as the author himself has indicated in the passage quoted from *Sandra Belloni*, demanded a seriousness of manner that precluded all appearance of satiric levity or extravagance of any kind. The style of the narrative is simple and direct, without any effort at phrase-making, and free from any palpable defect, unless it be an occasional rapidity of movement that taxes the reader's powers of apprehension. But the nervous strength that marks the expression throughout has no effect of monotony. As there is a wealth of variety in incident and characterisation, so there is the widest range of expression, from the highest eloquence to the most graceful daintiness of touch. Nowhere else shall we find such a happy combination of massive outline and delicate detail of workmanship. The march of an historic nation through blood to freedom is ever in our ears, yet there is time to follow with a strong personal interest the fortunes of the different actors in the drama, to note how great issues hang on trivial events, and how the interplay of motive among many types of character, grave and gay, noble and base, weaves a subtle web of destiny alike for the individuals concerned and for their country. The personality of Vittoria herself is the central point that at once forms the focus of the patriotic movement in its larger aspects, and supplies the concrete element that art demands. Apart from the dramatic success of the main study we are impressed by the completeness of knowledge, the penetration into the inner springs of action, the ardent and yet judicial temper, that give the book a high historical value in addition to its interest as a work of fiction. Meredith bears the weight of learning lightly, but his familiarity with the modes of thought and feeling, and with the manners and customs, civil and military, alike of Italians and Austrians,—nay, even with the details of the natural features of the country, and with the finer shades of expression in the languages of both nations,—is more than sufficient not only to convince the general reader, but to satisfy an exacting criticism.

It has been a constant ground of admiration with Meredith's critics that his warm enthusiasm for the cause of Italian liberty should in no instance have betrayed him into any lapse from the impartial attitude of the observer and the artist. Never was a more powerful impression made by so dispassionate, so impersonal a record. The Austrians get every justice; their point of view is fully represented, and their good qualities—their courage, their gallantry, their strength of purpose, their discipline and organizing power—are made clear to us. And there is no false glamour thrown over the struggles and aspirations of Italy. All is set down, nothing extenuated. It may be said, of course, that a novelist is no more than politic in holding the balance evenly between the conflicting forces in his story, so that the interest may not be one-sided or lacking in piquancy; but no consideration of advantage is enough to secure the necessary calmness of judgment and generosity of temper, if these qualities are not natural and constant possessions of the writer.

A study of the construction of this remarkable novel reveals the highest degree of skill alike in the general plan, in the treatment of the various scenes, and in the manipulation of the numerous figures that make up the *dramatis personæ*. Though there are over thirty characters that play a definite part in the story, there is not one that does not represent some distinctive type which is required to complete the picture. If, for example, we pass in review the names of the different Italian portraits, we shall find that while each figure is an undoubted creation of flesh and blood, it is at the same time an illustration in concrete form of some prevailing characteristic of mind or temperament. After the Chief, the most prominent and the most ideal of these is Vittoria's lover and husband, the youthful Carlo Ammiani, who with his ardent enthusiasm and high courage combines a delicate sense of personal honour and an appreciation of the heroine's nobility of character that win our ready sympathy. Nor is this sympathy alienated by the obstinate hardihood that in the relentless march of events brought about the tragedy of his death. We are scarcely able to blame him for the self-sufficiency that shut out from his counsels the saner influences of his loving wife; we can only pity him that he was borne onward in a relentless current that made everything easier than inactivity and obedience to reason. An effective contrast to Carlo's headstrong impetuosity is found in the more critical and reflective, while equally genuine, patriotism of Agostino, who supplies the element of half-humorous satire that forms an invariable ingredient in Meredith's novels. Other types are no less striking. Ugo Corte, the plain, blunt soldier, despising all finesse and compromise; Romara, the generous, brave-hearted friend; the brothers Guidascarpi, strenuous in their fanaticism up to the verge of mania; Count Medole, half enthusiast and half puppet of circumstances; and Barto Rizzo, the terrible demon of conspiracy in its sternest aspect,—all these add to our understanding of the problem at the same time that they fill up the spaces in the picture with a forcible appeal to our imagination. The Austrian figures are no less convincingly portrayed, especially Major Weisspriess and Anna von Lenkenstein, who may be taken as representing the distinguishing features of their race, its *élan*, its masterfulness, its contempt of conscientious or emotional scruple in reaching the desired end. In relation to these various groups are introduced effectively some of the English characters whom we knew as forming the heroine's environment in the years of her girlhood; and binding all together in a splendid whole is the personality of the heroine herself, whose fortunes we follow with breathless interest, from the fine opening scene when she meets the Chief on the Monte Motterone, through the glorious but futile triumph of the night at La Scala, and the terrible experiences of the fight in the Stelvio Pass, to the sad ending in her fateful and hopeless separation from her husband in spirit and in the flesh, though happily not in affection. Vittoria is the most elaborate of all Meredith's portraits. She is the subject of two of his longest novels, and he has recorded her history from her early maidenhood through the critical years of her development till she reached the fulness of experience brought by the stirring events of her high destiny. It is an exhaustive study of an artistic nature tried by the fires of disappointment and disillusionment, and purified from the dross of sentimentality, so that it stands out clear in its devotion to friendship, to art, to love of country.

Perhaps the only adverse criticism in connection with the character-drawing in *Vittoria* concerns the figure of Merthyr Powys. An intrepid critic of Meredith has called him "an insufferable incarnation of the prig". This judgment is not worth refuting seriously, but it may suggest to us the same comment that has been applied to the portraiture of Daniel Deronda. The nearer we come to the ideal, the more difficult is it to clothe the figure in the garb of our common humanity. It has been pointed out how in his younger heroes Meredith has departed little from the conventional standard. He has solved the problem partly by drawing his most ideal men after they have passed their youth, and partly by giving them an almost subordinate place on the canvas. This may sound like a shirking of the difficulty, but it is wonderful how effective a part he has succeeded in making such characters take in the action, in spite of their unobtrusive position. I have called Meredith the great master of the indirect, and it is one of his most characteristic devices in this direction to make the ideal element in his stories take the form of a figure of strength and courage and unselfishness, held more or less in the background, but manifestly winning for himself a high place in the confidence of the other persons in the drama, especially those of them who stand in need of help and counsel. In *Sandra Belloni* and *Vittoria* it is Merthyr Powys who fills this place of honour, just as in *Richard Feverel* it is Austen Wentworth; in *The Egoist*, Vernon Whitford; in *Beauchamp's Career*, Seymour Austen; in *One of Our Conquerors*, Dartrey Fenellan.

Altogether, *Vittoria* is a record of great events told with all the narrative skill of a practised historian, with all the wisdom and impartiality of a sociologist, and yet with the sympathy and imaginative insight of a poet.

In *The Adventures of Harry Richmond* the form of the title prepares us for some neglect of the unities; we are only to expect a record of adventures centring round the personality of the hero. But the time has gone past when a series of disconnected events, bound merely by the slender thread of their all happening to the same person, can claim to be a novel, and in the present case there is something approaching a definite *motif*. The book is really a study of the career of the adventurer Richmond Roy, Harry's father. It is he on whom the curtain is raised in that highly dramatic scene when he rouses Squire Beltham's house at dead of night and demands his boy; and it is on him the curtain falls in the no less impressive scene when he perishes in the flames of Riversley, the victim of affectionate but exuberant fancy, displayed in the theatrical welcome to Harry and his bride. Yet this unity of interest, genuine though it is, is not always strong enough to bridge over the transitions in the movement of the story; and we are hurried from one scene to another with such rapidity, and have to witness such curious episodes, that we scarcely know when we are touching solid ground and when we are lifted into the air. To those who do not object to be whirled about in this unceremonious fashion the exercise is certainly exhilarating, and many of the experiences well worth having. It is difficult to be very much interested in the individuality of the hero, who in himself is of rather a conventional pattern—high-spirited and generous, though with too great a share of self-confidence until the buffets of fortune take the conceit out of him; but in his relation to his wonderful father we have a study of the highest value. Richmond Roy is a portrait worthy to be placed along with the Countess de Saldar, and in some respects even more subtle and masterly. The author's power is shown in his winning our pardon and even our sympathy for a man who lives by his wits alone, who has no solidity of character, no self-restraint, no scrupulous regard for truth. It is his warm disinterested affection for his son that makes him attractive, and his irresistible personal *aplomb* that compels our admiration. We come to understand completely the extraordinary ascendency he established over Harry, who, in spite of his constant distrust and disapproval, never ceases to love his father and finds it almost impossible to oppose him. Though the hero is not a strongly distinctive figure, yet if we take him as a type of English boyhood and youth we can enjoy to the full the record of his varied experiences, which are related with a delightful buoyancy and humour. The happiness of his childhood was somewhat chequered by the blows of ill-fortune that occasionally plunged his father below the surface; but we can all envy him those bright gleams when Roy gave himself up to his entertainment with that magnificent abandonment to the spirit of the moment which no one of a less mercurial temperament could have been capable of.

Though *Harry Richmond* is not a satisfactory whole, it comes second to none in the success of its episodes. It is a series of effective scenes, some of them full of picturesque beauty and others inspired by rollicking humour, and yet others marked by strong portraiture and a pure command of dramatic presentation. There could not be more delightful reading than the record of Harry's experiences at Mr. Rippenger's school, with its early romance of hero-worship, or his adventures with the gypsy-girl Kiomi in their eventful runaway journey, and his compulsory voyage with Temple in the barque *Priscilla* under the remorseless providence of Captain Welsh, or the meeting with the little princess in the German forest. These scenes all dwell in the memory with the vividness of pictures from real life, invested with the glamour of poetic retrospect. The book has many points of effective contrast, most of which do not depend on any extravagance of conception. In scenery and surroundings we have the eminently pleasing variety of passing from the quiet country neighbourhood of Riversley, with its easy-going solidity of habit and opinion, to the unsubstantial excitements of a brilliant struggle to force open the portals of London society, and then again to the idyllic atmosphere of the quiet little German court, with its quaint mixture of artificial gaiety and conventional prejudices and romantic charm. It is in the strongly-marked contrasts of character, however, that the interest of the book chiefly lies. It is difficult to imagine a more striking antagonism of type than that between Squire Beltham, the incarnation of territorial respectability and narrow but common-sense obstinacy, and Richmond Roy, the imperturbable light horseman whose elasticity of spirit and wonderful rhetoric carry him bravely over all the slippery insecurities of his position. The different temperaments and points of view of the father and the grandfather are portrayed so sympathetically that we are able fully to understand how Harry's allegiance swayed between them, and to appreciate his difficulties in making good his responsibility for his own actions. The great scene towards the close where the opposing factions are all brought together, and the old squire expends his last strength in merciless denunciation of the adventurer whom the irony of fate has given him for a son-in-law, is a masterpiece of dramatic presentment. Keenly as we enjoy the terrible strength of his indictment, we never lose our feeling of sympathy for his victim. This is the highest achievement of the novelist, when he makes us wonder and learn and acquiesce, absorbing all our partiality and antagonism in the keenness of the psychological interest.

Besides the standing antagonism between these two salient figures, there is another strong continuous interest in the story in the relations of the hero to the two maidens whose fortunes are interwoven with his own. Ottilia is perhaps the most romantic of Meredith's heroines; she is a noble vindication of the high intelligence and emotional fervour that are combined in the Teutonic ideal, and may take a worthy place beside the French Renée, the Italian Vittoria, the Irish Diana, and the English Clara Middleton. It was no light task for the novelist to reconcile us to the decree that separated this ethereal creature from the youth in whose lot we had grown to be interested, particularly when her place was to be filled by a girl like Janet Ilchester, whose straightforward and matter-of-fact directness placed her at some disadvantage as a heroine of romance. But here again Meredith's insight and breadth of outlook compel our admiration. We are won round to the feeling that Janet's steadfastness and generosity and grasp of reality made her a fitting mate for Harry, and we are constrained to admit that if the *dénoûment* wears some of the sober colour of everyday prose, it is none the less likely to reach the highest faithfulness to probability.

Beauchamp's Career has the distinction of exciting greater differences of opinion as to its merits than any other of Meredith's novels, and that, as we have seen, is saying a great deal. Miss Lynch calls it his only dull book, and adds that "it would almost be unreadable, other than ... as an exhaustive political treatise, were it not for one or two successes in character-drawing". But if there is too much of politics for Miss Lynch's taste, there is too little to suit the demands of other critics. The following is the judgment of an able but perverse writer:—

"In *Beauchamp's Career* Mr. Meredith has, besides his usual ideal love-interest, the choice of the actual interest of politics. Characteristically, throughout the greater part of the book he hovers irresolutely between these two interests; but in the end, as might have been expected, the political interest becomes purely subordinate and, read in the light of the final chapter, might have been almost dispensed with. Mr. Meredith has been all along intent on the solution of the emotional problem. This is spun out to an inordinate length; and while the small motive of love and marriage is made out of elaborate psychologizing, what might have been the larger motive of the political interest—the reflection in the mind of an individual of the great mind of the nation—is handled in a merely perfunctory manner, and only made to serve as one of the factors in determining the course of the love-interest. Would any other of our great modern dramatic or fictive artists have been so lacking in the sense of psychological proportion as to contrast so imprudently matters of such vastly different degrees of importance, and finally to make the smaller motive bulk most largely?"

Now all this sounds plausible enough, yet it would perhaps be difficult to find another piece of criticism that contained so complete a misstatement of facts, and rested on so confused and baseless a mass of theory. Foolish as it is, the passage will serve well enough for a text. In the first place it may be suggested that as some readers find too much politics in the novel, and others too little, it is not unlikely that there may be just the right amount. Of course the degree of interest that we find in it must depend on the attractiveness that political problems have for us, but apart from the personal equation it should be possible to decide the point on purely artistic grounds. The question is really not so much of bulk as of relative importance. Meredith does *not*, as is asserted, "hover irresolutely" between the interests of love and politics. It was clearly his intention from the first to combine the two, and this is what he has succeeded in doing to the entire satisfaction of most of his readers. It is not the case that the political interest is "handled in a merely perfunctory manner", and the critic virtually refutes himself on this point by admitting a little further on that the book "contains the shrewdest political sense"; and finally, what is called the "smaller interest" is not made to "bulk more largely" at the close. But much more serious than these perversions of fact are the assumptions that underlie them as to the true sphere of the novel, and as to the place in life that belongs to the relations of the sexes. What is meant by calling love the ideal, the emotional, the smaller interest, in contrast with politics, which is the practical, the intellectual, the larger? The first antithesis, that of the ideal and the practical, is scarcely even intelligible in this connection. What can be more absolutely practical, both in regard to the life of the individual and the future of the race, than the courses of events that determine marriage? And where is there more room for the purest idealism than in the forces and tendencies that work out the solution of social and political problems? The contrast of the emotional and the intellectual is not so unaccountable, but it may easily be pushed beyond just limits. Surely the enthusiasm of the social reformers is as truly emotional in its own way as the passion of the lover. As to the "vastly different degrees of importance" that belong to the two interests we must dissent entirely. The welfare and progress of a community are of course of wider significance than the concerns of any individual. But the types that are presented to us in art are not individual in this narrow sense; they are generic. They prefigure the experiences of the great majority of human beings, and thus have as extended an application as any corporate institution of society. It matters comparatively little what Beauchamp in his private capacity may do, but when he represents each one of us his action becomes of supreme importance. And while this holds good, more or less, in every particular of his conduct, it is true above all in those personal relations that determine the very structure of society. A community is an aggregate not of individuals but of families. If the future of humanity is decided by the interaction of different races and states co-operating and competing with each other, it is equally true that the evolution of every nation, every society,—and therefore indirectly of the race itself—is the outcome of a conflict of forces that belongs to the history of family life. Whether we have special regard to the inexorable laws of hereditary transmission, or to the more easily discernible influences on character that pervade all the closer domestic relations, we cannot fail to be profoundly impressed by the momentous nature of the issues that depend on the choice of a husband or a wife. The subtle compound of conditions, physical and spiritual, that form the bonds of attraction between men and women, constitutes a theme that, so far from lacking serious practical importance, may almost be considered the main problem of life. I have already quoted in a former chapter George Eliot's eloquent vindication of the prominence the love-interest receives in her stories, but this is such a vital question in relation to the art of the novelist that it merits a more reasoned defence. No writer has any need to ask forbearance or to fear reproach on the ground that the subject of love bulks too largely in his pages. It is true that he touches it at his peril; there are many chances of darkening counsel to the one chance that he may have some wise guidance, some acute perception, some fresh quickening impulse towards the ideal, to contribute. It is a theme which it is fatally easy to treat unworthily; on every side there are temptations to levity, to grossness, to insincerity, to sentimentalism. But the great novelists who can weigh their responsibility aright may claim the utmost freedom in dealing with a problem which they recognise to be no mere excuse for exciting the ill-regulated emotions of the idle and the frivolous, but as a precious opportunity of giving artistic expression to scientific truths of the highest moment.

If we ask what is the *motif* of this book, the answer must be that it is a study of the conflict of ideas with the inertia of sentiment and tradition—a conflict that is presented to us with the same comprehensive sympathy and sense of justice that we noted in the author's account of Italy's struggles under the grasp of the Austrians. *Beauchamp's Career* is a demonstration of the difficulty, in a transition phase of progress, of reconciling the zeal of a reforming temper with the claims of a long-established order of society. The ultra-radical stand-point is of course represented mainly by the hero himself, but also very effectively by Dr. Shrapnel, whose detachment from social trammels and from the more direct forms of public responsibility give him the fullest freedom of expression. I can see no ground whatever for the assertion made by one critic that Dr. Shrapnel is "drawn in a spirit of gross caricature". It is true that his idiosyncrasies are noted with the observant humour that is never absent from Meredith's portrayal of character, whatever be the type; but it is perfectly clear that in its leading features the figure of the kind-hearted, strenuous old doctor is regarded with serious sympathy, and that his stand-point is held to be a position of vantage. It is, however, in the forces of the opposition that Beauchamp has to encounter that we find the greatest variety and happiness of characterisation. At the extreme verge of intolerant obscurantism comes his uncle Ronfrey, described as "in person a noticeable gentleman, in mind a mediæval baron, in politics a crotchety unintelligible Whig", who in spite of his unreasoning prejudices attracts our liking by his shrewdness, his strength of purpose, and his loyalty to his natural affection for his nephew, which survives even the severest strain. Three interesting intermediate representations of the Conservative type are Blackburn Tuckham, the worthy but unromantic young lawyer whose reasonableness and generosity keep us from disliking him, although he is placed in the highly invidious position of carrying off the heroine, whom we feel to be properly due to Beauchamp; Seymour Austen, the embodiment of calm strength, and restraint, and fair-mindedness; and Colonel Halkett, the excellently-drawn type of a well-meaning man, whose injustice and lack of sympathy are accounted for simply by his intellectual limitations, and the narrow bounds of his social horizon. On the same side must be numbered Cecilia herself, for the determining cause in her destiny lay within her own nature, or at least in the tyranny of her position, which she allowed herself to submit to. But lest we should incline to condemn her overmuch, let us hear the author's defence of her, in a passage to which we may give a wider reference as an expression of his sympathy with women in their disabilities.

"She could not write to Nevil . . . because she was one of the artificial creatures called women . . . who dare not be spontaneous, and cannot act independently if they would continue to be admirable in the world's eye, and who for that object must remain fixed on shelves, like other marketable wares, avoiding motion to avoid shattering or tarnishing. This is their fate, only in degree less inhuman than that of Hellenic and Trojan princesses offered up to the gods, or pretty slaves to the dealers. Their artificiality is at once their bane and their source of superior pride."

In *Beauchamp's Career* the interesting question arises whether it is possible to understand or respect a hero who, within a short space of time, if not simultaneously, is in love with three different women. This is a very superficial and indiscriminating way of characterising Nevil Beauchamp's relations to Renée, to Cecilia Halkett, and to Jenny Denham, but it is the form in which the question has been sometimes put. The record of the hero's attachments is a valuable assertion of the truth that while choice in marriage cannot be too careful, success is not bounded by a single chance. Renée or Cecilia could have made him happy as well as Jenny; each would have appealed in part to a different side of his nature, would have struck a different chord, though many of the notes would have been the same. There is perhaps no other notable work of fiction that illustrates this precise situation,—certainly there is none where it is portrayed with so much fulness and subtlety. It is quite another *motif* from the favourite device of making hero or heroine fall in love with the wrong person first, in order to give point to their falling in love with the right person afterwards; and if it is a less common experience, and one that does not flatter so much the sentimental notion of love as a predestined fate, it is at least entirely true to life, and affords a special opportunity for a searching scrutiny of the mysteries of the heart. The special difficulty that some may have felt in accepting Beauchamp's emotional experiences as compatible with the possession of ideal qualities, would arise of course in relation to the question of time. We can have little respect for a nature so shallow or unstable that it is not wholly and continuously absorbed by any passionate affection that it conceives. Though we may readily enough understand how one passion can succeed another, our instinct demands, and rightly demands, that they should not be numerous or come closely together. But any adverse criticism of Beauchamp in this respect would take no account of the difference of his feeling towards each of the three girls. It depends on opportunity whether an attraction will ripen into a strong attachment, and constancy can be demanded only when some profession of love has created an obligation. The hero's first romantic fancy for Renée was arrested before it had time to enlist the strength of his whole character, and it remained with him only as a tender memory appealing to his sense of chivalry. In Cecilia Halkett his maturer nature discovered a possible mate, whom early friendship and family influences and personal sympathy combined to recommend, but who drifted away from him, partly owing to the almost accidental perversity of events, partly owing to an inevitable antagonism between her surroundings and the *rôle* that her lover's social enthusiasm led him to adopt, and partly also owing to a wrong-headedness on his part that detracts from his heroic quality while it is wholly in keeping with his impetuous disposition. It is in the history of his relation to Cecilia as it is mirrored in her consciousness that the psychological value of the love-interest lies. In her mind we see what Beauchamp really was, and at the same time we get a masterly account of the struggle of a girl's affection with the tyranny of circumstance, both within and without her. Only after Cecilia was lost to him and he had gone through a severe illness and other sobering experiences did Beauchamp find that his sympathy with Jenny Denham had been transformed by gratitude into a tenderness of feeling that impelled him to seek her as his wife; and the reader is induced to acquiesce in this union as likely to yield quite as much satisfaction as any other. Even had the various episodes occurred in a closer succession than was really the case, there was nothing in the hero's varying phases of feeling that could be held inconsistent with constancy or depth of character. But it is nevertheless true that the solution does not altogether please us, and we suspect that this is not entirely due to a weak preference for a conventional winding up that would deal happiness all round in the form we have anticipated. Are we then to blame the novelist? A more careful study will make it clear that our disappointment in the issue of Beauchamp's love affairs is a necessary and significant part of the disappointment we are meant to feel in Beauchamp's career as a whole. He is not presented to us as an ideal hero, though he has enough of the qualities proper to such a part to enlist our sympathies in his failure to reach anything like an epic greatness. His was a strenuous nature that found no fitting opportunity for expansion. It was too hard a task for his wisdom and patience to reconcile obedience to the promptings of social enthusiasm with conformity to the code of behaviour that his aristocratic birth and surroundings imposed on him. He fought his fight so far with credit that his courage never failed him, and he made no compromise with his convictions; but it was inevitable that in his manful buffeting with the world he should lose some of his fine sensibility. Perhaps it may even be said that one who could persevere in the struggle under such conditions must have been from the first somewhat deficient in the more delicate refinements of character; of two opposite goods both cannot be fully possessed, and it is one of the tragedies of life that the widening of sympathy is so often accompanied by a loss of intensity in response to individual claims. The social reformer has to pay for his breadth of outlook by forfeiting his keen interest in personal relationships. This is the key to the story of Beauchamp's attachments. So far from being in love with three women he can scarcely be said to have been really in love with any. He had qualities that called forth admiration and affection, but he was too much enamoured of his own gospel and too much preoccupied with his mission to be able to make any adequate requital. "Does incessant battling keep the intellect clear?" was the question addressed to him by one of his best friends, and the answer must be—"No! it neither allows the intellect to be clear, nor the heart to be free". It is a part of the pathos of the situation that the emotional irresponsiveness that so often exasperates us is in most cases associated with traits in his character that we cannot but admire. It is hard to quarrel with him because in his generous discipleship for Dr. Shrapnel he was more anxious to read to Cecilia a part of his friend's letter, extreme though it might be, than to listen to the military band; yet there must have been a strange obtuseness in a lover who could not see what was the true policy of the moment. A man cannot of course be blamed for being unmusical, but we are forced to recognise that a nature given to storm and stress is almost sure to be deficient in susceptibility to artistic impressions, which are the avenues of emotional sympathy.

Much abuse has been heaped on Meredith's head for cutting short his story, or at least ending abruptly the imaginative prospect that the story opened out, by the untimely death of the hero. It is not of course demanded by any reasonable person that heroes and heroines should never die young, but we naturally expect that the tragedy shall follow with some appearance of necessity from the leading situations of the narrative. It is urged that in the present case the catastrophe was purely accidental and gratuitous, bearing no relation to the previous course of the story, and harrowing our feelings without any evident purpose. There is something to be said, however, in the author's defence. In the first place, it will be granted that Beauchamp's death by drowning, in the effort to save another's life, not only was wholly in keeping with his generous impetuosity of character and courageous disregard of consequences under the impulse of the moment, but took the form that harmonises most fittingly with our ideas of the gallant young naval officer, whose proper sphere of activity, in the opinion of many of his best friends, was the sea. But there is still more to be said. It is not beyond the province of the novelist to suggest general truths through the symbolism of a destiny in which no definite sequence of cause and effect may be traceable; and so long as the laws of probability are not transgressed, such an appeal to our imagination is surely to be welcomed. It is idle to say that Beauchamp was killed off because the author did not know what to do with him, for there was no need to do anything at all with him at that stage. The book might have been ended with a mere indication of some likely direction for his future, or the curtain might have been drawn, without any inartistic suddenness, on the early scenes of his married life; but our sense of fitness is really better satisfied as it is. The casual manner of the hero's end is meant to symbolise the lesson of his career. It is an indirect presentment of the double-edged truth that while on the one hand energy and fearlessness and disinterested enthusiasm will avail little without the rarer gifts of patience and wisdom and foresight, yet there is a saving grace in the instinctive sacrifice of self which the world will never cease to value and applaud.

In so far as we can draw any separating line between Meredith's earlier and his later manner, it may be placed between *Beauchamp's Career* and his next work, *The Egoist*. From this point onwards we find certain tendencies of style and treatment more or less prominently marked. In the later novels there is less direct presentation of the characters in action and speech, more exposition of their thoughts and feelings from observation and analysis. It is scarcely possible to decide in the abstract whether this represents an improvement in method or whether it is a step in the wrong direction. The novelist is in part a dramatist, in part a story-teller, and it depends on many things whether in any given case he should speak mostly in his own person, or let his creations tell their own tale. It is to be regarded, however, as a natural feature of a novelist's development that reflective description should tend to encroach on his faculty of immediate literal transcript from life, and this tendency will be all the more marked when, as in Meredith's case, the gift of analytical introspection is more remarkable than the power of reproducing living speech. No novel, of course, can afford to dispense altogether with the more palpable forms of action, of which in our day dialogue is perhaps the chief, and it is to be feared that too great a reliance on indirect modes of delineation is apt to keep the hand out of practice for the purely impersonal manipulation of the characters. All this will account for the fact which most readers of Meredith must have experienced, that in his last five novels we feel ourselves on firmer ground when we are following the author's searching scrutiny of thought and fancy and motive than when we are listening to the actual conversations of the figures of the drama.

I have placed *The Egoist* alongside *Vittoria* in the front rank of Meredith's novels, but for different reasons. In style and treatment the two stories are strongly contrasted, each representing the highest achievement in its own kind. While the tale of Italian freedom shows the author in his most impersonal mood, dealing with great issues in the history of outward events in a spirit of objective observation, and in a style of simple directness, *The Egoist* has for its subject-matter the anatomy of a single mind and heart, which is unfolded with a striking combination of penetrative insight and self-conscious humour, expressed with the greatest fastidiousness of phrase. The characteristics of Meredith's later manner are here displayed in their most favourable light, and the barriers that he has allowed to grow up between him and the public may as yet be surmounted without any painful effort, while the special graces of the earlier novels are still to be discerned. If there is a certain suggestion of artificiality in the framework which makes us hesitate to call it absolutely Meredith's finest work, it is at least certainly the most unique, the most wonderful, the most consistently artistic in plan and treatment. I have already quoted the passage in which the author explains and justifies his use of the sub-title "A Comedy in Narrative", but it should be further noted that if this is a plea for greater liberty, there is a faithful fulfilment of the bargain that the price of freedom in tone and manner shall be paid in obedience to the limitations of the dramatic form. The unities are carefully observed. The scene is laid entirely in a country house and its immediate neighbourhood; the action, after some passages of introduction, is limited to the space of a few weeks; and the whole interest centres round a single situation. There is no doubt that this unusual concentration of aim adds immensely to the force of the impression, and the slight feeling of unreality which may at first be associated with it tends to disappear as we learn to make allowance for the conditions. Every form of art must have its own conventions, without which it cannot produce its legitimate effects. The first time we go to the theatre we are inevitably disappointed at the incompleteness of the illusion. That is because we unconsciously expect the reality of nature to be merely imitated instead of transformed by art. As we come to understand the conditions of representation more fully, we cease to demand what the stage cannot offer, and are then able to appreciate rightly the effects that lie within its sphere. It is the same with a book like *The Egoist*, that is purposely cast in a form more artificial than belongs to ordinary forms of fiction. A first reading, while it cannot fail to leave a strong impression of brilliancy and power, bewilders us a little from the novelty of the structure; a second reading finds us in some degree prepared to make the necessary concessions and enjoy the special excellences that the form permits, and when, like Robert Louis Stevenson, we shall have read the book seven times, we may well believe that all unreasonable expectations will have finally melted away in the glow of an unrestrained enthusiasm.

Variety of interest is secured in spite of a *motif* of unexampled simplicity. The whole plot might be summed up in a single sentence. Clara Middleton is engaged to Sir Willoughby Patterne, and the engagement is broken off; that is the whole affair. Yet within these narrow limits there is enacted a drama of life of the deepest significance. As its title implies, the book is a study of the most refined form of selfishness, in the highly respectable person of Sir Willoughby, and no more searching analysis of the subtleties of motive has ever been given to the world. The moral diagnosis which discerns every shadow of a subterfuge, every grain of alloy, in the most generous instincts, and lays bare every hidden corner of the human heart, would be terrible in its mercilessness if it were not free from every suspicion of cynicism or pharisaic complacency. Yet with all its profound lessons the book never for a moment belies its pretension to be a comedy. It is a spirit of sympathetic laughter that runs all through it and recommends the offender to our mercy. It is not indignation at the Egoist that fills our minds; it is shame and humility and sorrow that such things should be characteristic of human nature—our own as well as that of others. Yet the book is very far from being sombre in effect. Light and shadow course through it, treading fast on each other's heels, and its happy ending gives us a welcome relief. Sir Willoughby is certainly Meredith's most elaborate and most subtly-drawn character, just as Clara Middleton is his most entirely beautiful and delightful heroine.

The Tragic Comedians is an imaginative and yet veracious record of the pathetic episodes that led to the humiliating death of the well-known social democrat, Ferdinand Lassalle. It is a painful study, but it is carried out in so large a spirit that our pity never reaches the sadness of despondency, and our condemnation has none of the bitterness of contempt. From the dramatic stand-point the figure of Alvan is one of Meredith's greatest achievements. The tremendous force of his personality is conveyed to us by every kind of indication. His words literally glow on the page; we are caught up with his fiery spirit as by a whirlwind. Never surely was there so irresistible a lover! Yet with all our submission to the charm of his impetuous buoyancy, there is always an undercurrent of misgiving that helps to prepare us for the issue. His fate is another illustration of the inevitable discomfiture of the egoist. For Alvan, with all his splendidly-endowed nature, deserves this name. His self-sufficiency, sublime though it was, betrayed him in the end, and his ordeal, like that of Richard Feverel, came to him in his relation to a woman. He fell because he profoundly misunderstood the place of women in the world.

"He would have stared like any Philistine" [we are told] "at the tale of their capacity to advance to a likeness unto men in their fight with the world. Women for him were objects to be chased, the politician's relaxation, taken like the sportsman's business, with keen relish both for the pursuit and the prey, and a view of the determination of his pastime. Their feelings he could appreciate during the time when they flew and fell, perhaps a little longer; but the change in his own feelings withdrew him from the communion of sentiment. This is the state of men who frequent the avenues of success."

In choosing a wife he was moved by the desire for those graces that would best set off his own personality, or add some new element to the store of his advantages. So he wooed a daughter of the Philistines, whose rank, and beauty, and wit, and ready sympathy captured his fancy, trusting to the force of his own nature not only to win her but to mould her to his requirements. The story of the tragedy lies in this, that his plans might easily have succeeded, and might have brought him the happiness he anticipated even though he was not wholly worthy of it, if his vanity and overweening confidence had only allowed them to carry these out with reasonable foresight. Clotilde was not of a heroic nature, or she could not have been so utterly vanquished by her parents' cruelty as to swallow all their deceptions; but she had it in her to respond bounteously to the stimulating affection of a man like Alvan, if the first steps had been made easy enough for her. Each failed the other in the hour of greatest need, and with both we can lay our finger on the spot of weakness that came to leaven the whole nature. Clotilde, like her lover, was a tragic comedian, a self-deceiver; her lack of the highest sincerity of nature was apparent from the first even in the self-consciousness of her wit. I cannot quite decide whether the author means to expose her mercilessly in the terribly silly affectations of her speech about the letter to the baroness, or whether we may suppose that he has a sneaking tolerance for such misplaced ingenuity; but at least we feel ourselves at one with him in his broad estimate of the type, and we recognise the creation as one of great boldness in design and finish in execution.

Like *The Tragic Comedians, Diana of the Crossways* is based upon fact, but not with anything like the same degree of closeness in regard to the incidents. The heroine is intended to represent the Hon. Mrs. Norton, the well-known grand-daughter of Sheridan, whose beauty and wit and personal charm made so strong an impression on the society of sixty years ago. In some of the determining facts of her life, such as the separation from her husband, following on his unsuccessful suit for divorce, her friendship with Lord Melbourne, and her success in making a career for herself by her pen, the real historical figure is accurately reflected in the portrait of the heroine in the novel, but in other respects the author has used the liberty of the artist in adapting the situations to his purpose. The most important change is that which allows a happy ending to Diana's sorrows in her marriage with the devoted lover whose belief in her nobility of character remained unwavering through good and evil report. The real Mrs. Norton was not set free by her husband's death till she was over sixty years of age.

After all, however, the biographical interest of the novel is its smallest claim to appreciation. Its undying value lies in the wonderful intensity of colour with which the study of the heroine is presented. The highest testimony to the power of the portraiture lies in the fact that the extraordinary vividness of the impression is scarcely in any degree dimmed by two very serious difficulties that our sympathy has to encounter. One of these concerns Diana's manner of speech. Her conversation is too clever for anything. We have only two alternatives—either boldly to disbelieve that she could ever have said all these brilliant things, or else humbly to accept them with the admission that such unusual gifts place their possessor in an entirely different category from ordinary human beings. If we prefer to be sceptical, we impose on the author the hard task of persuading us of the truth of his creation through our grasp of its broader outlines alone, while the outer garb remains unfamiliar to us. This is a burden that Meredith often lays on himself, and it is surely a marvel of art to convince us, as he so frequently does, that the characters are not only acting naturally, but *saying* substantially the things they would say, when their *manner* of saying them does not appeal to our sense of reality. It is all very well, however, to reduce the difficulty by a counterbalancing strength on other sides, but no novelist can afford to neglect the witchery of illusion that lies in the artistic reproduction of living speech. It is interesting to speculate what Meredith's power would have been if his dialogue had always been as realistic as it is in his best moments. There is still, however, the alternative of conceding that Diana may have spoken as she did, being on an intellectual pedestal that we poor mortals can only gaze at from afar. But it is doubtful whether this is a more satisfactory way of escape; for besides the break of sympathy that the interval of mental capacity causes, there rises the further question—Even if Diana were able to frame polished epigrams with such ease and rapidity that whenever she opened her lips one dropped out, would she have used her unexampled powers with so little restraint and discrimination? There are serious questions of taste that arise in relation to the exercise of a gift that ministers so directly to personal vanity. We cannot help a feeling that there is more affectation and love of display in the constant war of wits which the heroine wages with everyone who crosses her path than is consistent with the essential simplicity of her character. It is of course possible that the habit of condensed metaphorical expression may become so much of a second nature that it is accompanied by no marked degree of self-consciousness. It is said, indeed, by those who have had the privilege of hearing Meredith's own conversation, that it sparkles with witty sayings such as he has put into the mouth of Diana, but notwithstanding all that may be said in this line of defence, our admiration for this most dazzling of all the author's heroines would have been greater if she had uttered fewer epigrams.

The second difficulty is a still more serious one. It concerns Diana's conduct at a most critical point of the story—her betrayal for money of the political secret confided to her by her lover. This has proved a rock of offence to many readers. Could she have done it? And if she did, is it possible to feel any further sympathy for her? Even if this incident had been a genuine transcript from the life of the Hon. Mrs. Norton, there would be no force in the plea that it actually occurred. The novelist's business is to convince his reader of the consistency of his characters as he conceives them. If there are parts which we cannot reconcile with each other, there is some failure of art. Those who maintain that there is no excessive improbability in Diana's action are bound to persuade us that a high-minded woman may under the stress of money difficulties be guilty of deliberate treachery in order to retrieve her position. In the abstract no one can profess to find this easy of belief, but a great deal, of course, will depend on the nature of the circumstances. In the present case there is no help to be got by any suggestion of a difference of degree in integrity; for Diana, with all her faults, was the last person in the world who could be suspected *à priori* of any approach to dishonourable dealing. Nor is there any mitigation to be found in the nature of the act itself. To betray the confidence of a friend on a matter of the highest moment is bad enough, even if the motive be laudable; to do this for money to serve one's personal ends seems unpardonable indeed. By what device can we unite these two conditions in our imagination? Does Meredith succeed in any degree in making us understand how his noble heroine came to do this evil thing? Readers of the novel will probably be found to represent all stages of acquiescence on this point, from the absolute negative of incredulity to the most subservient assent. Those who are almost persuaded to believe may doubt whether the author has possessed himself of every coign of vantage. The main defence must rest on three general truths. The first is that we all have moments of moral aberration, when we do wrong things with the utmost innocence, only seeing them to be wrong when we look back on them. We speak of absence of mind, which is quite compatible with the highest intelligence; must we not also recognise an occasional absence of conscience, when some strong emotion seems to dispossess the sense of right even in the most scrupulous? As the author says in reference to Diana's marriage: "There must be a spell upon us at times. Upon young women there certainly is." The second point is that under the pressure of money difficulties people will do things that, when temptation is absent, they would regard with horror. And finally, careful observers have noticed that in the days when Diana lived, the sense of honour in women was as yet imperfectly developed. We must beware of applying the ethical standard of to-day to the problems of a less enlightened age! These considerations will certainly go a long way to smooth over the difficulty, and a close study of the masterly scene in which she is abased before the bitter reproaches of Dacier and the condemnation of her own better judgment, will help to carry conviction to many minds. The one point where one may venture to express a doubt is in the analysis of Diana's consciousness while she was carrying out her impulse to sell her information. We are led to suppose that the suspicion never even crossed her mind that she had no right to tell the secret. This seems scarcely possible; surely it would have been natural, and equally serviceable, to have made her at least partly conscious of what would be thought of her action, and yet able to stifle the feeling by sophistical reasoning.

The next question is, whether, if we accept the heroine's dishonourable deed as credible, we can continue to feel any further sympathetic interest in her. There must be few readers who would not side with Diana in this as in every other crisis of her life, not in the sense of freeing her from blame, but in holding to their belief in the essential purity and goodness of her nature. But this notable effect of the author's presentation is not gained by any loading of the dice. There is no ground for the contention that Diana is Meredith's own favourite among his heroines, and that he espouses her cause openly against the world, lashing her enemies with his satire, and portraying her with the tender mercy of a lover rather than the impartial candour of a biographer. This is Miss Lynch's view, and she would evidently find no fault with the author for such an attitude. But, fortunately for his reputation as an artist, Meredith is here guilty of no lapse from his uniformly impersonal pose. Satire is abundant, of course, but the heroine has her full share of it. If we love her, it is for what she is and in spite of what she does—not because she is presented to us in rosy hues.

The two most beautiful features of the book are the ideal friendship between Diana and her friend Emma Dunstane—a friendship which survives many serious strains on the affections from the waywardness of the wild Irish girl,—and the patient constancy of Tom Redworth, who represents a different type of hero from those of the earlier novels. It is to be noted that in all the later works the man who is rewarded with the love of the heroine is of a distinctly higher stamp than the impetuous self-confident youths of the earlier period. It is no longer a Richard Feverel, a Harry Richmond, or an Evan Harrington, but a political enthusiast like Beauchamp, a cultivated scholar like Vernon Whitford, a resolute man of action like Redworth, a strong self-restrained nature like Matthew Weyburn.

It has been remarked that in Meredith's later novels he has shown an increasing tendency to side with women in their battle against men. Put in this bald form the statement might very readily be misunderstood. There could be no greater mistake than to suppose that this great investigator of human nature has lent the slightest sanction to those crude and baseless imaginations, so prevalent of recent years, that pretend to ignore the essential distinctions of sex. The extreme advocates of what are called women's rights, who, under the unfortunate stress of the struggle for freedom from mischievous disabilities, cry out for changes that would imply not only an equality, but a practical identity with men in nature and position, will look in vain for support in the pages of Meredith. He is far too subtle a psychologist to miss the profound significance of those feminine characteristics of thought and feeling that are the inner counterpart of structural features which science is ever helping more and more to discern and explain. With him they are exceptional persons indeed who, like the Baroness von Crefeld, in *The Tragic Comedians*, "after a probationary term in the character of woman, become men". If the later novels show an increasing interest in the problems that specially concern women, it is not from any sympathy with the champions of that wonderful creature the New Woman, but rather from a keener appreciation of the qualities that distinguish "the everlasting feminine". It is not the sordid struggle of the sexes to rival or dispossess each other on the same ground that engages his attention, but the efforts of women and their friends to claim the recognition and influence to which they are entitled by the very fact of their distinctive nature. To a large extent, of course, the battle must be for freedom on the same pathways that are trod by men, and in so far as this has to be won by combating unreasoning prejudices and traditions, Meredith lends his powerful aid, as in the passage quoted from *Beauchamp's Career*, where Cecilia's helplessness under the bonds of convention is bewailed with sympathetic satire. But no reader of the later novels (or even of the earlier ones) can doubt for a moment that the author's conception of the ideal of womanhood would imply a development of character and functions in which the divergence from a masculine standard is no less marked than the approach to a common level.

It is in *One of Our Conquerors* that the problem of the position of women is most deliberately dealt with, but there is no talk there of the extension of the franchise.

The question is—How are women to be esteemed by men? How can social opinion be moved to grant to women the power to realise their influence? The book has a *motif* of singular effectiveness, combining elements of the greatest dramatic strength with the enforcement of a weighty lesson in social morality. It is a special feature in the plan, moreover, that the central situation develops naturally into another in which a complementary or corrective truth is illustrated. From a structural point of view this double *motif* has the great additional advantage that it allows a hopeful ending to relieve the pathetic burden of the story. In its main aspect, the novel is a study of the tragic issue that is to be reckoned with when those who are capable of a sincere allegiance to social laws fall under the temptation to make their own path pleasant in selfish blindness to existing claims. The situation is broadly similar to that of George Eliot in her relations with Lewes, but differs in the nature of the ties that were severed. It is of course impossible that either in real life or in art we should be induced to sympathise in any degree with a breach of the marriage laws where an appreciable wrong is done to innocent members of the family that is broken up. There must be the strongest reasons to urge in extenuation of the step before we will consent even to pass from the question of individual injury to the wider social aspect of the matter. In the case of George Eliot's union the special circumstances, viewed apart from the observance due to social needs, were all in her favour. For an artistic presentment of the position, it was necessary to have some definite personal obligation to give dramatic point to the Nemesis; and yet, as I have said, it was equally necessary that our sympathy should be conciliated by features in the case that would seem to enlist the laws of nature on the side of the rebels. This is the problem that Meredith has proposed to himself in both of his last novels, but he has somewhat unaccountably offered very different, if not absolutely contradictory, solutions in what are substantially similar cases. The treatment of the *motif* in *Lord Ormont and his Aminta* will invite our criticism presently; its development in *One of Our Conquerors* demands our highest admiration from the standpoint alike of artistic impressiveness and of social ethics. The figure of Mrs. Burman succeeds at once in touching our compassion sufficiently to quicken our sense of the justice of her attitude, and in throwing the weight of our sympathy into the scale of the youth whom she bribed to enter an unnatural marriage, and the maiden whose love opened his eyes to the terrible mistake. Judgment and feeling are so evenly balanced that we follow the issue with the deepest interest, at one time echoing the lovers' hopes for a release that would enable them to face the world openly, and again acquiescing in the inevitableness of the suffering that belongs to their false position. The force of the tragedy lies in the pitiless demonstration that in such momentous relations one wrong step may poison the whole life, and that the finer the nature the heavier will be the retribution. It is Nataly, the pure-hearted woman, the loving helpmeet, the devoted mother, who is borne down to earth under the load of shame and anxiety and suspicion, while Victor, who is made of somewhat coarser clay, is enabled by his irrepressible hopefulness and self-assertion to offer a bold face to the world, until he too is struck down through his affection for the woman who has thrown in her lot with his. The excuses we may make for him are largely tempered by our irritation at his insensibility to the more delicate aspects of the position as they were only too keenly apprehended by Nataly, especially when his ill-judged ambitions lead him into an equivocal relation with Lady Grace Hally. But yet there is true pathos in the spectacle of a man of such generous impulses and impressive personality wrestling manfully against the chances of social obloquy that threatened the splendid success of his outward career, only to be hopelessly defeated just when the goal of his wishes was almost reached. The most penetrating enforcement of the lesson, however, is to be found in the tale of Nataly's suffering unto death under a burden that made itself felt in every relation of her life, undermining her courage and paralysing her judgment. It destroyed her helpfulness to Victor, in the imperative need to preserve their affection even at the cost of mutual confidence and influence. It shadowed her friendships by the call for a mask to hide her consciousness of dark desires that required all her strength to control them. And—sorest trial of all—it separated her in spirit from her child at the crisis of her fortunes, by fostering a morbid distrust of the springs of Nesta's independence of thought and feeling. The whole history of Nataly's conflict with the world is a terrible warning to those who are tempted to persuade themselves that there can be any gain in combating the forces of social opinion when the motive is not free from every taint of self. Such rebels must be worsted in the strife with the constraining wisdom of the ages, and they perish without any of the consolations of heroism. Victor and Nataly fell by the weapons they had forged for themselves, but their love was not without a splendid fruition, though it was denied to them to realise its fulness. Their daughter Nesta is second to none among Meredith's heroines. She may not have all the engaging grace of Clara Middleton, or the brilliant piquancy of Diana, but she stands apart from these and all the others in the fearless strength and calm deliberate purpose that she unites with a personality that is full of charm. It was no doubt easier for her than for Cecilia Halkett to break through conventional trammels in the determination to widen the horizon of her life; but if opportunity favoured, at least it was fitly matched in the high courage, the quick insight, the passionate ideality of the young girl who stood out bravely from the shadow of her birth in her ardent pity for justice to the unfortunate of her sisters. We get a vivid glimpse of her in the following description:—

"Nesta's Arcadian independence likened her somewhat in manner to the Transatlantic version of the English girl. Her high physical animation and the burden of themes it plucked for delivery carried her flowing over impediments of original self-consciousness, to set her at ease in the talk with men; she had not gone through the various nursery exercises in dissimulation; she had no appearance of praying forgiveness of men for the original sin of being woman; and no tricks of lips or lids or traitor scarlet on her cheeks, or assumptions of the frigid mask, or indicated reserve-cajoleries. Neither ignorantly nor advisedly did she play on these or other bewitching strings of her sex after the fashion of the stamped innocents, who are the boast of Englishmen and matrons, and thrill society with their winsome ingenuousness."

If there is a suggestion of over-strenuousness in our final impression of Nesta Radnor that slightly veils her from our sympathy, we may well remind ourselves of the saddening experiences that met her in cruel succession on the threshold of womanhood, eclipsing her natural joyousness, and throwing the serious qualities of her nature into strong relief. At least we have the comfort of rejoicing in her happiness in the love of a man like Dartrey Fenellan—the one man she knew whom she could trust for his "respect for women—for all women, not only for those who were fortunate".

Though all the leading characters of this remarkable book are drawn in the author's best manner, the greatest achievement is the portrayal of Victor Radnor. He has the leading part in the drama; it is on his vitality that our conviction of the truth of the story depends. The task is no light one, but is fulfilled with triumphant success. The reader is borne along irresistibly on the stream of his sanguine persuasiveness, to the full understanding of the unique effect he produced on those around him. The subtle influence of his temperament is well conveyed in the following paragraph of analysis, describing Nataly's feeling when he was trying to induce her to share his renewed hopefulness that Mrs. Burman was about to grant them freedom by suing for a divorce:—

"The histrionic self-deceiver may be a persuasive deceiver of another, who is again, though not ignorant of his character, tempted to swallow the nostrums which have made so gallant a man of him: his imperceptible sensible playing of the part, on a substratum of sincereness, induces fascinatingly to the like performance on our side, that we may be armed as he is for enjoying the coveted reality through the partial simulation of possessing it. And this is not a task to us when we have looked our actor in the face, and seen him bear the look, knowing that he is not intentionally untruthful; and when we incline to be captivated by his rare theatrical air of confidence, when it seems as an outside thought striking us, that he may not be altogether deceived in the present instance; when suddenly an expectation of the thing desired is born and swims in a credible featureless vagueness on a misty scene; and when we are being kissed and the blood is warmed. In fine, here as everywhere along our history, when the sensations are spirited up to drown the mind, we become drift-matter of tides, metal to magnets. And if we are women, who commonly allow the lead to men, getting it for themselves only by snaky cunning or desperate adventure, credulity — the continued trust in the man—is the alternative of despair."

It is a reasonable desire that the sum of an artist's achievement should present a definite progress and culminate in a climax of success, and in this aspect *Lord Ormont and his Aminta* is disappointing, not because the author's cunning had in any degree forsaken him, but mainly because the general plan of the novel has not the necessary proportions for a monumental work. It is not that the eccentricities of style that belong to Meredith's later manner had become increasingly obtrusive, for the book is written with comparative simplicity, and is eminently readable and interesting. The dialogue, moreover, is on the whole decidedly more natural than in *Diana* or *One of Our Conquerors*, while the characters, with perhaps the exception of Aminta's aunt, are drawn with all the old firmness of handling and show no diminished insight. There are abundant examples, too, of the author's delicate humour and happy phrase-making, as when a decorous lady, in the effort to open conversation with a French boy, is described as "taking a slide on some French phrases". But notwithstanding all these subsidiary graces there is an impression of slightness about the structure that detracts from the effect of the whole. In short, we have the feeling that we could have done without the book; and that, in the case of anything written by Meredith, is to say a good deal. It is not only, however, because the novel is not indispensable that it is disappointing. There are more positive grounds for dissatisfaction in the curious fact that the solution of the problem raised by the *motif* is not only of doubtful value in itself, but is opposed to the lesson so powerfully enforced in the novel that immediately preceded it. Is there any sufficient distinction in the circumstances to prepare us for the entirely different *dénoûment*? It is not a question merely of the course of events; what we are concerned to know is the author's reading of the situation as it is expressed in the experience of his characters. With Victor and Nataly the rebellious step led by slow but sure steps to a catastrophe; with Matthew Weyburn and Aminta it was the beginning of happiness. The contrast is not explained by saying that the author is here showing us the reverse of the picture. If exactly opposite issues are both possible from the same situation, then all tracing of cause and effect is vain. The position must have been different then. But where? There is no doubt that Meredith means to justify his heroine in leaving the husband who withheld from her the status of a wife, and joining her fortunes with those of Weyburn, and in the weighty words of caution that he puts into the latter's mouth, in anticipating the difficult conditions of their proposed life in Switzerland, he evidently means to express his sense of the serious responsibility incurred by those who take the law thus into their own hands. Both Matthew and Aminta are represented as acting with full deliberation and without any apparent strain of conscience, and as they form the ideal figures of the story, our sympathy is manifestly claimed for them in this momentous choice. Few will agree with Meredith in defending, or even palliating, the step. Granted that there is more to be said for the lovers here than in *One of Our Conquerors*, still there is not enough. Even in such cases as George Eliot's, where the marriage bond had been already broken on the other side, the paramount claims of a general social law force us to condemn the breach, though we may discriminate as to the extent of our blame. Much more clearly may we refuse our sanction in those cases where, as in this novel, the impulse to sever the bond is born of an opportunity that confuses the judgment by the clamorous desire to enter into a new relation. To fly from a husband to the protection of a lover is an act to be held in suspicion, not only by the world that cannot make subtle distinctions, but by the two most intimately concerned, who know all the circumstances, if they would hope to keep any pretence of dealing honestly with themselves. That Aminta should have resolved to leave Lord Ormont was natural, and may have been right; but that the step should have been taken without warning, and in the one way that could not be retraced, was entirely unjustifiable. We may hesitate to say that no conjunction of events short of her husband's death could have excused her and Weyborn for eventually coming together, but the situation demanded that at the very least some time should elapse. If it be thought that in all this we should be saddling the author unwarrantably with responsibility for the conduct of his creations, we may take refuge on the surer artistic ground of questioning the consistency of the characterisation. We cannot believe that Matthew Weyborn and Aminta, being, as we readily acknowledge, essentially noble and honourable, would have allowed their passion to involve them in any breach of contract that was deliberate on their side and precipitate as regards the other party to the bond.

Of course this criticism is not to be taken as impugning in any degree the loftiness of Meredith's ethical standard. The decision of a point of this kind involves no question of moral rectitude, but only of the soundness of sociological judgment. Even on this more controversial ground one would naturally speak with diffidence in differing from so acute a thinker, were it not that we have the teaching of the earlier novels to support us. We can appeal from Philip drunk to Philip sober, from the Meredith of *Lord Ormont* to the Meredith of *One of Our Conquerors*.

After the disappointments of *Lord Ormont* it is reassuring to find that in his latest novel Meredith regains his normal level of tone and sentiment. *The Amazing Marriage* is not in the very forefront of his achievement, but it is undoubtedly a powerful and highly interesting work, and if it should remain the last fruit of the author's genius, it would form no unworthy close to a splendid series. In some respects, indeed, the book is equal to the best of its predecessors. Though the mask of cynicism is assumed in an occasional interlude for the sake of the free outlook it affords, there is no lack of seriousness in the general treatment, while the manner of the narrative is more than usually piquant. In point of style, moreover, there is little to try the patience of those readers who have learned to accept certain mannerisms of expression as familiar symbols that can be almost automatically translated into their equivalents in the current forms of speech. When one has grown accustomed to the idiosyncrasies of Meredith's language, it almost ceases to seem unnatural that his characters should reflect them in their conversations. The absence of the usual inversion of words in questions, the suppression of the *if* in hypothetical clauses, the omission of connective particles, the elliptical transitions from one subject to another,—all these well-known mannerisms, which are not out of keeping with the author's modes of thought, come to form part of a special medium, through which, by making an instinctive allowance for refraction, we see the figures in the drama in their true lineaments. The illusion indeed is not perfectly maintained throughout the novel, but this is not due to any failure in the manner of telling the story. Indeed so convincing is the presentation, alike in the analysis of the motives of the chief actors, in the supply of illustrative matter from the impressions of the onlookers, and in the subjective comments of the narrator, that the reader can scarcely help accepting the book as an authentic account of actual events. The *motif* could not have been endowed with greater *vraisemblance*, and it is only when we subject it to a critical examination that we discover its defects as a theme for artistic treatment. It has already been suggested that *The Amazing Marriage* affords part of the evidence for a charge against Meredith of too strong an attraction towards a *tour de force*. It is right for the competent artist to choose a difficult theme, which will draw forth all his powers, but he must steel himself to resist the snare of a subject so perverse that it cannot be made to wear the aspect of reality without a sacrifice of the ideal features required by art. In the present case the author has undertaken to trace the history of a marriage arranged at a first interview, and completed without any further opportunity of meeting. No doubt this is what happens in many a *mariage de convenance*, but the characteristics of an ordinary union of this type could not offer the kind of interest that was desired. It was necessary that the agreement should be freely made, and that both parties to it should be of a nature to attract the sympathy of the reader. Here indeed was a task to try the mettle of the most skilful artist! It is only just to acknowledge that no writer of fiction could have come nearer success than Meredith has done, but this very tribute to his genius implies some condemnation of his judgment, for if *he* has fallen short of a triumphant issue, there is the strongest presumption that the endeavour was hopeless. The portrayal of the bridegroom, indeed, is admirably executed; his eccentricity is sufficiently explained by his situation and surroundings. But this was the easier half of the problem. We can readily accept one such character without too severe a stretch of sympathy, especially when it is the man, in whom a greater degree of instability may be pardoned. The difficulty was to account for the coincidence of two natures in whom such precipitate and ill-considered action could seem conceivable, without forfeiting the reader's respect for one or other. Meredith has cut the knot by simply leaving the heroine's part in the earlier scenes unexplained. Our attention is directed to the course of the drama after the initial stages have been assumed, and it will be generally admitted that from that point onwards there is very little strain on the sense of probability. If we are prepared to regard the *motif* as restricted to the chastening influence of a strong and simple nature on one more subtly compounded of good and evil, in a relation at once intimate and full of misunderstandings, without enquiring closely into the genesis of so singular a situation, then we may glean almost unmixed satisfaction from the story. But the indulgence that is granted to the exigences of the dramatist, who must raise his curtain at a more or less arbitrary point, cannot be lightly claimed by the novelist, who is bound to share with his audience the vantage-ground of some conception of the previous history of his characters. In *The Amazing Marriage* the author has not wholly evaded this expectation; he has been careful to state the facts of Carinthia's heredity and upbringing which throw light on her individuality, and he has given us a vivid picture of the girl herself at the moment when she leaves the primitive surroundings of her youth to confront the world in a more sophisticated form. But the preparatory insight into her character only adds to our bewilderment when we find her plighting her troth to a stranger on meeting him for the first time in a ball-room, and holding him to his word, in spite of undoubted evidence that he had speedily repented of his rashness. Inexperienced though she was in social manners, she is represented from the first as possessed of a singularly clear apprehension of the realities of life, and it is quite impossible to believe that she would have deliberately entered into so momentous a relation without satisfying herself as to the prospect of happiness it afforded to both parties concerned. This is the really "amazing" element in the marriage, and nothing in the sequel helps to make it more credible. Only by shutting our eyes to this fatal defect in the *motif*, and confining attention to the masterly analysis of the various steps in the moral regeneration of the young earl, can we draw any lasting satisfaction from the story. It cannot be accepted as an artistic whole, but apart from the one serious inconsistency, the execution is admirable, the development of the tragedy following its relentless course with the inevitableness of that most tyrannous of destinies which lies in the very nature of the actors in the drama. It is no just criticism to object that the story need not have ended so sadly. A final reconciliation would have been out of keeping with the character of the heroine, whether we regard it in the uncertain light in which her precipitate betrothal makes it appear, or fashion it anew for ourselves irrespective of that doubtful episode. With all her ideal features Carinthia had the defects of her qualities. Her courage, her sincerity, her steadfastness, her generous ardour, were associated with a certain lack of sensibility. Her somewhat egoistic attachment to her brother, which led her to leave her child to the care of others, as soon as it ceased to be immediately dependent on her, was merely one expression of a nature deficient in the finer shades of imaginative sympathy. We may feel that, with all the justification she had for the death of her love towards her husband, a more tender heart would have learnt to forgive the wrongs that were not wholly without excuse, and had been expiated by suffering and repentance; but the author was undoubtedly faithful to the truth in his reading of the situation, and we are constrained by his portrayal to acquiesce in the tragic issue.

It is natural, before taking leave of George Meredith, to suggest some points of comparison between his total work and that of George Eliot. In regard to both it may be said that the nature of their task has been conceived in a spirit which was foreign to any of their predecessors. They have certainly been literary craftsmen, like the others, making their bread out of an honourable career. They have been also artists, speaking out of the fulness of their hearts, with a delight in exercising the gift of expression for its own sake. But beyond all this they have been leaders of thought and teachers, scientific observers unfolding the significance of conduct, practical moralists and sociologists, giving us lessons, none the less urgent that they are indirect, for the actual guidance of life. Their success in all these aspects has been secured by their exceptional fulfilment of the conditions under which alone a great work of fiction can be produced. Their choice of themes has been comprehensive in its range and uniformly exalted in standard; their characters and situations have been imagined and described with the keen observation of the naturalist, and the presentative faculty of the true artist; they have shown an unusual mastery of the technical skill in the use of words that is specially required from the writers of prose fiction; and they have known how to illustrate and adorn their narratives with a rare wealth of suggestive wisdom and poetry and wit.

There are of course differences of degree in their display of these excellences, but neither has failed signally in any one of the necessary qualities. In the case of George Eliot no particular failure is generally charged, though points of weakness in a few individual instances, such as one may find in the work of all dramatists and novelists, may readily be admitted. It is the rank which her total achievement entitles her to take, that to my mind is as yet scarcely recognised; and I have sought to vindicate for her a place of unique interest and importance among all artists in prose fiction, ancient and modern, British and foreign. With Meredith it is otherwise. He is still more or less on his trial, in regard not only to the total value of his work and the rank it will eventually give him, but to his right to be called a great novelist at all, in view of the alleged fact that in certain requisites of his art he is hopelessly deficient. The two special elements of weakness that are singled out by adverse critics, and are accepted by that section of the public that wishes an excuse for avoiding books that demand any mental effort, are his lack of constructive skill and his repellent style. It has been urged in these pages that the defects in the plan of his stories are so few and inconsiderable in contrast with his brilliant successes as to form no ground for any definite charge, while the difficulties and drawbacks of his style are greatly exaggerated.

A word or two may be hazarded of more direct comparison between the two writers. Meredith cannot be placed quite on the same level as George Eliot. He has not the same invariable truth to reality, the perfection of detail, the massive proportion, the well-defined theory of life. On the other hand, there are aspects in which Meredith must be ranked above the older writer, and indeed above all other novelists. No one has shown so great a range of power or so fertile an imagination. He is the only writer of fiction besides George Eliot who inspires an absorbing and passionate interest in life as a whole. In spite of all the difficulties that surround the appreciation of his meaning, and all the faults of art that may be imputed to him, he raises us into a new and wonderful and beautiful world, where every fibre of the soul is set quivering to strange and ravishing harmonies. Other writers, with a more vivid sense of proportion and fitness, may captivate us for a time by their success in appealing to one or another faculty or inclination in us, but there are few indeed who can hold us, body and soul, with so resistless a grasp as this great master of fiction.

Chapter VIII.

R. Louis Stevenson.

In a short critical essay entitled "A Gossip on Romance", and its sequel, "A Humble Remonstrance", Stevenson distinguishes three kinds of novels—the novel of incident, the novel of character, the novel of passion; and he urges that there is a proper tone and treatment appropriate to each. He does not hesitate to avow—and indeed the avowal was scarcely necessary, for his practice sufficiently attests it—that it is the first description, the novel of incident, that he holds to be, if not the highest, at least the most desirable form of fiction. In his view the greatest triumph of the novelist is the power to create so perfect an illusion, to represent situations of interest with so irresistible an appeal to the imagination, that the reader shall for the moment identify himself with the characters of the story, and seem to experience their adventures in his own person. This is the true poetry of romance, and, as he makes out, it is not only independent of character and passion, but it is even inconsistent with them. The interest lies in the succession of moving incidents, and any individuality in the *dramatis personæ* beyond what is needed to keep them distinct from each other, only serves to distract attention from the thread of the narrative. It is not quite clear how far Stevenson would carry this separation of aim and method, but it would almost appear that he would have every novel choose to be exclusively one of these three kinds; though in his own case he has scarcely carried out his theory with entire rigour. There is no question indeed but that the place he wishes to fill is pre-eminently that of a writer of romances; but if he had done nothing more than attain this ambition, he would assuredly never have reached his present rank. In truth we must join issue with him at the outset in regard to his theory of fiction, which is certainly extreme and one-sided. As the matter has an importance beyond the estimate of any single writer, it will be worth our while to consider it with some care

It may be granted that according to a logical analysis the interest we take in any work of fiction depends partly on the incident, partly on the characterisation, and partly on our sympathy with the emotions of the actors. But it is one thing to be able to separate these elements in our thought, and quite another thing to insist on this separation in the concrete presentment of the story. It is surely possible to combine two of these kinds of interest, or even all three, in the same impression. We are not less strongly moved to imaginative delight in romantic incidents because we have become interested in the individuality of the persons who are experiencing them, nor are we more able to sympathise deeply with moods of strong passion when they are represented without the characteristic traits that distinguish personality from type. Indeed we may go much further than this, and say that when these various kinds of interest are united there is more than the ordinary effect of combination,—there is even a *cumulative* effect. It is in fact our appreciation of the character of the actors, and our sympathy with them, that lends more than half the charm to the pictures we form of the circumstances in which they are found, and the emotions that affect them. For Stevenson is surely wrong in supposing that most readers are either capable or desirous of being so carried out of themselves by the illusion of the story as to lose the sense of their own individuality. "There never was a child", he writes, "but has hunted gold, and been a pirate, and a military commander, and a bandit of the mountains; but has fought and suffered shipwreck and prison, and imbued his little hands in gore, and gallantly retrieved the lost battle, and triumphantly protected innocence and beauty." Now children certainly have a wonderful faculty of making-believe, but it is very doubtful whether in many cases it amounts to the completeness of illusion that would be needed for Stevenson's argument. It is doubtful whether many ordinary boys have lived through these varied experiences, except with a tolerably clear consciousness of the unreality of the whole affair. And what about girls? Have they also imagined themselves pirates and warriors? The mere fact that the fancy of children takes entirely different directions according to sex is enough to disprove the contention that our pleasure in a work of art depends in any degree on the momentary forgetfulness of our own identity. The mistake seems to lie in the confusion of imaginative experience in our own persons with imaginative sympathy with the experiences of others. This will appear evidently enough from the following passage.

"While we read a story" [says Stevenson] "we sit wavering between two minds, now merely clapping our hands at the merit of the performance, now condescending to take an active part in fancy with the characters. This last is the triumph of romantic story-telling; when the reader consciously plays at being the hero, the scene is a good scene. Now in character-studies the pleasure that we take is critical; we watch, we approve, we smile at incongruities, we are moved to sudden heats of sympathy with courage, suffering, or virtue. But the characters are still themselves; they are not us, it is incident that woos us out of our reserve. Something happens as we desire to have it happen to ourselves; some situation that we have long dallied with in fancy is realized in the story with enticing and appropriate details. Then we forget the characters; then we push the hero aside; then we plunge into the tale in our own person and bathe in fresh experience; and then, and then only, do we say we have been reading a romance."

The more one thinks of this passage, the more astonishing does it seem that a writer of successful novels, who is an excellent critic into the bargain, should be so completely astray in estimating the effect of fiction upon the average reader. For it may be said boldly that when we read a story we are *not*, as Stevenson asserts, either judging of its merit or identifying ourselves with the characters, but that, on the contrary, for by far the greater part of the time we are really occupied in sympathising with the characters, loving them, hating them, pitying them, admiring them, despising them. In two important respects Stevenson underrates the intelligence of his audience. He says that fiction is to grown people what play is to children, and that is true enough if it means that the more it lifts them outside the bounds of everyday life, the more successful it is.

But he forgets that the conditions of absorbing interest are different, except for those who remain at the intellectual level of children. To the young, variety of character has little significance; to older people who are possessed of any cultivation of mind or heart, it means a very great deal, and incident will always be subordinate to it and dependent on it. In the second place, he loses sight of the fact already explained, that incident is tending more and more to become inward. The conditions by which our life is determined are no longer mainly those of visible action and adventure; the leading factors in our circumstances are the thoughts and feelings of those around us. Thus the key to the course of events lies largely in the reading of character. It does not of course follow that because stirring outward events are growing comparatively rare in real life we should cease to be interested in hearing about them; in some ways just the opposite would be the case. For the imagination rebels against the restrictions of modern existence, and loves to roam into regions that are no longer familiar to our experience. But the pleasures of such freedom are short-lived. Those who have grappled with realities soon grow dissatisfied with the irresponsible fancies of the pure romancer, and begin to demand that the pictures presented to them shall have some tangible relation to actual present fact. The supernatural atmosphere of *The Arabian Nights* is not the only kind of unreality in fiction; a story like Stevenson's *Treasure Island*, realistic as it is in its treatment, is just about as far removed from the range of possible experience, as regards its readers, as the *History of Sindbad the Sailor*. It may be said that such books are written avowedly for boys. We may criticise them on that assumption, but it cannot be entirely accepted. For though Stevenson modestly puts his tales of adventure forward with some such profession, it is very clear from his tone in the papers referred to that he believes the appreciation of young people to be the best touchstone of the success of a romantic novel. He takes for granted that we all envy the more complete illusion of children, and there is no doubt a charm to older people in recovering for a brief space the crude delight in reminiscences of semi-civilised conditions of life. There are still traces of our savage ancestry in each one of us, and the barbarous instincts of unrestrained violence and greed can be appealed to with success. But it is another question whether it is a worthy service for art to perform, to rouse even in the most indirect way impulses which it is the whole trend of social progress to destroy. It would be a mistake to say that such feelings should be ignored, for there must be no moral pedantry in the artistic selection of material, but it cannot be held unreasonable to demand that the lower inclinations shall as far as possible be represented in no greater proportion than that in which they actually exist. Tried by this test, such stories as *Treasure Island* cannot be justified. The skill of narrative with which it is told may blind us to its significance. There is so much art in the manner of it that it does not occur to us, till we close the book, to apply any standard to its general effect. The grim horrors of the situations; the strong excitement of the sanguinary struggles; the terrible figures of Black Dog and Pew, and Long John; the interest in the discovery of the treasure; the fascinating swing of the sailor's chorus—

" Fifteen men on the dead man's chest,
 Yo! ho! ho! and a bottle of rum";

—these triumphs of workmanship keep our judgment in abeyance till we reach the end, which we most of us do at a single sitting. Stevenson would probably have considered this the highest possible tribute to his success. It is a tribute to his power indeed, but not to his judgment in its use. The immediate effect of a work of art is not the entire measure of its greatness; we can say nothing more damaging about a book than that our appreciation of it was greater while we read it than when we looked back on it, and that we have no inclination to read it again. Not many people would think of reading *Treasure Island* a second time. When the experiment is made one is surprised to find how much the glamour of it has vanished and how repellent the sordid motives and vicious characters have become. As a children's book it is about as bad as it could be. There is not a particle of beauty in any part of it; the whole atmosphere is one of unscrupulous greed, meeting a reward which it not only does not deserve, but which in the circumstances it was most improbable it should receive. Further, there is no character-drawing in the book at all, and of the figures, such as they are, there is not one in which we can take any interest for its own sake. Fortunately for the author's own reputation this book stands almost alone among his stories. Some of the tales in his *New Arabian Nights* are not much higher in aim, and one or two stories, such as *The Wrong Box* and *The Wreckers*, for which he is at least partly responsible, are not higher at all; but in his later works we have a much juster proportion between the different kinds of interest to which the writer of fiction may appeal. But in spite of its inadequate and unsatisfactory motive, *Treasure Island* has excellences which must not be passed over. In particular it shows to the fullest advantage the author's unrivalled power of narrative. It would be difficult to find any more perfect example of the story-teller's art, free from any complication of other ends. Not a phrase, not a word, either too few or too many; every incident is presented to us as a vivid picture, and the impressions follow each other with entire subservience to the end in view. It is a model of constructive art, but all the greater is the pity that the story was not more worth telling.

In *The Black Arrow* we have hardly less skill in narrative, and if the excitement of the incidents is not so intense, there is the additional interest of the historical setting, to say nothing of the undoubted advantage from a romantic point of view of introducing, however incidentally, the element of love. In *Kidnapped*, however, we find ourselves on a distinctly higher level. Here we have no mere tale of violence and bloodshed and unworthy avarice. There is plenty of exciting incident in the story, but the adventures of the hero are made duly subsidiary to higher kinds of interest. We are led to value the book as a masterly picture of the political and social condition of Scotland after the rebellion of 1745, and in the types of character that are presented to us, we gain insight into many subtle intricacies of humour and temperament. David's uncle, who did him such an evil turn, is a notable study of malignant eccentricity, and in all the minor figures there is proof of the author's unusual faculty of conferring individuality by a few unerring touches. But the crowning excellence of the story is the character of Alan Breck, in whom the virtues and failings of the Highlander are so admirably represented.

It is certainly a tribute to the author's powers that our interest should be held so successfully throughout a book in which the feminine element is entirely absent that it is only the incidental reference to the girl who rows the travellers over the ferry at the close of the story which reminds us of the omission, but Stevenson evidently felt that such an experiment could not be hazarded again, and in the sequel, *Catriona*, while the other elements of romance are not wanting, there is the additional interest of a love-story. Of the heroine herself, and of the companion picture of Barbara Grant, something may be said presently. To the novel as a whole very high praise must be given. There are many readers who find it, like almost all sequels, disappointing in comparison with the story it continues, but these must surely be of the class that grows impatient when any study of character seems to interrupt even for a moment the record of sensational incident. There is enough of action in *Catriona* to satisfy any reasonable person, and the portraiture, while no less happy than in *Kidnapped*, covers a wider range.

Before we come to consider *The Master of Ballantrae* and *Weir of Hermiston*, in which are to be found the finest fruits of Stevenson's genius, the more important of his remaining novels may be rapidly passed in review. Of *The Ebb-tide* it may be said that it is a powerful study of a sordid phase of life that was scarcely worth transcribing, and of *St. Ives* that it is a good-going story of *The Black Arrow* type, but little more. *Prince Otto* and *Dr. Jekyll* claim a little more attention. The former deals with a different class of subject from any of the others, and is a proof of his freedom with comparatively unfamiliar material. The scene is laid in a small German principality, and the atmosphere is mainly that of court intrigue, relieved by the beauty of the affection between the prince and his wife, which is realised after much misunderstanding and mistrust. It was a new field for Stevenson, but the attempt was well justified. The interest lies chiefly in the development of the two leading characters under the discipline of events; and the analysis of the subtle gradations of feeling in their motives is almost worthy of even the greatest searchers of the human heart. At a first reading the rapidity of the narrative is a little bewildering, but the book grows on acquaintance, and will well repay a more careful study. Like all the author's works it is finished with the greatest care in detail. The secondary figures are admirably sketched and the various stirring scenes are highly dramatic. This is a noteworthy tribute to Stevenson's versatility, for the excitement here is of quite a different order from the shipwrecks and bloody fights that we are accustomed to in many of his other stories. It is a war of wits, of finesse, of moral ascendency,—in short, it is incident and adventure of the inward kind that lies somewhat outside the author's theory of romance. Nor is it wanting in many of the graces that we associate with a refined comedy. In the doubtful strategy of the Countess von Rosen we have all the stage advantages of a complicated intrigue; in the outspoken wit of Dr. Gotthold, the caustic irony of Sir John Crabtree, and the pitiable but ridiculous subserviency of the old Chancellor there are elements of various humour; and the excellent local colouring affords an affective scenic background. It is the moral interest, however, that remains pre-eminent. The relations of Otto to his wife, to his cousin, to the Countess von Rosen, are treated as only a wise and good man could treat them, and we close the volume with a stronger faith in the cheering doctrine that "all's right with the world".

In the powerful but not quite satisfactory study, *Dr. Jekyll and Mr. Hyde*, the force of the narrative, the charm of the style, the strength of the portraiture, are no less persuasive than in any of the other novels, but the distinctive character of the book lies in the attempt to deal with a grave problem of moral psychology through the form of a work of fiction. In itself there can be no more worthy aim than this, and indeed almost every really noble work of literary art may be defined in terms of such an endeavour. But it is the manner of it in this case that calls for criticism. In the transformation which forms the basis of the story our sense of reality is so strained that we can only escape the acceptance of supernatural conditions by agreeing to interpret the tale as a parable. Now from an artistic point of view this is a vicious dilemma. The realism of the treatment almost forbids the half-unconscious suspension of judgment under which alone the supernatural can be tolerated in narrative, and we seek refuge in the alternative of allegory, where no true refuge is to be found. The moralist in art must frankly profess what medium of suggestion he intends to adopt; he cannot with impunity trifle with the understanding of his readers. The uncertain sense in which the conclusion is to be received forces us to the judgment that the book, if it achieves an artistic result at all, achieves it only at the sacrifice of the moral impression. But at least it may be granted that under these almost impossible conditions the author has had a certain triumph. For, even with those who cannot accept the illusion, he has not failed to suggest imperious questionings on the momentous problem of the higher and lower self.

In *The Master of Ballantrae* the higher note that was heard in *Kidnapped* and *Catriona* is repeated to still greater purpose. It is not a longer story,—indeed all Stevenson's stories are comparatively short. This, however, does not mean slightness of structure or a restricted scope. The canvas is large, but there is no crowding; the strokes are few and telling. No author with so much individuality has ever obtruded himself less in his artistic work. We know from his poems and his essays that he has very definite and significant judgments on men and things, but very seldom, if ever, do these appear in his stories. Such reticence is not, of course, necessarily a merit; the abundant comments of George Eliot and Meredith are the channels of a richer and wider influence than can be exercised by those who deny themselves this privilege of the novelist. But it is an essential part of the method that Stevenson has chosen, that his narrative should be as vivid and forcible and restrained as he can make it. He imposes on himself, in short, more of the conditions of the dramatist than almost any other writer of fiction has done, and if he has thereby sacrificed something in fulness of impression, at least he has gained in the clearness and directness with which the characters disclose themselves to us in their deeds and in their speech. *The Master of Ballantrae* is not long, as novels go, but it is at least conceived and executed in the grand style. The *motif* is a weighty one, dealing with events of national importance in their bearing on the destinies of a house which is a battlefield of strong character and ill-fortune. It is a dark picture, but in its gloom there is nothing cynical or pessimistic. The pity of it all is what strikes us most deeply; and the power of the evil is not more borne in upon us than a profound sympathy with those who suffered rather than sinned. No more convincing portrait has ever been drawn than that of the terrible Master himself, whose existence was a perpetual nightmare to those whose lot was bound up with his, and there is a wonderful art in the way in which the dread of him is communicated to the reader. In the following scene there is the happiest blending of striking incident with vivid and powerful portraiture as well as the portrayal of strong passion. It is being discussed in the castle of Durrisdeer which of the two brothers is to join the Jacobite army in the rising of 1745. The story is told by Mr. Mackellar the steward:

" My lord, Miss Alison, and Mr. Henry all held the one view; that it was the cadet's part to go out; and the Master, what with restlessness and vanity, would at no rate consent to stay at home. My lord pleaded, Miss Alison wept, Mr. Henry was very plain-spoken; all was of no avail.

" ' It is the direct heir of Durrisdeer that should ride by his king's bridle,' says the Master.

" Mr. Henry went and walked at the low end of the hall without reply, for he had an excellent gift of silence. Presently he came back.

" ' I am the cadet and I should go,' said he. ' And my lord here is the master, and he says I *shall* go. What say you to that, my brother? '

" ' I say this, Harry,' returned the Master, ' that when very obstinate folk are met, there are only two ways out: blows— and I think none of us would care to go so far; or the arbitrament of chance, and here is a guinea piece. Will you stand by the toss of the coin?'

"'I will stand or fall by it,' said Mr. Henry. 'Heads I go, shield I stay.'

"The coin was spun, and it fell shield.

"'So this is a lesson for Jacob,' said the Master.

"'We shall live to repent of this,' says Mr. Henry, and flung out of the hall.

"As for Miss Alison, she caught that piece of gold which had just sent her lover to the wars, and flung it clean through the family shield in the great painted window.

"'If you had loved me as well as I loved you, you would have stayed,' cried she.

"'I could not love you, dear, so well, loved I not honour more,' sang the Master.

"'Oh,' she cried, 'you have no heart—I hope you may be killed!' and she ran from the room, and in tears, to her own chamber.

"It seems the Master turned to my lord with his most comical manner, and says he, 'This looks like a devil of a wife.'

"'I think you are a devil of a son to me,' cried his father, 'you that have always been the favourite, to my shame be it spoken. Never a good hour have I gotten of you since you were born; no, never one good hour,' and repeated it again the third time. Whether it was the Master's levity or his insubordination, or Mr. Henry's word about the favourite son, I do not know; but I incline to think it was the last, for I have it by all accounts that Mr. Henry was more made up to from that hour."

Short as this scene is, it is enough to bring before us the whole atmosphere of the house, dominated by the combined fascination and cynical selfishness of the elder son, the old lord submitting with the helpless bitterness of unrequited affection, the younger son struggling to repress his natural sense of injustice, but losing his peace of mind in the effort, the girl loving and yet distrusting the Master, and wronging in her heart the man whose whole life is devoted to her service. There are very few writers indeed who could in a couple of pages give us an epitome of such a tragedy by a direct presentation of the words and deeds of the actors; yet how quiet and restrained is the manner of it all! We see the picture through the eyes of the observant but unimpassioned steward, and in the contrast between the calm of the description and the repressed force of the emotions described we have a kind of impression which only a great artist can produce. How far such a passage is removed from the mere narrative of adventure, ignoring character and passion, which Stevenson defended by anticipation in 1882, and afterwards illustrated in the production of *Treasure Island*!

Although the *Master of Ballantrae* must on the whole be ranked as the finest work of art which Stevenson produced, there are signs of an even higher reach of power and a fuller maturity in the romance which the untimely death of the author left unfinished. *Weir of Hermiston* cannot, of course, be judged as if it were a completed work, for not only does the story break off in the middle, but even those chapters that we possess had not the benefit of the author's revision. There are certain aspects, however, in which it may fairly be brought under criticism, and if we should find in it any illustration of tendencies that are characteristic of Stevenson's work as a whole, we may have the greater confidence in treating them as essential features of his artistic method. In the first place, it is worthy of notice that in this novel, which there is evidence that he himself looked upon as his most important effort, besides laying the scene in his own country he chose for almost the only time a period belonging to his own century. We may trace here a somewhat tardy recognition on Stevenson's part of the truth that art is fulfilling its highest function when it is dealing with contemporary material. Before he could reach this position he had a long way to travel from his earlier doctrines, and indeed it must be said that the journey was never wholly completed.

The *motif* of the book is found in a study of the difficulties that may arise in the relations between a father and a son through incompatibility of temperament. In its general form, of course, this theme is peculiar to no age or country, but Stevenson was naturally attracted to it through its special application to the conditions of Scotland in the nineteenth century. There is perhaps no race that affords more possibilities of tragedy in such a relation than our own, in which the repression of all signs of strong feeling has become a traditional habit, and where convictions are carried into action with uncompromising rigour while they are conscientiously held, but are liable to be expelled from the mind with the utmost logical consistency if they are once discredited by reason. There is here unusually full opportunity for the inevitable gulfs in thought and feeling between one generation and another to be indefinitely widened by misunderstanding; and at no period of our history was there such ample scope for breaches of sympathy that seemed even more serious than they were, as in the earlier half of the present century, when marked changes in sentiment and belief were trying the tolerance of a generation brought up under a more stable *régime*. In the notorious Lord Braxfield, Stevenson had an excellent model for the portrait that forms the most impressive feature of the book, but some exception must be taken to the means by which he has secured the strength of the contrast between the father and the son. Mr. Sidney Colvin has pointed out that the period of the novel has been placed about a quarter of a century later than the historical setting would justify, and though in some respects this may be immaterial, in so far as it has any bearing on the development of the story it must be disapproved. A good deal of the piquancy of the contrast between Archie and his father arises from the differences of feeling and taste that are reflected in the tone of their speech; but it is not a permissible artistic device to exaggerate these differences by ignoring the changes in manners, and even in thought, that came about in a generation of no little significance in social history. It was part of the author's plan that the younger Weir should be essentially modern, so Lord Hermiston was forcibly transplanted from last century into this, and unfair capital was made of the historical trappings of his habits and manners. It is not like Stevenson to load his dice, and we may readily acquit him of any deliberate intention of heightening his emotional effects by falsifying history, especially as a more obvious explanation is to be discerned in the incompleteness of his journey out of the land of romanticism into the highest realms of art. He wished his book to be in the main a psychological study, the record of an inward drama involving problems that are specially acute in our own time, but he could not be satisfied with the amount or the kind of outward incident that would be in natural keeping with such a *motif*. Even amidst the milk and honey of the promised land he hungers after the flesh-pots of Egypt, and so there is introduced into his plot not only the old-time figure of the "hanging judge", but a good deal of the atmosphere of the days of border-raiding, with the surely much-belated incident of the rescue of the hero from the hands of the law by storming the county jail! This latter piece of melodramatic stage-business was never indeed actually written, and we may hope that the author would himself have perceived its incongruity with the treatment appropriate to his subject, before giving the book to the world, if he had lived to complete it, but it is instructive to know that at least it formed part of his original plan.

One or two other points of interest arise in connection with the intended *dénoûment* of the story as it has been outlined by the editor, though in making them the subject of criticism it would be unfair to press any objection in regard to matters that never received the author's final sanction. One comment that must occur to many readers is that Stevenson had proposed to himself an exceedingly difficult task if he hoped to retain our sympathy for a heroine who, while she is still in love with a man whom she respects, could allow herself even in the revulsion of pique and wounded vanity to be wronged by another man for whom she had no affection whatever, and whose shallowness of heart and insincerity she had wit enough to discover. It cannot be said, of course, that the situation is in itself wholly unnatural. We cannot even say that it was impossible for a great artist so to treat the episode that it should not detract from the ideal quality of the heroine sufficiently to alienate our sympathy altogether. But the venture would have been indeed a bold one, and it is not easy to imagine for it a wholly successful issue. A further remark may be made about the nature of the ending. There are books, as Stevenson himself says elsewhere, that begin to end badly, and others that begin to end well. We may fully agree with this judgment, and yet differ in regard to any particular case. Stevenson goes on, for instance, to mention *Richard Feverel* as a novel that ends tragically when it was begun to end well. Many readers would hold strongly to the opposite view, and will feel no less strongly that *Weir of Hermiston* was begun to end badly if any book ever was. One cannot therefore get reconciled to the idea that the hero and heroine should eventually come together to start a new life in America, and presumably to live happily ever after.

It is an interesting question how far the completed portion of this work seems to disprove the charge, so often made against Stevenson, of failure in the presentation of women. If it is true that when tried by this searching test of a novelist's quality he is found wanting, and that the ripest production of his art does little or nothing even to suggest that there was in him the possibility of worthy achievement in this direction, then we must admit a serious detraction from his greatness. Though we may not admit that such a charge can be made good in a general and absolute form, it must be granted that the author has laid himself open to it. We cannot disregard the negative evidence to be gathered from almost all his books. In some of them female figures are altogether absent; in a good many others they are introduced in a purely conventional and perfunctory way, to help out the action; and only in two or three do they appear as really important persons of the drama. These facts afford sufficient proof either that the portrayal of the "eternal feminine" offered little attraction to Stevenson, or that he distrusted his powers in dealing with it. Perhaps both conclusions are to some extent justified. If the mysteries of a woman's nature had lain open to his scrutiny as clearly as they did to that of George Eliot, or Meredith, or Tolstoi, he would have shown more interest and confidence and power in making them the subject of artistic treatment. But this is a very different thing from saying that he failed to be true to nature in the portraits of women that he has given us. It may be maintained, on the contrary, that his fault has lain in an excess of diffidence, that he has wronged his readers by too sensitive a shrinking from the danger of even a comparative unsuccess in a realm where the very loftiness of his ideal made achievement seem especially difficult. In support of this judgment one might point to the characterisation of the five women whom he has drawn life-size—Princess Otto, Catriona, Barbara Grant, and the two Christina Elliots. There is not one of these figures of whom it could not truly be said that it is at once a genuine type of womanhood and an ideal creation. There are people who do not approve of Catriona, but in the judgment of most readers she must be looked on as one of the most charming heroines in fiction. Indeed the conception of this character alone would go infinitely further than is necessary to scout the author's deprecatory self-criticism that his girls " all turned to barmaids on his hands ". *Weir of Hermiston* illustrates in a typical way both Stevenson's strength and his weakness in regard to feminine portraiture. His lack of confidence is shown in a rather exasperating fashion in his unwillingness to bring young Kirsty sufficiently on the stage to impress us with her personality. We recognise of course that she is not meant as a type of a strong nature, but the account of her first interview with Archie at Cauldstane Slap is enough to interest us completely in the natural freshness of her character, and we are keenly disappointed to find, when she next comes into view, that the intermediate scenes of courtship, at one or two of which we should so much have liked to be present, have all taken place off the stage. On the other hand, there is more than one indication of greater power and freedom in drawing the portraits of women than can be found in any of the preceding stories. The thoughts and feelings of the young girl throughout the memorable day when she first sees Archie Weir are analysed with an insight and subtlety that are new with Stevenson, who is in general content to rely solely on dialogue and narrative for the understanding of his characters; while the figure of the elder Kirsty, though it shows no remarkable originality, is not only firmly conceived, but is presented with an unusual fulness of sympathy and strength of touch. Nothing, for example, could exceed the vividness of the impression we get from the scene where Kirsty tells her story to Archie:

" 'And, my dear Mr. Erchie, ye mauna think that I canna sympathize wi' ye. Ye mauna think that I havena been young mysel'. Lang syne, when I was a bit lassie, no twenty yet,—clean and caller, wi' a fit like the hinney-bees,—I was aye big and buirdly, ye maun understand; a bonny figure o' a woman, though I say it that suldna,—built to rear bairns— braw bairns they suld hae been, and grand I would hae likit it! But I was young, dear, wi' the bonnie glint o' youth in my een, and little I dreamed I'd ever be tellin' ye this, an auld, lanely, rudas wife! Weel, Mr. Erchie, there was a lad cam courtin' me, as was but naetural. Mony had come before, and I would nane o' them. But this yin had a tongue to wile the birds frae the lift, and the bees frae the foxglove bells. Deary me, but it's lang syne! Folk have dee'd sinsyne, and been buried, and are forgotten, and bairns been born and got merrit and got bairns o' their ain. . . . And here I'm still, like an auld droopit craw—lookin' on and craikin'! But, Mr. Erchie, do ye no think that I have mind o' it a' still? I was dwallin then in my faither's house and it's a curious thing that we were whiles trysted in the Deil's Hag. And do ye no' think that I have mind of the bonny simmer days, the lang miles o' the bluid-red heather, the cryin' o' the whaups, and the lad and the lassie that was trysted? Do ye no' think that I mind how the hilly sweetness ran about my hairt? Ay, Mr. Erchie, I ken the way o't—fine do I ken the way how the grace o' God takes them, like Paul of Tarsus, when they think it least, and drives the pair o' them into a land which is like a dream, and the world and the folks in't are nae mair than clouds to the puir lassie, and heaven nae mair than windlestraes, if she can but pleasure him! Until Tam dee'd —that was my story; he dee'd, and I wasna at the buryin',— but while he was here, I could take care o' mysel'. And can yon puir lassie?'"

The most impressive figure in the book, however, and, as far as it goes, perhaps the most powerfully-drawn of all Stevenson's characters, is Lord Hermiston himself, whose appearances in the story affect us almost with the vividness of personal contact, though comparatively little of his actual speech is recorded. It is a subtle and well-executed artifice of the novelist to suggest the features of the rough, coarse, upright judge rather by the reflection of the effect he produces on others than by direct presentation, but in the scene where he disposes of his son's future we come face to face with the brutal frankness of address that almost belies the sound sense of his decision.

"'You're a young gentleman that doesna approve of Caapital Punishment. Weel, I'm an auld man that does. I was glad to get Jopp haangit, and what for would I pretend I wasna? You're all for honesty, it seems; you couldna even steik your mouth on the public street. What for should I steik mine upon the bench, the King's officer, bearing the sword, a dreed to evil-doers, as I was from the beginning, and as I will be to the end! Mair than enough of it! Heedious! I never gave twa thoughts to heediousness, I have no call to be bonny. I'm a man that gets through with my day's business, and let that suffice. . . . You've been reading some of my cases, ye say. But it was not for the law in them; it was to spy out your faither's nakedness, a fine employment in a son. You're splairging; you're running at lairge in life like a wild nowt. It's impossible you should think any longer of coming to the Bar. You're not fit for it; no splairger is. And another thing; son of mine's, or no son of mine's, you have flung fylement in public on one of the Senators of the College of Justice, and I would make it my business to see that ye were never admitted there yourself. There is a kind of decency to be observit. Then comes the next of it—what am I to do with ye next? Ye'll have to find some kind of a trade, for I'll never support ye in idleness. What do ye fancy ye'll be fit for? The pulpit? Na, they could never get diveenity into that blockhead. Him that the law of man whammles is no likely to do muckle better by the law of God. . . . Na, there's no room for splairgers under the fower quarters of John Calvin. . . . And I would send no man to be a servant to the King, God bless him! that has proved such a shauchling son to his own faither. . . . There's no splairging possible in a camp; and if you were to go to it, you would find out for yourself whether Lord Wellington approves of Caapital Punishment or not. You a sodger! Ye auld wife, the sodgers would bray at ye like cuddies! . . . There's just the one thing it's possible that ye might be with decency, and that's a laird. Ye'll be out of hairm's way at the least of it. If ye have to rowt, ye can rowt amang the kye; and the maist feck o' the caapital punishment ye're like to come across 'll be guddling trouts.'"

Chapter IX.

Rudyard Kipling and I. Zangwill.

Neither Rudyard Kipling nor Israel Zangwill has yet reached the age of thirty-five, and it may seem unreasonable to bring them forward for discussion, to the disregard of other novelists who have come to their maturity, and have the bulk of their life-achievement to show in evidence of their powers. But in another aspect it is this very circumstance that gives them their advantage. The older writers of the day have had their chance, and must be judged by the use they have made of it. If they have failed to gain the front rank according to critical opinion, —for merely popular vogue counts, of course, for very little,—they must be content with something short of the highest consideration. In their case no allowance can be made for possibilities as yet unfulfilled. We may be practically certain that Thomas Hardy, for instance, if he should write any more novels, will not show any greater capacity for sustained and consistent portraiture than he has done in the past, and we are therefore entitled to decide that in spite of his many subsidiary gifts he can never claim a place among the greatest artists. But if we should find among the younger writers of fiction any outstanding figures, where there is enough of actual accomplishment to form a sound basis of judgment, and where the quality of work gives promise of high achievement, it is surely right to turn our eyes in their direction in the hope of finding the most significant signs of the probable development of the art. There will of course be a margin of uncertainty in our forecasts, and any estimate of the final place in literature of such comparatively untried writers that is suggested by the association of their names with those of the great masters, must be taken as merely provisional.

The most interesting fact about Mr. Rudyard Kipling's work is his preference for the short story. This may have been largely due to the fact that he began his literary life as a journalist, contributing tales and sketches to a weekly newspaper in India. Whether he would have chosen this form apart from the pressure of opportunity to turn his gifts to immediately profitable account, it is scarcely possible to say, but there can be little doubt that he has found in it the fullest scope for his special capacity. Indeed the highest tribute to his success in adapting his materials to the limits of his form is that he makes us wonder sometimes whether the short story is not destined to supersede the novel of one or more volumes. What we can certainly say is, that henceforth a more honourable place must be found for it as an art-form of high possibilities. It was not, of course, originated by Kipling; he has had three worthy predecessors in our tongue, who curiously enough are all Americans —Edgar Allan Poe, Hawthorne, and Bret Harte. But though each of these contributed valuable elements to strengthen and enrich its resources, it has assumed with the English writer a more definite character and a greater range. In one respect, indeed, the short story is placed at a somewhat serious disadvantage. Convenience of publication demands that a number of tales should be bound up together, and when these are of different lengths, of different classes of subject, and of different degrees of importance, there is a sense of abruptness and incongruity in passing from one to another which largely interferes with their impressiveness. The only way to appreciate them fully is to read them with distinct intervals between.

One of the chief sources of Kipling's strength lies in the originality of his themes. His earliest literary conquest was India; he has laid before us with striking vividness the romance of that wonderful land whose fortunes are so closely bound up with our own. The wealth of interest that lies in its strange medley of races, of faiths, of civilisations, in its dark problems of influence and administration, in the conflict of heroic endeavour with the well-nigh hopeless difficulties of maintaining order and justice in spite of imperfect sympathy and adverse physical conditions;—all this boundless treasury of romantic interest lay unsuspected, till the magic touch of the young writer transformed it into current coin. Even apart from the artistic opportunity he has found there, it would have been a great and memorable achievement, for there can be few social services so valuable as to help in any material degree to give a governing nation a deeper understanding of the people they govern, and the conditions under which the task has to be carried out. No one can fairly charge Mr. Kipling with writing in order to expound any theory of government, but all faithful pictures must point a moral, and the political lessons of his stories are a part of their legitimate effect. The impression we get of life in India is not a cheerful one, but it is none the less likely to be true on that account, while it is all the more important that if improvement is possible we should realise vividly where it is most needed. The author's outlook certainly inclines to pessimism, but the occasional bitterness of his tone is not the cynicism of the man who has come to doubt the reality of goodness and truth; it is really a cry of pity and righteous anger and injured hope. There could be no more biting satire than is contained in his merciless exposure of the vanities, the follies, the wickednesses of Anglo-Indian life at a place like Simla, where those who have been for months exposed to the disappointments and dangers of service in outlying districts, meet together for a season of respite, and too frequently, in the reaction from solitude and hardship, forget the restraints of self-respect, and set at naught the bonds of social morality. Yet all the redeeming points of this perilously artificial life are no less persuasively brought before us, and our sympathies are invariably enlisted on the right side. Even Mrs. Hawksbee, the very embodiment of worldliness, is conquered by the "second-rate woman" she had despised for her dowdy dress, and sheds blessed tears when the child she had befriended is saved from death by the other's courage. We are made to feel in subtle fashion that the conquest is typical of the final triumph of what is good and beautiful over all the evil that flaunts itself in the high places of Simla.

And with what tender sympathy does Mr. Kipling portray the courage and endurance, and sense of duty, of those on whom the responsibility is cast of spreading the benefits of a higher civilisation, such as it is, through the vast territory that has so strangely come into our keeping! India may in some respects be a doubtful school of morals for the governing race, but in others it certainly must call out the best qualities that average human nature can show. There can scarcely be a deeper pathos than in the spectacle of patience and unselfishness and conscientiousness enduring through every kind of discouragement, and finally overborne by the incurable pitilessness of the climate.

But this is not the only kind of heroism of which Mr. Kipling has to tell. He has warm sympathies for the military side of Indian life, and his experience as a war-correspondent has given him a marvellous insight into the idiosyncrasies of Tommy Atkins, the British soldier of the ranks. Never surely were figures represented with more dazzling vividness than those of Mulvaney, Ortheris, and Learoyd, "the soldiers three", who in their own characters embody all the typical vices and virtues and humours of the whole army. Their adventures may not always be wholly reputable, but we shall hesitate to turn away our eyes when we have the chance, that comes too rarely, of looking at pictures that are pulsating with life and reality. There is pathos, too, of no ordinary kind in "The Courtship of Dinah Shadd", and "On Greenhow Hill", in which Mulvaney and Learoyd tell their love-stories, looking dimly back through years of cloudy strife and self-indulgence to the one bright spot of romance in their lives; while an even higher note is struck, in the praise of military devotion, in such tales as "The Drums of the Fore and Aft" and "Only a Subaltern".

Nor are his Indian pictures limited to the different classes of English; he seems to have just as full and intimate a knowledge of the manners and customs, the thoughts and feelings, the shortcomings and redeeming features of the native population. Mussulman or Hindu, Bengali or Afghan, men, women, and children,—all alike have come within the range of his unerring vision, and stand before us with convincing clearness of outline in his pages. He has evidently no illusions about these native races; he does not think them, and he does not paint them, either better or worse than they are. His judgment is in no way deflected by prejudice or sentiment, but when he esteems them most he does not forget their limitations, and when he exposes their weaknesses he does not lose his sympathy.

India proved to be no narrow field for the exercise of Mr. Kipling's artistic powers. Many and various are the aspects in which he has presented it to us, and it is clear from the evidence of such stories as "The Bridge Builders", "The Tomb of his Ancestors", and "William the Conqueror" in his latest volume that the vein is by no means exhausted. But his conquests there were not enough to satisfy his ambition or absorb his energies. The young writer set out to subdue new worlds, and his marked success in other realms of interest has placed it beyond a doubt that the impression of his genius is not dependent on any fortunate accident in his opportunities of acquiring material. Wherever he has travelled, over the face of the outer world, or beneath its forms and shadows to the inner recesses of the spirit, he has shown the same unerring penetration, the same grasp of the realities of life, the same imaginative insight, the same wonderful power of vivid representation. In his recent books there are one or two entirely new developments of an interesting kind that may be considered separately.

Most closely akin to the tales of Indian life are those that unfold the romance of the sea. If Kipling was not the first to discover the artistic possibilities in the picture of the deep waters and the life of those that go down to the sea in ships, no one at least has ever treated the subject with the same wealth of resource. He might have been a seafaring man from his youth upwards, to judge from his evident knowledge alike of the anatomy of every kind of vessel afloat, and of the humours and characteristics of those who sail them. None but an expert could venture to discuss the internal economy of a steamship with the fulness and freedom which he shows in such stories as "The Ship that Found Herself", "The Devil and the Deep Sea", or "Bread upon the Waters", and this faculty of minute observation and assimilation is matched by the range of his knowledge. He seems equally at home on the Indian Ocean and in the English Channel, in the Malay Archipelago and on the Banks of Newfoundland, on the estuary of an African river and among the seals in the Behring Sea. But his special note in the treatment of such material is something more remarkable than can be accounted for by any degree of completeness in his equipment of information. He has compelled the sea, as no one had ever done before, to yield up the secrets of its power and its charm; he has dived below its surface to bring up treasures of greater value than the pearls that lie hidden there; he has learned to understand and interpret the life that is moulded by its strange and mighty forces, and to trace the subtle influences of its varying moods on the characters of the men who live within its grasp. The most conspicuous example of Kipling's power in this region is *Captains Courageous*, which is almost an ideal book of adventure, not only for boys, but for "children of a larger growth". A comparison of this story with Stevenson's *Treasure Island* would soon disclose the superiority of the younger writer's work. In *Captains Courageous* we have the romance of adventure presented in its genuine form, namely, by the artistic rendering of scenes and experiences that are at once real and interesting and unfamiliar. In Stevenson's book a quasi-realistic treatment only partially conceals the wildly improbable character of the situation and its remoteness from any conceivable conditions of everyday life. Moreover, as has been already urged, there is no character-drawing in the story, and if any lesson is to be gathered from it, it is a false and a bad lesson. *Captains Courageous*, on the other hand, while it in no degree falls short in vivid description of detail and variety of incident, has at the same time the supreme merit of showing human beings in real living relations, and its lesson is the truest and the best that anyone can ever learn, namely, that the highest discipline of character is to be found in hard work under the necessary conditions of co-operation with others.

Two other developments of Mr. Kipling's art deserve special notice, and they must so far be taken together—his imaginative interpretation of the conscious side of animal life, and his indirect reflection of human character and destiny through the medium of allegory. The figure of Mowgli, the boy who was nurtured among the wolf's litter, and grew up in the jungle to learn the ways of all its four-footed inhabitants, appears first in one of the stories in *Many Inventions* entitled "In the Rukh", but without any direct suggestion of fable. This became the germ of the well-known *Jungle Books*, which of course were primarily put forward as pure fairy tales, but probably had from the first a deeper significance in the author's intention. However little defined this *arrière pensée* may have been, we must now judge these fanciful animal stories by the natural impression they have produced. It is not too much to say that they have opened up a new world of imaginative sympathy, the importance of which had hitherto been quite unsuspected. It may not be a very large world, and it does not seem to contain the possibilities of much development, but it is a genuine extension of the sphere of fiction for which we cannot but be grateful. It is the function of art to enrich our life by revealing and transfiguring every element of experience round which emotion can be made to play, and it is not to be denied that in the community of nature between ourselves and the lower animals there are opportunities of sympathetic interest that the artist may turn to excellent account. This field has never been entirely neglected. From Æsop downwards many have sought to endow the brute creation with an imaginary consciousness, but it had never been more than a palpable device to convey a moral by indirect suggestion from purely fictitious circumstances, until Mr. Kipling out of the fulness of his knowledge of the life of animals, and the abundance of his sympathy with them for their own sakes, taught us to recognise the essential unity of the whole animate world.

We may gladly admit the genuineness and value of such a contribution to the resources of fiction, and yet we may venture to doubt whether there is not some hazard of humouring the tendency beyond its legitimate limits. It is difficult to avoid some misgivings in this regard when we count the number of stories in the author's latest volume, *The Day's Work*, in which the naturalistic stand-point has been abandoned for the region of pure imagination. It is true that the boundaries of artistic realism are not to be hastily determined, but there are certain restraints which even the highest genius must observe. In the fanciful attribution of consciousness to creatures or things outside the pale of human life there is a point where the chords of imaginative sympathy will snap, unless the treatment has been of a kind to suggest a merely allegorical interpretation from the beginning. There is a certain atmosphere that is appropriate to pure allegory, which Mr. Kipling has admirably produced in his singularly beautiful tale in an earlier volume, "The Children of the Zodiac", and the only alternative to this atmosphere by which the sympathy of the reader can be retained is a frank avowal at the outset of the special conditions assumed. In quite half of the stories in *A Day's Work* the element of what may be called the "extra-natural" is more or less dallied with, and this may seem a disproportionate number in a miscellaneous collection of tales. But two or three of these are certainly proof against any adverse criticism on the grounds I have suggested. The greatest purist in such matters must admit the eminent success of such *jeux d'esprit* as "A Walking Delegate", where a number of horses discuss their grievances at the hand of man; or "The Maltese Cat", where the ponies in a polo match are represented as consciously sharing in the fortunes of the play. Most readers will be prepared to justify the author in his still more daring attempt to confer an intelligent individuality on locomotives; but surely the limit of what may be termed *allegorical realism* is passed in the story of "The Ship that Found Herself", where there is an indiscriminate endowment of life and personality on every individual bolt and rivet. Mr. Kipling must really be warned to stay his hand, all the more that there are signs that even in dealing with themes of another class he is losing the sureness of his foothold by giving too much ear to the calls of his wayward fancy, as in the story of "The Brushwood Boy", which is beautifully written, but is vitiated by the confusion of an allegorical and a realistic *motif*.

Considering as a whole, however, the short stories

that make up the bulk of the author's work in prose fiction, we cannot fail to be powerfully impressed by the high degree of creative art they represent. A few are trivial or unpleasant in subject; others show traces of misplaced flippancy or an affectation of cynicism, or an inclination to approach too nearly the line that separates coarseness and brutality of plain speaking from the realism of expression that has been duly chastened for the purposes of art; and one or two press the demands on the sympathetic imagination of the reader to an extreme limit. But the stories to which exception could fairly be taken on any of these grounds are few in number, and scarcely detract from the importance of the total achievement. It may be said, however, that in keeping almost entirely to short stories Mr. Kipling escapes the chief difficulties of the novelist,—those, namely, of construction and characterisation. It is true that he has seldom attempted to paint on a large canvas, and that his success in his more pretentious efforts has not been such as to place it beyond a doubt that he will come to be ranked with the great masters. *The Naulahka* indeed is a work of very great merit, on which alone a considerable reputation might be founded, but as it is a joint-production of Mr. Kipling and his brother-in-law, Mr. Balestier, it is unfortunately impossible to apportion the credit to which they are severally entitled. The only direct evidence we possess as to Kipling's capacity for writing a novel in the ordinary sense is to be found in *The Light that Failed*, and this evidence is both meagre and inconclusive. The book is, after all, little more than an extended sketch, an elaborate study of a single character, in relation to which the two or three subsidiary figures are only a somewhat neutral background. It is undoubtedly a powerful study, but the power is more manifest in the impressive colouring of the detail than in the general conception. The atmosphere is too oppressively Bohemian to favour any true dignity of treatment in the development of the tragedy, and our interest is not keenly enough aroused in the personality of the leading figure to induce us to follow his fortunes with much sympathy. It is scarcely comprehensible that a man of Dick Heldar's kind should have staked his happiness on the favour of a cold-hearted egoist like Maisie, and if he did, we cannot feel much pity for him in his inevitable disappointment. Nothing in this book can save us from the admission that Mr. Kipling has as yet written nothing in the grand style. Are we then to assume that he is excluded from the higher realms of prose fiction,—that there is little hope of his making any contribution that is imposing in mass to the permanent treasure of ideal beauty in the art he serves? It would not be just to decide that he is incapable of treating the interplay of character through continuous experiences, without taking full account of such faculty in this regard as the scale of his work has allowed him to exercise. It should be remembered, in the first place, that many of the short stories are really united by the thread of a common figure or set of figures appearing in them. Mulvaney and his two friends are presented to us in so many different lights that their individuality is made perfectly definite, and all the while their consistency is admirably maintained. Moreover, looked at even as separate scenes, the stories are so thoroughly dramatic that it is difficult to believe the same hand could not construct a continuous narrative with an equal sense of fitness. Further, with Mr. Kipling ten pages will go for fifty pages of many novelists. Every sentence, every phrase, every word almost, tells its own tale. If the strokes are few, there is yet no vagueness in the sketch, for every line is placed where it is most significant. There can be no question that the types he has presented to us are wonderfully individual, as well as vivid and various, but there remains to ask whether the variety is that of outward habit and circumstance only, or whether his insight is equally penetrating below the superficial differences of rank and occupation. Can he distinguish and portray those subtleties of the human heart that defy any outward category and only yield their secrets to the inward eye? Perhaps this question can best be put through another, namely,—Is he equally at home in dealing with men, women, and children? There can be no surer test of combined breadth and depth of vision. His outstanding success in the characters of men will be undisputed, and those who have read *Wee Willie Winkle* will have no doubt about the children; but the evidence as to women may be thought conflicting. On the one hand, it must be granted that in Maisie, Badalia, Ameera, Minnie Gadsby, and Mrs. Hawksbee we have characters all of marked individuality, very various in type, and each conceived with great subtlety of appreciation. On the other hand, it is said with truth that the author has drawn no really fine Englishwoman. Is this enough to condemn him? Hardly. It is one thing to attempt ideal portraits and fail, and quite another thing to refrain from the attempt. In the latter case we must look for reasons before we give judgment. Part of the defence may be that the conditions of Anglo-Indian life and society, from which most of the author's experience is drawn, do not commonly produce characters of ideal beauty either in men or in women, and that any elements of the heroic that can be discovered are sadly mixed with baser metal. It cannot be said that Mr. Kipling has shown any lack of understanding of the place that women may hold in life, and his championship of the native women is a proof of essentially chivalrous feeling. Lastly, it may be urged that his abundant satire of women is really an inverted expression of a demand for the noble qualities they fail to show. When we take all the evidence into account, we must decide that it is not unreasonable to expect from Mr. Kipling some important contributions to the treasury of prose fiction that will clearly affirm his title to be accounted one of the representative masters of his art in this generation.

The claim of Israel Zangwill to be placed in the front rank of the younger writers, along with Rudyard Kipling, may be demurred to, and it may be granted that his books do not yield the same impression of instinctive unconscious power. He has not the same unfailing sureness in realistic technique, whether of dialogue or of narrative; he cannot paint so vivid a picture with so few touches. But these are the special gifts of workmanship in which Kipling excels not only all his contemporaries but all his predecessors as well, and though they make up a 'good deal of that intangible quality which we like to designate as genius because it is difficult to analyse, they by no means exhaust the equipment of the artist. Their possession, as we have seen, is compatible with certain positive weaknesses and with some lack of command over the larger effects. Perhaps the fullest justice can be done to Mr. Zangwill's powers by suggesting points of likeness and difference between his achievement and that of his companion writer. Like Kipling he has discovered a new field of imaginative material, and he has created, or given importance to, a new literary form. He has caught the public ear by his revelation of the inner life of the wonderful race to which he belongs—a race that in its unique history embodies almost every element of sympathetic interest, alike in the romance of its outward fortunes, and in the subtle mysteries of its spiritual inheritance. The first indication of the possibilities for artistic treatment that lay in the character and destiny of the Jewish people may have come from George Eliot, but she could only deal with the subject experimentally and from the outside. The true secret of the theme could only be revealed by one who was himself a Jew of the Jews, by birth, by upbringing, by sympathy, and who was at the same time free from the illusions peculiar to his race. Never before our own time, perhaps, would it have been possible to find the due combination of intellectual detachment and congenital enthusiasm for spiritual ideals. Nor would it have been enough that the historical spirit should have captured the more enlightened members of the Jewish race, and enabled some of them at least to bring a dispassionate judgment to bear on the forms of their traditional faith, without alienating their sympathy from the aspirations which were expressed in them. To the passionate ideality of the enthusiast, the judicial temper of the critic, the clear vision of the thinker, there had to be added the presentative power of the artist. The hour had come in its fulness, and with it, fortunately, came the man. Those who have read *The Children of the Ghetto*, *Ghetto Tragedies*, *The King of Schnorrers*, and *Dreamers of the Ghetto*, do not need to be reminded with what pre-eminent success Mr. Zangwill has laid before us the romance of his race. There can be no question that it has proved a genuine discovery of treasure for imaginative use. It is not indeed so wide a region as those into which Mr. Kipling has led the way, but its resources are ample for its possessor, and the approaches are well guarded against usurpers. It is not necessary, however, to bespeak appreciation of Mr. Zangwill on the ground of his good fortune in finding a new field of interest for poetic creation. It is true that but for his distinctively Jewish note he would probably have had to wait somewhat longer for his popularity, but his genius would sooner or later have compelled recognition, whatever class of subject he had been led to choose. His books may challenge criticism on the merits of his workmanship alone, and it is in that aspect that they may be rapidly passed in review. It has been said that he may be held to have created a new literary form, and his latest book, *Dreamers of the Ghetto*, in which this is embodied, may first be touched upon. The studies of Jewish character of which it is composed represent a daring, but brilliantly successful, attempt to lend dramatic movement to historical figures that had become dim and shadowy in the formal annals of a distant past, or in the sober atmosphere of authentic biography. It is a happy extension of the plan of Landor's *Imaginary Conversations*, giving fuller scope to the fancy by the suggestion of an idealised setting to memorable deeds and scenes. In these pages Uriel Acosta, Spinoza, Heine, Lassalle, and other striking representatives of the Jewish race, are raised from the dead to pass before our eyes in their true semblance as men who live and move and have a real being. Such an achievement may be no more than a by-product in the evolution of the art of fiction, but it is one that claims acknowledgment not only for its originality but for the strength of its emotional appeal.

None of Mr. Zangwill's Jewish books can be judged as an ordinary work of fiction. *The King of Schnorrers* is an exceedingly able picture of a characteristic side of Hebrew life, but it is too much of an extravaganza to be tried by accepted canons, while the plan of *The Children of the Ghetto* seems to require for it a special category on other grounds. The latter work must be regarded rather as a succession of scenes somewhat slightly bound together by the thread of continuous narrative. The interest is too much dispersed among different groups of characters to allow a complete unity of effect, and the larger outlines are somewhat obscured by a superabundance of illustrative detail. But notwithstanding these difficulties, which are not diminished by the break of several years that is interposed between the first and the second part, we are strongly impressed by the evidence of the author's power of dramatic presentation, which appears not only in the highly effective treatment of individual episodes, but in the strength and consistency of the portraiture throughout the entire texture of the story. In fact, though Mr. Zangwill has not embodied his pictures of the life of his own people in any work that can be regarded as a model of prose fiction, he has shown in dealing with this special subject all the various qualities of the novelist's art in a high degree of perfection. Even had he written nothing else, it might have been safely predicted that when experience brought a fuller control of his resources and a finer sense of proportion he would produce works in the front rank of importance.

But this has not been left a matter of conjecture; there is ample proof not only that his power is independent of any authority that belongs to him as the exponent of a special subject, but further, that he can fashion works of art in what has been called the "grand style". In support of this contention no stress can be laid on such *jeux d'esprit* as *The Celibates' Club*, clever and interesting though such pieces of deliberate persiflage may be. The book on which Mr. Zangwill's fame as a novelist can as yet be most securely based is undoubtedly that which he has entitled *The Master*. In this story he has broken entirely new ground, finding his *motif* in the life-history of a Nova-Scotian lad, who, impelled by the instinct of the artist within him, fights his way through manifold difficulties to the summit of his ambition, but finds his hardest task in the conquest of himself in face of the temptations he encounters, appealing alike to his higher and to his baser self. It cannot be claimed that this novel is wholly free from fault. In its general plan there is too great a violation of the dramatic unities of time and place, which no work of fiction, even in the narrative form, can afford altogether to ignore. It is scarcely possible to trace the whole career of a leading character from youth to manhood, without giving an impression of abruptness in the necessary transitions from one significant episode to another, and the selection of the episodes themselves is apt to seem arbitrary, or at least not absolutely inevitable. It may be suggested further that the book shows traces of the author's besetting sin—the over-elaboration of detail. Some of the hero's experiences would have been better omitted, not because they were irrelevant, but simply because, not being indispensable, their presence weakens the general effect. This latter defect, arising from an over-abundance of imaginative material and an insufficiently chastened facility of expression, may be readily pardoned in a writer who may still be thought of as in the period of exuberant youth; while the lack of unity in design must of course be regarded as incidental to a plan that has undoubted advantages of its own. It would certainly be hard, for the reader as well as for the author, if the early scenes of Matt Strang's boyhood had to be pruned away, for they are full of admirable description, and show a wonderful creative gift in a writer who had only indirect means of assimilating local colour. It is not, however, mainly for the masterly skill shown in details of execution that this book is memorable; its greatness is established by the powerful treatment of the leading theme. It is interesting to compare this novel with Kipling's most pretentious effort, *The Light that Failed*, which happens to deal with a similar subject. In both we have the story of an artist who reaches fame after a struggle, and fails to find happiness in his success. In point of skill in narrative and dialogue there is little to choose between them, Kipling having the advantage in rapidity of movement and incisiveness of touch, while Zangwill excels in wealth of description and suggestion; but in all the larger aspects of treatment *The Master* is incomparably the finer work. It would be unjust, of course, to take the least satisfactory production of the one author along with the other's masterpiece, as an adequate basis for a comparative estimate of their total merits, but the contrast may at least serve to bring into relief the special strength of Mr. Zangwill's achievement. We have in *The Master* a profound reading of the ultimate facts of life. The subtler problems of human destiny are convincingly presented through the medium of artistic creations, and are solved by the light of a sane and high philosophy. In Matthew Strang's rejection of the promptings of the world, the flesh, and the devil, that come to his long-suffering spirit in the guise of ministering angels—a rejection achieved through the unconscious influence of the woman who represents for him the constraining forces of duty and the need for sacrifice of self to the claims of others,—there is expressed the true ideality of an artist whose creative gift is informed by wise thought and noble feeling. In Mr. Zangwill's appreciation of moral beauty is to be found the distinctive quality of his work which enables him to enter the higher regions of imaginative effort. A clear vision of the eternal verities is no guarantee of æsthetic perception or artistic capacity, but it is the imperative condition of the consecration of these gifts to the worthiest ends, and it rarely fails to impress itself as surely on the smaller elements of literary technique as on the general features of the construction and the portraiture.

Mr. Zangwill's poetic temperament and his well-rounded theory of life are vividly reflected in the idiosyncrasies of his style, which not only has the flexibility that fits it to every opportunity of description and dramatic speech, but is capable of rising to the highest eloquence under the stress of strong emotion. The following passage may be taken in illustration:—

"The more London refused him, the more his consciousness of power grew. As he tramped the teeming streets a thousand ideas for great pictures jostled in his sick brain, a thousand fine imaginings took form and shape in beautiful colour-harmonies and majestic groupings. In the ecstatic frenzy of moments of hysterical revolt against the blind forces closing in upon him like a tomb to shut him out for ever from

the sunlight, he grew Titanic to his own thought, capable
of masterpieces in any and every kind of art—great heroic
frescoes like Michael Angelo's, great homely pictures like those
of the Dutch, great classic canvases like Raphael's, great
portraits like Rembrandt's, great landscapes like Turner's,—
not to say great new pictures that should found the school of
Strang, combining all the best points of all the schools, the
ancient poetry with the modern realism. Nay, even literary
impulses mingled with artistic in these spasms of nebulous
emotion, his immature genius not having yet grasped the
limitations of the paintable. Good God! what did he ask?
Not the voluptuous round of the young men whose elegant
silhouettes standing out against the black silent night from
the warm lighted windows of great houses athrob with joyous
music filled him with a mad bitterness; not the soft rose-
leaf languors of the beautiful white women who passed in
shimmering silks and laces from gleaming spick-and-span
carriages under canvas awnings over purple carpets amidst
spruce obsequious footmen; not the selfish joys of these
radiant shadows dancing their way to dusty oblivion, to be
trodden under foot by the generations over which he would
shine as a star, serene, immortal; but bread and water, and a
little money for models and properties, and a top-light straight
in touch with heaven, and a few pounds to send home to his
kith and kin; but to paint, to paint, to joy in conception and
to glory in difficult execution, to express the poetry of the
ideal through real flesh and real shadows and real foliage,
and find a rapturous agony in the search for perfection; to
paint, to paint, to exult fiercely in the passing of faces, with
their pathos and their tragedy, to catch a smile on a child's
face, and the grace of a girl's movement, and the passion in
the eyes of a woman; to watch the sunrise consecrating tiles
and chimneys, or the river, mirroring a thousand night-lights,
glide on, glorifying its own uncleanness; to express the
intense stimulus of the wonderful city, resonant with the
tireless tread of millions of feet, vibrant with the swell of
perpetual currents of traffic, pulsating with the rough music
of humanity — roaring markets, shrilling trains, panting
steamships; to record in pigment not only the romance of
his dreams, or the glamour of the dead past, but the poetry of
the quick—the rich full life of the town, the restless day and
the feverish night, with its mysterious perspectives of fitful

gleams; to paint, to paint, anything, everything, for the joy of eternalizing the transient beauty that lurked everywhere, in the shimmer of a sunlit puddle, in the starry heaven, in the motions of barefoot children dancing to a barrel-organ, in the scarlet passing of soldiers, in the play of light on the fish in a huckster's barrow, in the shadowy aisles of city churches throbbing with organ-diapasons; O the joy of life! O the joy of art that expresses the joy of life!"

Index.

Æsthetics, philosophy of, 2.
Arnold, M., quoted, 73.
Art, appreciation of, 1.
— origin of, 3.
— place in life of, 4.
Austen, Jane, 24–30, 63, 82, 86.

Balzac, 24.
Birrell, A., on J. Austen, 28.
Blind, M., on *Romola*, 110.
Boccaccio, 13.
Brontë, Charlotte, 64–77, 82.
— *Jane Eyre*, 67–69, 72, 74–77.
— *Shirley*, 67, 74–77.
— *Villette*, 67–69, 74–76.
Brontë, Emily, 64.
Brown, Dr. John, on Thackeray, 52, 60.
Browning, Oscar, on *Romola*, 110.

Carlyle, T., 16, 20, 40, 60.
Cervantes, 13.
Colvin, Sidney, 222.

Dante, 13.
Defoe, 13.
Dickens, Charles, 30–47, 51, 55, 56, 57, 58, 63, 82, 86, 159.
— *Barnaby Rudge*, 44.
— *Bleak House*, 38, 45, 46.
— *Christmas Carol*, 45.
— *Dombey and Son*, 33, 45.
— *Hard Times*, 32, 37.
— *Nicholas Nickleby*, 33, 46.
— *Old Curiosity Shop*, 45.
— *Oliver Twist*, 33, 34, 36–40.
— *Pickwick Papers*, 33, 46.
— *Tale of Two Cities*, 34, 40–44.

Drama, rise of, 7.
— decay of, 9–10.

Eliot, George, 28, 71, 78–143, 160, 195, 201, 206–208, 218, 225, 241.
— *Adam Bede*, 85, 91, 93.
— *Daniel Deronda*, 83, 85, 87, 116, 120, 129–143.
— *Felix Holt*, 85, 112–116.
— *Middlemarch*, 83, 84, 85, 87, 116–129.
— *Mill on the Floss*, 84, 88, 91, 95–99, 120.
— *Romola*, 83, 101–112.
— *Scenes of Clerical Life*, 83, 90–91.
— *Silas Marner*, 83, 99–101, 102.
Epic, rise of, 7.

Fiction, early history of, 7.
Fielding, H., 13, 24, 84, 106.
Fortnightly Reviewer on Meredith, 152.

Goldsmith, O., 24.

Hardy, Thomas, 229.
Harrison, Frederic, on George Eliot, 80–82.
Harte, Bret, 230.
Hawthorne, Nathaniel, 72, 82, 86, 230.
Hugo, Victor, 24.

James, Henry, 80.

Kipling, Rudyard, 229–241.
— *Captains Courageous*, 235.

Victorian Novelists.

Kipling, Rudyard, *Jungle Books*, 235–236.
— *The Light that Failed*, 238–239, 245.

Landor, W. S., 145, 243.
Lassalle, F., 186.
Lewes, G. H., 78, 195.
Lynch, Hannah, on Meredith, 165, 173, 193.

Macaulay, Lord, on J. Austen, 25.
Martineau, Harriet, on Thackeray, 52.
Mazzini, on *Romola*, 102.
Meredith, George, 86, 87, 122, 139, 143–208, 218, 225.
— *Amazing Marriage*, 151, 202–206.
— *Beauchamp's Career*, 151, 170, 173–183, 194.
— *Diana of the Crossways*, 151, 188–193.
— *Egoist*, 147, 151, 153, 158, 170, 183–186.
— *Evan Harrington*, 151, 157–161.
— *Harry Richmond*, 151, 153, 170–173.
— *Lord Ormont*, 153, 199–201.
— *One of our Conquerors*, 151, 153, 170, 194–199, 202.
— *Rhoda Fleming*, 146, 161–164.
— *Richard Feverel*, 146, 149, 151, 153–157, 170, 224.
— *Sandra Belloni*, 149–151, 153, 164, 170.
— *Shaving of Shagpat*, 146.
— *Tragic Comedians*, 186–188, 194.
— *Vittoria*, 150, 153, 164, 165–170, 184.
Merivale, H., on Thackeray, 52.
Milton, 137.
Music-drama, 8, 144.

Norton, Hon. Mrs., 188–189.

Poe, E. A., 230.
Prose Fiction, origin of, 4.
— position of, 6.
— future of, 12.

Rabelais, 13.
Richardson, S., 13, 24.
Rossetti, D. G., on *Romola*, 102.
Ruskin, John, 34, 38, 88–90, 95–96.

Sand, George, 24.
Scott, Sir Walter, 12, 14–24, 29, 82, 84, 86, 93.
— *Abbot*, 23.
— *Antiquary*, 17, 19, 21.
— *Bride of Lammermuir*, 15.
— *Guy Mannering*, 17.
— *Heart of Midlothian*, 15–16, 21.
— *Ivanhoe*, 21, 103.
— *Legend of Montrose*, 15.
— *Pirate*, 17.
— *Redgauntlet*, 16, 21.
— *St. Ronan's Well*, 16.
— *Woodstock*, 23.

Shakespeare, 11, 88, 129, 135, 163.
Smollett, T., 13.
Stephen, Leslie, 80, 101.
Stevenson, R. L., 18, 185, 208–229.
— *Black Arrow*, 215.
— *Catriona*, 215, 225–226.
— *Dr. Jekyll*, 217–218.
— *Ebbtide*, 216.
— *Kidnapped*, 215.
— *Master of Ballantrae*, 216, 218–221.
— *Prince Otto*, 216–217.
— *St. Ives*, 216.
— *Treasure Island*, 212–214, 221, 235.
— *Weir of Hermiston*, 216, 221–228.
Swift, Dean, 13.
Swinburne, A., 70, 71, 89, 97–98, 138.

Taine, H., on Thackeray, 53–55, 58, 60.

Index.

Thackeray, W. M., 47, 82, 84, 86, 106.
— *Barry Lyndon*, 55, 56, 161.
— *Esmond*, 55, 56, 58, 60–61.
— *Newcomes*, 55, 61.
— *Pendennis*, 55, 57, 59, 60.
— *Philip*, 55, 60.
— *Vanity Fair*, 55, 56, 60.
— *Virginians*, 55, 56.

Tolstoi, L., 225.
Tourgénieff, 120.

Zangwill, Israel, 229, 241–247.
— *Children of the Ghetto*, 243.
— *Dreamers of the Ghetto*, 242–243.
— *King of Schnorrers*, 243.
— *The Master*, 244–247.

www.ingramcontent.com/pod-product-compliance
Lightning Source LLC
Chambersburg PA
CBHW031350230426
43670CB00006B/487